16.95

THE SUPREME COURT AND THE MASS MEDIA

THE SUPREME COURT AND THE MASS MEDIA

Selected Cases, Summaries, and Analyses

Douglas S. Campbell

PRAEGER

New York
Westport, Connecticut
London

Library of Congress Cataloging-in-Publication Data

Campbell, Douglas S.
The Supreme Court and the mass media : selected cases, summaries, and analyses / Douglas S. Campbell.
p. cm.
Includes bibliographical references (p.
ISBN 0-275-93421-7 (alk. paper) ISBN 0-275-93549-3 (pbk. : alk. paper)
1. Mass media—Law and legislation—United States—Digests.
I. Title.
KF2750.A59C36 1990
343.73'099—dc20
[347.30399] 89-26567

Library of Congress Catalog Card Number: 89-26567
ISBN: 0-275-93421-7 (hb.)
0-275-93549-3 (pbk.)

First published in 1990

Praeger Publishers, One Madison Avenue, New York, NY 10010
An imprint of Greenwood Publishing Group, Inc.

Printed in the United States of America

The paper used in this book complies with the Permanent Paper Standard issued by the National Information Standards Organization (Z39.48-1984).

10 9 8 7 6 5 4 3 2 1

For Beverly, my wife, and

Christopher, David, and Channing, my three sons

Contents

Cases Related to Libel

Cases Related to Privacy

Cases Related to First Amendment Issues

Preface

I shall never forget part of the lecture given at the first meeting of my first graduate class. The instructor inveighed against most modern critics of Ralph Waldo Emerson. What these critics are criticizing, he asserted, is not Emerson but the Emersonians. These are lazy scholars, in his opinion, who simply repeat what others say of Emerson or what the followers of Emerson say. They do not read Emerson for themselves. Later, I heard this evaluation of scholars commenting on Walt Whitman, John Calvin, and many others.

The same can be said of a good portion of the scholarly comments on the United States Supreme Court's rulings on libel, privacy, and the First Amendment. Often scholars will base their statements about these opinions solely on what other scholars have said. It should be said in defense of such academicians that time may not allow them to read all the cases they comment on. Moreover, a long established scholarly tradition rests upon the confidence that critics place in an opinion repeated by revered authorities in their field of study. Still, in the end, there exists no acceptable defense for commenting on an unread case.

Because there are voluminous collections of court cases, jurists, over time, have developed many ingenious methods for finding the cases relevant to the needs of the researcher. Some are better than others. For the most part, these methods depend on extremely concise summaries of relevant legal concepts or practices. While such methods save much time for someone interested in tracing a narrow legal notion, they are of little help to one who wishes to understand the case as a whole.

In fact, mistaken understandings of cases, not surprisingly, commonly result from cursory summaries because readers naturally, even if wrongly, assume that there is little more of value in a case than what appears in the summary. This book is a rare attempt to present comprehensive summaries including, not only succinct salient points of law, but also full arguments of the justices, all important points, and all dissenting as well as concurring opinions.

These summaries grew out of my many and varied responses to the struggles of my communication law students with the wise but upon occasion obtuse words of nine justices. At times the students struggled just to discover who "won" and who "lost." At other times they grappled with the meaning of a Latin word, a technical legal term, or a rule of civil procedure. Sometimes they lost the thread of the argument, and sometimes they were unclear about the chain of events leading up to the law suit.

So, I began to write summaries and analyses of the cases in order to save class time for other matters. With the grateful assistance of student evaluations, I added and deleted over the years various parts of these documents to make them more useful. Now, I share these oft-revised abstracts with others, hoping that they too may benefit from summaries that do more than highlight disjunctive key points.

Two brief notes about style are necessary. First, docket numbers made no reference to years until 1974. Therefore, I added the year to the all docket numbers composed before that date. Thus, those docket numbers with the year added use all four numbers for the year: e.g., 1919-437. Those numbers with the year included by the Court use only the last two digits of the date: e.g., 86-636. Second, for those cases not yet published in the United States Reporter, I have cited page numbers from the Lawyer's Edition.

I close with a few words of thanks. I confess these comments reflect my human inadequacy to express all the assistance I received, but they are sincere and heart-felt. First, I wish to thank Saundra K. Hybels, colleague, office mate for a few years, respected author, and, most of all, friend, who encouraged me to collect my writings into a book. Secondly, I thank the members of my department, who, without ever complaining, allowed me to come in late some days or to leave early others in order to go home and pound the key board of my computer, safely away from the office telephone. Frank and Dorothy Vaughn deserve special mention for their friendship and unflagging support and for helping me keep track of the many details necessary to lubricate the machinery of an academic department. Nor should I forget Craig Dean Willis, an extremely rare university president, who not only fully supported my research efforts, but also took a genuine personal interest in my work.

I owe a debt of gratitude to many, many librarians. I mention first Ester Jane Carrier, research librarian par excellence. I am sure she must have been tempted to hide every time I walked into the university's library reference section, but she always greeted me with a smile and she always found what I was seeking. Joan Gallagher and Stevenson Library director Robert Bravard were also very helpful. Reference Librarian at the Dickinson School of Law, Gail Partin, gave me the same kind of thorough and competent help she gave to her own faculty.

Cases Listed by Full Title: Chronological Order

CASES RELATED TO LIBEL

(1) 1964 *New York Times Company* v. *L. B. Sullivan*, Docket No. 1964-39
Ralph D. Abernathy v. *L. B. Sullivan*, Docket No. 1964-40
376 U.S. 254, 11 L.Ed.2d 686, 84 S.Ct. 710

(2) 1964 *Jim Garrison* v. *State of Louisiana*, Docket No. 1964-04
379 U.S. 64, 13 L.Ed.2d 125, 85 S.Ct. 209

(3) 1965 *Henry* v. *Collins*, Docket No. 1965-89 and
Henry v. *Pearson*, Docket No. 1965-90
380 U.S. 356, 13 L.Ed.2d 892, 85 S.Ct. 992

(4) 1966 *William C. Linn* v. *United Plant Guard Workers of America, Local 114*, Docket No. 1966-45
383 U.S. 53, 15 L.Ed.2d 582, 86 S.Ct. 657

(5) 1966 *Alfred D. Rosenblatt* v. *Frank P. Baer*, Docket No. 1966-38
383 U.S. 75, 15 L.Ed.2d 597, 86 S.Ct. 669

(6) 1966 *Steve Ashton* v. *Kentucky*, Docket No. 1966-619
384 U.S. 195, 16 L.Ed.2d 469, 86 S.Ct. 1407

(7) 1967 *Beckley Newspapers Corporation* v. *C. Harold Hanks*,
Docket No. 1967-467; 389 U.S. 81, 19 L.Ed.2d 248, 88 S.Ct. 197

(8) 1967 *Curtis Publishing Company* v. *Wallace Butts*, Docket No. 1976-37
and *Associate Press* v. *Edwin A. Walker*, Docket No. 1967-150
388 U.S. 130, 18 L.Ed.2d 1094, 87 S.Ct. 1975

(9) 1968 *Phil A. St. Amant* v. *Herman A. Thompson*, Docket No. 1968-517
390 U.S. 727, 20 L.Ed.2d 262, 88 S.Ct. 1323

(10) 1970 *Greenbelt Cooperative Publishing Association* v. *Charles S. Bresler*, Docket No. 1970-413; 398 U.S. 6, 26 L.Ed.2d 6, 90 S.Ct. 1537

(11) 1971 *Monitor Patriot Co.* v. *Roselle A. Roy*, Docket No. 1971-62 401 U.S. 265, 28 L.Ed.2d 35, 91 S.Ct. 621

(12) 1971 *Time Incorporated* v. *Frank Pape*, Docket No. 1971-109 401 U.S. 279, 28 L.Ed.2d 45, 91 S.Ct. 633

(13) 1971 *Ocala Star-Banner Company* v. *Leonard Damron*, Docket No. 1971-118; 401 U.S. 295, 28 L.Ed.2d 57, 91 S.Ct. 628

(14) 1971 *George A. Roosenbloom* v. *Metromedia, Inc.*, Docket No. 1971-66 403 U.S. 29, 29 L.Ed.2d 296, 91 S.Ct. 1811

(15) 1974 *Old Dominion Branch No. 496, National Association of Letter Carriers, AFL-CIO* v. *Henry M. Austin*, Docket No. 72-1180 418 U.S. 264, 41 L.Ed.2d 745, 94 S.Ct. 2770

(16) 1974 *Elmer Gertz* v. *Robert Welch, Inc.*, Docket No. 72-617 418 U.S. 323, 41 L.Ed.2d 789, 94 S.Ct. 2997

(17) 1976 *Time, Inc.* v. *Mary Alice Firestone*, Docket No. 74-944 424 U.S. 448, 47 L.Ed.2d 154, 96 S.Ct. 958

(18) 1979 *Anthony Herbert* v. *Barry Lando*, Docket No. 77-1105 441 U.S. 153, 60 L.Ed.2d 115, 99 S.Ct. 1635

(19) 1979 *Ronald R. Hutchinson* v. *William Proxmire* and *Morton Schwartz*, Docket No. 78-680; 443 U.S. 111, 61 L.Ed.2d 411, 99 S.Ct. 2675

(20) 1979 *Ilya Wolston* v. *Reader's Digest Association, Inc.*, Docket No. 78-5414; 443 U.S. 157, 61 L.Ed.2d 450, 99 S.Ct. 2701

(21) 1984 *Kathy Keeton* v. *Hustler Magazine, Inc.*, Docket No. 82-485 465 U.S. 770, 79 L.Ed.2d 790, 104 S.Ct. 1473,

(22) 1984 *Iain Calder* and *John South* v. *Shirley Jones*, Docket No. 82-1401 465 U.S. 783, 79 L.Ed.2d 804, 104 S.Ct. 1482

(23) 1984 *Bose Corporation* v. *Consumers Union of United States, Inc.*, Docket No. 82-1246; 466 U.S. 485, 80 L.Ed.2d 502, 104 S.Ct. 1949

(24) 1985 *Dun & Bradstreet, Inc.* v. *Greenmoss Builders, Inc.*, Docket No. 83-18; 472 U.S. 749, 86 L.Ed.2d 593, 105 S.Ct. 2939

(25) 1986 *Jack Anderson* v. *Liberty Lobby, Inc.* and *Willis A. Carto*, Docket No. 84-1602; 477 U.S. 242, 91 L.Ed.2d 202, 106 S.Ct. 2505

(26) 1986 *Philadelphia Newspapers, Inc.* v. *Maurice S. Hepps*, Docket No. 84-1491; 475 U.S. 767, 89 L.Ed.2d 783, 106 S.Ct. 1558

(27) 1988 *Hustler Magazine* and *Larry C. Flint* v. *Jerry Falwell*,
Docket No. 86-1278; 56 Law Week 4180
485 U.S. ---, 99 L.Ed.2d 41, 108 S.Ct. 876

(28) 1989 *Harte-Hanks Communications, Inc.* v. *Daniel Connaughton*,
Docket No. 88-10; 57 LW 4847
491 U.S. --, 105 L.Ed.2d 562, 109 S.Ct. 2678

CASES RELATED TO PRIVACY

(1) 1967 *Time, Inc.* v. *James J. Hill*, Docket No. 1967-22
385 U.S. 374, 17 L.Ed.2d. 456, 87 S.Ct. 534

(2) 1974 *Margaret Mae Cantrell* v. *Forest City Publishing Co.*,
Docket No. 73-5520; 419 U.S. 245, 42 L.Ed.2d. 419, 95 S.Ct. 465

(3) 1975 *Cox Broadcasting Corporation* v. *Martin Cohn*, Docket No. 73-938
420 U.S. 469, 43 L.Ed.2d. 328, 95 S.Ct. 1029

(4) 1977 *Hugo Zacchini* v. *Scripps-Howard Broadcasting Company*,
Docket No. 76-577; 433 U.S. 562, 53 L.Ed.2d. 965, 97 S.Ct. 2849

(5) 1989 *The Florida Star* v. *B.J.F.*, Docket No. 87-329, 57 LW 4816
491 U.S. ---, 105 L.Ed.2d 433, 109 S.Ct. 2603

CASES RELATED TO FIRST AMENDMENT ISSUES

(1) 1919 *Charles T. Schenck* v. *United States of America*, Docket No. 437
Elizabeth Baer v. *United States of America*, Docket No. 438
249 U.S. 47, 63 L.Ed. 470, 39 S.Ct. 247

(2) 1919 *Jacob Abrams* v. *United States*, Docket No. 1919-316
250 U.S. 616, 63 L.Ed. 1173, 40 S.Ct. 17

(3) 1925 *Benjamin Gitlow* v. *People of the State of New York*,
Docket No. 1925-19; 268 U.S. 652, 69 L.Ed. 1138, 45 S.Ct. 625

(4) 1927 *Charlotte Anita Whitney* v. *People of the State of California*,
Docket No. 1927-03; 274 U.S. 357, 71 L.Ed. 1095, 47 S.Ct. 641

(5) 1931 *J. M. Near* v. *State of Minnesota Ex Rel. Floyd B. Olson*,
Docket No. 1931-91; 283 U.S. 697, 75 L.Ed. 1357, 51 S.Ct. 625

(6) 1942 *Walter Chaplinsky* v. *State of New Hampshire*,
Docket No. 1942-255; 315 U.S. 568, 86 L.Ed. 1031, 62 S.Ct. 766

(7) 1951 *Eugene Dennis, John B. Williamson, Jacob A. Stachel, Robert G. Thompson, Benjamin J. Daves, Jr., Henry Winston, John Gates, Irving Potash, Gilbert Green, Carl Winter,* and *Gus Hall* v. *United States*, Docket No. 1951-336
341 U.S. 494, 95 L.Ed. 1137, 71 S.Ct. 857

(8) 1957 *Oleta O'Connor Yates, Henry Steinberg, Loretta, Starvus Stack* v. *United States of America*, Docket No. 1957-06 and *William Schneiderman* v. *United States of America*, Docket No. 1957-07 and *Al Richmond* and *Philip Marshall Connelly* v. *United States of America*, Docket No. 1957-08
354 U.S. 298, 1 L.Ed.2d 1356, 77 S.Ct. 1064

(9) 1969 *Clarence Brandenburg* v. *State of Ohio*, Docket No. 1969-492
395 U.S. 444, 23 L.Ed.2d 430, 89 S.Ct. 1827

(10) 1988 *Hazelwood School District* v. *Cathy Kuhlmeier*, Docket No. 86-836
484 U.S. ---, 98 L.Ed.2d 592, 108 S.Ct. 562

(11) 1989 *Texas* v. *Gregory Lee Johnson*, Docket No. 88-155
491 U.S. ---, 105 L.Ed.2d 342, 109 S.Ct. 2533

Cases Listed by Full Title: Alphabetical Order

CASES RELATED TO LIBEL

(1) *Anderson* v. *Liberty Lobby, Inc.*
Jack Anderson v. *Liberty Lobby, Inc.*, and *Willis A. Carto*, Docket No. 84-1602; 477 U.S. 242, 91 L.Ed.2d 202, 106 S.Ct. 2505 (1986)

(2) *Ashton* v. *Kentucky*
Steve Ashton v. *Kentucky*, Docket No. 1966-619
384 U.S. 195, 16 L.Ed.2d 469, 86 S.Ct. 1407 (1966)

(3) *Beckley Newspapers Corp.* v. *Hanks*
Beckley Newspapers Corporation v. *C. Harold Hanks*, Docket No. 1967-467; 389 U.S. 81, 19 L.Ed.2d 248, 88 S.Ct. 197 (1967)

(4) *Bose Corp.* v. *Consumers Union of U.S., Inc.*
Bose Corporation v. *Consumers Union of United States, Inc.*, Docket No. 82-1246
466 U.S. 485, 80 L.Ed.2d 502, 104 S.Ct. 1949 (1984)

(5) *Calder* v. *Jones*
Iain Calder and *John South* v. *Shirley Jones*, Docket No. 82-1401
465 U.S. 783, 79 L.Ed.2d. 804, 104 S.Ct. 1482 (1984)

(6) *Curtis Publishing Co.* v. *Butts*
Curtis Publishing Company v. *Wallace Butts*, Docket No. 1976-37 and *Associate Press* v. *Edwin A. Walker*, Docket No. 1967-150
388 U.S. 130, 18 L.Ed.2d 1094, 87 S.Ct. 1975 (1967)

(7) *Dun & Bradstreet* v. *Greenmoss Builders*
Dun & Bradstreet, Inc. v. *Greenmoss Builders, Inc.*, Docket No. 83-18
472 U.S. 749, 86 L.Ed.2d 593, 105 S.Ct. 2939 (1985)

(8) *Garrison* v. *Louisiana*
Jim Garrison v. *State of Louisiana*, Docket No. 1964-04
379 U.S. 64, 13 L.Ed.2d 125, 85 S.Ct. 209 (1964)

(9) *Gertz* v. *Welch*
Elmer Gertz v. *Robert Welch, Inc.*, Docket No. 72-617
418 U.S. 323, 41 L.Ed.2d 789, 94 S.Ct. 2997 (1974)

(10) *Greenbelt Coop. Pub. Asso.* v. *Bresler*
Greenbelt Cooperative Publishing Association, Inc. v. *Charles S. Bresler*, Docket No. 1970-413; 398 U.S. 6, 26 L.Ed.2d 6, 90 S.Ct. 1537 (1970)

(11) *Harte-Hanks Communications, Inc.* v. *Connaughton*
Harte-Hanks Communications, Inc. v. *Daniel Connaughton*, Docket No. 88-10; 57 LW 4847
491 U.S. ---, 105 L.Ed.2d 562, 109 S.Ct. 2678 (1989)

(12) *Henry* v. *Collins*
Henry v. *Collins*, Docket No. 1965-89 and *Henry* v. *Pearson*, Docket No. 1965-90,
380 U.S. 356, 13 L.Ed.2d 892, 85 S.Ct. 992 (1965)

(13) *Herbert* v. *Lando*
Anthony Herbert v. *Barry Lando*, Docket No. 77-1105
441 U.S. 153, 60 L.Ed.2d 115, 99 S.Ct. 1635 (1979)

(14) *Hustler Magazine* v. *Falwell*
Hustler Magazine and *Larry C. Flint* v. *Jerry Falwell*, Docket No. 86-1278; 56 Law Week 4180
485 U.S. ---, 99 L.Ed.2d 41, 108 S.Ct. 876 (1988)

(15) *Hutchinson* v. *Proxmire*
Ronald R. Hutchinson v. *William Proxmire* and *Morton Schwartz*, Docket No. 78-680 ;443 U.S. 111, 61 L.Ed.2d 411, 99 S.Ct. 2675 (1979)

(16) *Keeton* v. *Hustler Magazine, Inc.*
Kathy Keeton v. *Hustler Magazine, Inc.*, Docket No. 82-485
465 U.S. 770, 79 L.Ed.2d 790, 104 S.Ct. 1473 (1984)

(17) *Letter Carriers* v. *Austin*
Old Dominion Branch No. 496, National Association of Letter Carriers, AFL-CIO v. *Henry M. Austin*, Docket No. 72-1180
418 U.S. 264, 41 L.Ed.2d 745, 94 S.Ct. 2770 (1974)

(18) *Linn* v. *United Plant Guard Workers*
William C. Linn v. *United Plant Guard Workers of America, Local 114*, Docket No. 1966-45; 383 U.S. 53, 15 L.Ed.2d 582, 86 S.Ct. 657 (1966)

(19) *New York Times Co.* v. *Sullivan*
New York Times Company v. *L. B. Sullivan*, Docket No. 1964-39 and *Ralph D. Abernathy* v. *L. B. Sullivan*, Docket No. 1964-40,
376 U.S. 254, 11 L.Ed.2d 686, 84 S.Ct. 710 (1964)

(20) *Ocala Star-Banner Co.* v. *Damron*
Ocala Star-Banner Company v. *Leonard Damron*, Docket No. 1971-118
401 U.S. 295, 28 L.Ed.2d 57, 91 S.Ct. 628 (1971)

(21) *Patriot Co.* v. *Roy*
Monitor Patriot Co. v. *Roselle A. Roy*, Docket No. 1971-62
401 U.S. 265, 28 L.Ed.2d 35, 91 S.Ct. 621 (1971)

(22) *Philadelphia Newspapers, Inc.* v. *Hepps*
Philadelphia Newspapers, Inc. v. *Maurice S. Hepps*,
Docket No. 84-1491
475 U.S. 767, 89 L.Ed.2d 783, 106 S.Ct. 1558 (1986)

(23) *Rosenblatt* v. *Baer*
Alfred D. Rosenblatt v. *Frank P. Baer*, Docket No. 1966-38
383 U.S. 75, 15 L.Ed.2d 597, 86 S.Ct. 669 (1966)

(24) *Rosenbloom* v. *Metromedia*
George A. Roosenbloom v. *Metromedia, Inc.*, Docket No. 1971-66
403 U.S. 29, 29 L.Ed.2d 296, 91 S.Ct. 1811 (1971)

(25) *St. Amant* v. *Thompson*
Phil A. St. Amant v. *Herman A. Thompson*, Docket No. 1968-517
390 U.S. 727, 20 L.Ed.2d 262, 88 S.Ct. 1323 (1968)

(26) *Time, Inc.* v. *Firestone*
Time, Inc. v. *Mary Alice Firestone*, Docket No. 74-944
424 U.S. 448, 47 L.Ed.2d 154, 96 S.Ct. 958 (1976)

(27) *Time* v. *Pape*
Time Incorporated v. *Frank Pape*, Docket No. 1971-109
401 U.S. 279, 28 L.Ed.2d 45, 91 S.Ct. 633 (1971)

(28) *Wolston* v. *Reader's Digest Assn., Inc.*
Ilya Wolston v. *Reader's Digest Association, Inc.*, Docket No. 78-5414
443 U.S. 157, 61 L.Ed.2d 450, 99 S.Ct. 2701 (1979)

CASES RELATED TO PRIVACY

(1) *Cantrell* v. *Forest City Pub. Co.*
Margaret Mae Cantrell v. *Forest City Publishing Co.*,
Docket No. 73-5520
419 U.S. 245, 42 L.Ed.2d. 419, 95 S.Ct. 465 (1974)

(2) *Cox Broadcasting Corp.* v. *Cohn*
Cox Broadcasting Corporation v. *Martin Cohn*, Docket No. 73-938
420 U.S. 469, 43 L.Ed.2d. 328, 95 S.Ct. 1029 (1975)

(3) *The Florida Star* v. *B.J.F.*
The Florida Star v. *B.J.F.*, Docket No. 87-329, 57 LW 4816
491 U.S. ---, 105 L.Ed.2d 443, 109 S.Ct. 2603 (1989)

(4) *Time* v. *Hill*
Time, Inc. v. *James J. Hill*, Docket No. 1967-22
385 U.S. 374, 17 L.Ed.2d. 456, 87 S.Ct. 534 (1967)

(5) *Zacchini* v. *Scripps-Howard Broadcasting Co.*
Hugo Zacchini v. *Scripps-Howard Broadcasting Company*,
Docket No. 76-577
433 U.S. 562, 53 L.Ed.2d. 965, 97 S.Ct. 2849 (1977)

CASES RELATED TO FIRST AMENDMENT ISSUES

(1) *Abrams* v. *United States*
Jacob Abrams v. *United States*, Docket No. 1919-316
250 U.S. 616, 63 L.Ed. 1173, 40 S.Ct. 17 (1919)

(2) *Brandenburg* v. *Ohio*
Clarence Brandenburg v. *State of Ohio*, Docket No. 1969-492
395 U.S. 444, 23 L.Ed.2d 430, 89 S.Ct. 1827 (1969)

(3) *Chaplinsky* v. *New Hampshire*
Walter Chaplinsky v. *State of New Hampshire*, Docket No. 1942-255
315 U.S. 568, 86 L.Ed. 1031, 62 S.Ct. 766 (1942)

(4) *Dennis* v. *United States*
Eugene Dennis, *John B. Williamson*, *Jacob A. Stachel*,
Robert G. Thompson, *Benjamin J. Daves, Jr.*, *Henry Winston*, *John Gates*,
Irving Potash, *Gilbert Green*, *Carl Winter*, and *Gus Hall* v. *United States*,
Docket No. 1951-336
341 U.S. 494, 95 L.Ed. 1137, 71 S.Ct. 857 (1951)

(5) *Gitlow* v. *New York*
Benjamin Gitlow v. *People of the State of New York*,
Docket No. 1925-19
268 U.S. 652, 69 L.Ed. 1138, 45 S.Ct. 625 (1925)

(6) *Hazelwood School Dist.* v. *Kuhlmeier*
Hazelwood School District v. *Cathy Kuhlmeier*, Docket No. 86-836
484 U.S. ---, 98 L.Ed.2d 592, 108 S.Ct. 562 (1988)

(7) *Near* v. *Minnesota Ex Rel. Olson*
J. M. Near v. *State of Minnesota Ex Rel. Floyd B. Olson*,
Docket No. 1931-91; 283 U.S. 697, 75 L.Ed. 1357, 51 S.Ct. 625 (1931)

(8) *Schenck* v. *United States*
Charles T. Schenck v. *United States of America*, Docket No. 437 and
Elizabeth Baer v. *United States of America*, Docket No. 438
249 U.S. 47, 63 L.Ed. 470, 39 S.Ct. 247 (1919)

(9) *Texas* v. *Johnson*
Texas v. *Gregory Lee Johnson*, Docket No. 88-155; 57 LW 4770
491 U.S. ---, 105 L.Ed.2d 342, 109 S.Ct. 2533 (1989)

(10) *Whitney* v. *California*
Charlotte Anita Whitney v. *People of the State of California*,
Docket No. 1927-03
274 U.S. 357, 71 L.Ed. 1095, 47 S.Ct. 641 (1927)

(11) *Yates* v. *United States*
Oleta O'Connor Yates, Henry Steinberg, Loretta Starvus Stack v.
United States of America Docket No. 1957-06 and
William Schneiderman v. *United States of America*,
Docket No. 1957-07 and
Al Richmond and *Philip Marshall Connelly* v. *United States of America*,
Docket No. 1957-08
354 U.S. 298, 1 L.Ed.2d 1356, 77 S.Ct. 1064 (1957)

CASES RELATED TO LIBEL

New York Times Co. v. Sullivan

New York Times Company v. L. B. Sullivan
Docket No. 1964-39

Ralph D. Abernathy v. L. B. Sullivan
Docket No. 1964-40

376 U.S. 254, 11 L.Ed.2d 686, 84 S.Ct. 710 (1964)
Argued January 6, 1964. Decided March 9, 1964.

BACKGROUND

In many ways this case is as much about the civil rights movement of the late 1950s and the 1960s as it is about libel. The main tactic used by blacks to oppose racial discrimination at the time that L. B. Sullivan, a commissioner for Montgomery County, filed his suit was nonviolent civil disobedience. This tactic is the subject of five books by the Rev. Dr. Martin Luther King. It is based on the thoughts of Henry David Thoreau and the nonviolent social action practiced by Mohandas Karamchand (Mahatma) Gandhi in South Africa from 1893 to 1915 in opposition to racial discrimination there and later in India as part of the struggle to win independence from Britain.

Aided in part by the Rev. Ralph D. Abernathy, King began his civil rights crusades in 1955 when he led a boycott of the buses in Montgomery, Alabama, to protest the requirement that Blacks must sit in the back of the city buses. Two years later, King, Abernathy, and other black citizens founded the Southern Christian Leadership Conference (SCLC). King was named the first president. After he was murdered in April 1968, Abernathy became president.

Few persons today would argue against the proposition that Commissioner Sullivan's real purpose in filing the lawsuit was to punish the *New York Times* (as an "outside agitator") for its role in calling the attention of the rest of the United States to race relations in Alabama. Indeed, by the time this case reached the U.S. Supreme Court, 11 libel actions had been filed against the *Times*, seeking a total of $5,600,000.

CIRCUMSTANCES

Until this case, libel law was pretty much a local matter governed by individual state laws. Then an advertisement entitled "Heed Their Rising Voices" was published in the March 29, 1960 edition of the *New York*

Times. Among other things, the advertisement described the police response to black students demonstrating at Alabama State College against segregation. Although six years had passed since the Supreme Court declared segregated public schools unlawful, not one black student was enrolled in another public college or university in Alabama.

Included in the list of 20 persons whose names appeared at the bottom of the advertisement as "endorsers" were four black clergymen: Ralph D. Abernathy, Fred L. Shuttlesworth, S. S. Seay, Sr., and J. E. Lowery. Sullivan filed a libel suit against the *Times* and the four clergymen, claiming that the advertisement's charges of police misbehavior reflected adversely on him in his capacity as the county commissioner who supervised the fire and police forces.

Among other things, Sullivan objected to these words from the advertisement:

> [The students] were expelled from the school, and truckloads of police armed with shotguns and tear-gas ringed the Alabama State College Campus. When the entire student body protested to state authorities by refusing to re-register, their dining hall was padlocked in an attempt to starve them into submission. (257)

Judge Walter Burgwyn Jones, who had earlier published a leaflet entitled "The Confederate Creed," presided over the trial. He allowed some jurors to take their seats wearing Confederate uniforms, and seating in the courtroom was segregated.

In Judge Jones's charge to the members of the jury, he told them that the advertisement was libel *per se* (on the face of it), and that, to find in favor of Sullivan, the jury had only to be satisfied that the statements in the advertisement did indeed refer to the commissioner. The jury gave Sullivan everything he asked for-$500,000, the largest libel judgment in Alabama's history. The four clergymen were also held responsible even though their names had been used without permission. Jones ordered the cars and other property of the four be attached to help pay damages.

The Supreme Court of Alabama upheld the judgment.

SUMMARY OF THE COURT'S ANALYSIS

Justice William J. Brennan, Jr., writes for the Court.
Chief Justice Earl Warren and Justices Tom C. Clark, John M. Harlan, Potter Stewart, and Byron R. White join.

In delivering the opinion for the Court, Brennan asserts that the Fourteenth Amendment applies the First to all forms of state actions. He says the fact that this lawsuit is based on a dispute between private parties is not important. The relevant issue here is that the authority of state law in some form is being exercised.

Next, Justice Brennan admits there were errors in the advertisement. He notes, for example, "The campus dining hall was not padlocked . . . . Although the police were deployed in large numbers on three occasions, they did not at any time 'ring' the campus" (259). In addition, Brennan points out that the *Times* received the advertisement from a well-known advertising agency and that A. Philip Randolph, chairman of the advertisement's signatory committee, was known to the advertisement department of the *Times* as a responsible person. In short, even though no one checked the accuracy of the advertisement, the newspaper followed its standard practice.

One of the first points the Court makes is that the document in question is an "editorial," not a "commercial," advertisement because it "communicated information, expressed opinion, recited grievances, protested claimed abuses, and sought financial support on behalf of a movement whose existence and objectives are matters of the highest public interest and concern" (266). Consequently, Brennan asserts, as an "editorial advertisement" (266), the information is entitled to First Amendment protection.

The next question for the Court is "whether it [the advertisement] forfeits that protection by the falsity of some of its factual statements and by its alleged defamation of respondent [Sullivan]" (271). In approaching the idea of false information, Brennan revives some famous words from an earlier case [*NAACP* v. *Button*, 371 U.S. 415, 9 L.Ed.2d 405, 83 S.Ct. 328 (1963)] when he writes, "Erroneous statement is inevitable in free debate, and . . . it must be protected if the freedoms of expression are to have the 'breathing space' that they need . . . to survive" (271, 272).

Another question is whether or not the advertisement loses its constitutional protection because it defames a public official. To this notion Brennan responds, "Criticism of their [public officials'] official conduct does not lose its constitutional protection merely because it is effective criticism and hence diminishes their official reputation" (273).

Should there be a requirement, then, that criticism of public officials at the least must be true? To avoid any doubt, Brennan reaffirms the Court's answer:

> A rule compelling the critic of official conduct to guarantee the truth of all his factual assertions--and to do so on pain of libel judgements virtually unlimited in amount--leads to a comparable "self-censorship." (279) Under such a rule, would-be critics of official conduct may be deterred from voicing their criticism, even though it is believed to be true and even though it is in fact true, because of doubt whether it can be proved in court or fear of the expenses of having to do so. (279)

Having cleared up these two issues, Brennan goes on to state the most famous words in modern libel litigation:

> The constitutional guarantees require, we think, a federal rule that prohibits a public official from recovering damages for a defamatory falsehood relating to his official conduct unless he proves that the statement was made with "actual malice"-that is, with knowledge that it was false or with reckless disregard of whether it was false or not. (279, 280)

This new "federal rule" of "actual malice" has since come to be known by a variety of names: Among them are the *New York Times* test or rule, the Sullivan test or rule, and the *New York Times* privilege. Brennan takes care to point out here that the Court did not make up this rule or privilege in order to decide this particular case, but that such a rule already existed in some state courts. A Kansas judge, he notes, for example, instructed a jury in a libel case involving a public official with these words:

> Where an article is published . . . for the sole purpose of giving what the defendant believes to be truthful information concerning a candidate for public office . . . the article is privileged, although the principle matters contained in the article may be untrue in fact and derogatory to the character of the plaintiff; and in such a case the burden is on the plaintiff to show actual malice in the publication of the article. (280, 281)

The privilege spoken of here is the constitutional right to publish false defamatory statements criticizing the official actions of public officials as long as the writer believes the statements to be truthful or does not hold a reckless disregard of their truth. Writes Brennan, "We conclude that such a privilege is required by the First and Fourteenth Amendments" (283).

As part of its analysis, the Court takes a fateful action, one that is repeated continually in reviews of later libel cases. Brennan introduces the Court's important step this way:

> Since respondent [Sullivan] may seek a new trial, we deem that considerations of effective judicial administration require us to review the evidence in the present record to determine whether it could constitutionally support a judgement for respondent [Sullivan]. This Court's duty is not limited to the elaboration of constitutional principles; we must also in proper cases review the evidence to make certain that those principles have been constitutionally applied. (284, 285)

In short, the Court asserts that, whenever necessary, it will review the evidence in each case to determine if the speech involved was granted proper constitutional protection. This very process of reviewing the evidence itself became an issue in a later libel case. (See *Anderson* v. *Liberty Lobby*, 1986.)

Nor should the Court's response to its review of the evidence be overlooked. Brennan writes, "We consider that the proof presented to show actual malice lacks the convincing clarity which the constitutional standard demands" (285, 286). The words "convincing clarity" were used often by the Court in later decisions as the standard of evidence needed to show actual malice. The normal civil standard of proof--preponderance of evidence--in effect is replaced here by a standard of convincing clarity.

In the Court's analysis of damages, Brennan eventually focuses on the requirements to demonstrate what is the "fault" of the *Times* for printing false statements. Almost in passing he points out a "state-of-mind" requirement that eventually becomes very important in libel cases. He writes:

> The mere presence of the [accurate] stories [that could have corrected the errors of the advertisement] in the files [of the Times] does not, of course, establish that the Times "knew" the advertisement was false, since the state of mind required for actual malice would have to be brought to the persons in the Times' organization having responsibility for the publication of the advertisement. (287)

In later libel cases, persons bringing suit did indeed attempt to show the "state of mind" of "the persons . . . having responsibility for the publication." (See *Herbert* v. *Lando*, 1979.)

The Court's characterization of the fault as more than negligence has equally important implications. Brennan writes, "We think the evidence against the Times supports at most a finding of negligence in failing to discover the misstatements, and is constitutionally insufficient to show the recklessness that is required for a finding of actual malice" (287, 288).

Over time negligence is contrasted with "actual malice" in libel and privacy cases when the Court attempts to define the level of fault needed to support various forms of damage. (See especially *Gertz* v. *Welch*, 1974.)

Moreover, the Court would eventually focus rather sharply on the standard set forth in this case that evidence of actual malice must be presented with "convincing clarity." This "convincing clarity" standard is used here by the Court to dismiss libel charges against the four black clergymen. Brennan says this of the four:

> Even assuming that they could constitutionally be found to have authorized the use of their names on the advertisements, there was no evidence whatever that they were aware of any erroneous statements or were in any way reckless in that regard. The judgment against them is thus without constitutional support. (286)

In ruling that the statements about the actions of the police did not refer to Sullivan, the Court raises another important issue. Brennan points out that converting criticism of the police into personal criticism of a public official, like Sullivan, wrongly changes criticism of public actions into personal libel. He writes, "We hold that such a proposition may not constitutionally be utilized to establish that an otherwise impersonal attack on government operations was a libel of an official responsible for those operations" (292). The Court says here that public officials cannot claim that criticism of their official actions constitutes personal criticism of them as a private person. This analogy to seditious libel (libel of the government) is cited by the Court in *Curtis Publishing Co. v Butts*, 1967, to be one very important basis for establishing the actual malice rule.

RULING

Brennan writes:

> We hold that the rule of law applied by the Alabama Courts is constitutionally deficient for failure to provide safeguards for freedom of speech and of the press that are required by the First and Fourteenth Amendments in a libel action brought by a public official against critics of his official conduct. (264)
>
> The judgment of the Supreme Court of Alabama is reversed and the case is remanded to that court for further proceedings not inconsistent with this opinion. (292)
>
> Reversed and remanded. (292)

Justice Hugo L. Black writes a concurring opinion.
Justice William O. Douglas joins.

Black and Douglas believe that the constitution provides an "absolute, unconditional constitutional right"--not just a limited privilege--for publishing criticism of public officials. They do not feel that, in order to be protected by the First Amendment from libel actions filed by public officials, journalists should have to demonstrate in court that they believe their criticism of official conduct to be true.

Black writes, "I base my vote to reverse on the belief that the First and Fourteenth Amendments not merely 'delimit' a State's power to award damages to 'public officials against critics of their official conduct' but completely prohibit a State from exercising such a power" (293).

Black's next words have become famous because they correctly predicted that the "actual malice" protection has turned out not to be as strong as the Court thought it to be at this time. He writes, "The requirement that malice be proved provides at best an evanescent protection for the right critically to discuss public affairs and certainly does not measure up to the sturdy safeguard embodied in the First Amendment" (293). He adds, "In my opinion, the Federal Constitution . . . [grants] the press an absolute immunity for criticism of the way public officials do their public duty" (295). He continues, "These officials are responsible to the people for the way they perform their duties. To punish the exercise of this right to discuss public affairs or to penalize it through libel judgments is to abridge or shut off discussion of the very kind most needed" (297).

Justice Arthur J. Goldberg writes a concurring opinion.
Justice William O. Douglas joins.

Echoing Black, Goldberg asserts, "In my view, the First and Fourteenth Amendments . . . afford . . . the press an absolute, unconditional privilege to criticize official conduct despite the harm which may flow from excesses and abuses" (298). He adds, "If the rule that libel on government has no place in our Constitution is to have real meaning, then libel on the official conduct of the governors likewise can have no place in our Constitution" (299).

Departing from Black, though, Goldberg next takes care to point out a distinction between criticism of official conduct and criticism of private matters:

> This is not to say that the Constitution protects defamatory statements directed against the private conduct of a public official or private citizen. Purely private defamation has little to do with the political ends of a self-governing society. The imposition of liability for private defamation does not abridge the freedom of public speech. (301, 302)

Goldberg's distinction caused some mischief later, however, because public officials soon began to assert that defamatory statements about them were directed at their private, not their public, actions. On several occasions the Court overruled such assertions. (See, e.g., *Garrison* v. *Louisiana*, 1964; *Henry* v. *Collins*, 1965; and *Patriot Co*. v. *Roy*, 1971.)

Goldberg also notes that the absolute privilege he advocates "does not leave the public official without defenses against unsubstantiated opinions for deliberate misstatements" (304). He writes, quoting in part from *Wood* v. *Georgia* 370 U.S. 375, 8 L.Ed.2d 569, 82 S.Ct. 1364 (1862), "Counter argument and education are the weapons available to expose these matters (305). The public official certainly has equal if not greater access than most private citizens to media of communication" (305).

His statement about access to the media eventually becomes a central concept in libel litigation. Eventually, a distinction is drawn between public and private figures partly on the basis that public figures have "greater access" to the mass media and so have a better chance to present counter argument. (See especially *Curtis Publishing Co*. v. *Butts*, 1967.)

SIGNIFICANCE

This case is significant for a number of reasons, but clearly the most important is the limited privilege it created for printing criticism of the official conduct of public officials. This rule or privilege (which has several names, e.g., the *Times* test, but is most often referred to simply as "actual malice") asserts, in brief, that the First Amendment protects reporters (and presumably any other citizens who disseminate false defamatory statements) from libel actions based on criticism of official conduct of public officials, as long as the journalists believe what they print is true or do not hold a reckless disregard for its truth.

Since the privilege protects only criticism of public officials, this decision set off a long series of clarifications of what is a public official, a process that may never be finished. Attempts to develop clear definitions center on the elements that must be present to invoke the actual malice privilege. These elements reside in two basic concepts. One concept says that libel plaintiffs must overcome the actual malice privilege whenever circumstances giving rise to a libel case concern matters of public interest. The other says the test centers not on the public or private nature of the circumstances, but on the public or private nature of the persons defamed.

For the most part--*Rosenbloom* v. *Metromedia* (1971) is one notable exception--the Court uses some combination of the two: subject matter and nature of person defamed.

In addition, since the privilege requires knowing what reporters believe about the truth of their statements, this decision eventually results in attempts by lawyers to determine a journalist's state of mind. Indeed, some reporters today destroy their notes, on the theory (probably mistaken) that they are eliminating evidence that might someday be used against them in an application of the *Times* test.

The standards or levels of fault have also become issues as a result of this case. Lower courts have been forced to draw distinctions between those actions that constitute actual malice and those that constitute lesser forms of fault. The Court makes clear time and time again that "mere failure to investigate" may constitute negligence, but it does not constitute actual malice. The justices also continually assert in later cases that actual malice must be demonstrated with "clear and convincing" evidence. A mere preponderance of the evidence is insufficient. (See especially *Anderson* v. *Liberty Lobby*, 1986.)

Another area needing continual clarification is the official, in contrast to private, conduct of a public official. The Court said that converting criticism of the police into personal criticism of a public official, like Sullivan, wrongly changes criticism of public actions into a personal attack. Nevertheless, many times the Court was forced to reassert this position because public officials could not resist the temptation (encouraged in part by Goldberg's dissent) to convert criticism of their public duties into attacks on their private character.

Nor did libel plaintiffs find it easy to give up falsity as sufficient evidence to win damages. Time and time again, the Court would repeat its assertion in this case that, where criticism of the government is concerned, the First Amendment requires some false ideas to be protected in order to guarantee that the full truth is heard. The Court said that error is inevitable in any vigorous debate and so some error must be tolerated in public debates in order to avoid deterring attempts to express unpopular but truthful statements. Taking words from another case (*NAACP* v. *Button*, 1963) the court termed this concept of tolerating some falsity "breathing space."

One of the first and most commonly overlooked points the Court made in this case is that an "editorial advertisement" is entitled to First Amendment protection. This distinction between commercial and editorial advertisements was one of a series of steps that expand First Amendment protection to various forms of "commercial speech." (See especially *Dun & Bradstreet* v. *Greenmoss Builders*, 1985.)

Anderson v. Liberty Lobby

Jack Anderson
v.
Liberty Lobby, Inc. and Willis A. Carto

Docket No. 84-1602
477 U.S. 242, 91 L.Ed.2d 202, 106 S.Ct. 2505 (1986)
Argued December 3, 1985. Decided June 25, 1986.

BACKGROUND

When the *Sullivan* decision was first announced, many journalists felt that eventually it would reduce the economic burden of defending libel suits by allowing an increasing number of these suits to be dismissed in summary judgment before trial. These journalists thought that it would be extremely difficult for public officials to prove actual malice. Consequently, judges, they reasoned, would throw out most suits on the basis that the defamed persons plainly could not prove the defamation was published with knowing falsity or with reckless disregard for the truth.

As time passed, however, attorneys became expert at showing actual malice even to the point of probing a journalist's state of mind (cf. *Herbert v Lando*, 1979). Thus, over the years fewer and fewer cases were thrown out in summary judgment. One result of this phenomenon was an inevitable sharpening of the tactics used to defend and attack motions for summary judgment.

When such a motion in this case was dismissed on grounds much different from those used previously by most other courts, however, the Court granted *certiori*. This particular appeals court caught the attention of the Court when it ruled that the *Sullivan* requirement of showing actual malice with clear and convincing evidence did not have to be addressed at a hearing for a summary judgment motion.

The question raised by the appeals court and addressed here by the Court itself is a highly technical question of law, demonstrating how sophisticated post-*Sullivan* libel litigation had become by 1986. Essentially, the Court faced the question of whether or not the *Sullivan* requirement of clear and convincing evidence needed to demonstrate actual malice also applied to Rule 56 of the *Federal Rules of Civil Procedures*, which said a summary judgement must be granted if "there is no genuine issue as to any material fact." In other words, the question is this: Do persons opposing a summary judgment have to show with "clear and convincing clarity" that a genuine issue does indeed exist?

CIRCUMSTANCES

A magazine published by Jack Anderson, called the *Investigator*, printed three articles in October 1981 that "portrayed" Willis A. Carto and his Liberty Lobby as "neo-Nazi, anti-Semitic, racist, and fascist" (245). Carto sued, claiming "that some 28 statements and 2 illustrations in the three articles were false and defamatory" (245). In addition to Anderson, he named "Bill Adkins, president and chief executive officer of the Investigator Publishing Co., and . . . Investigator Publishing Co, itself" as defendants (245).

After the discovery process was complete, Anderson asked for dismissal of the case in summary judgment, basing his request on Rule 56 of the *Federal Rules of Civil Procedure*. This rule says that summary judgment "'shall be rendered forthwith if the pleadings, depositions, answers to interrogatories, and admissions on file, together with the affidavits, if any, show that there is no genuine issue as to any material fact and that the moving party is entitled to a judgment as a matter of law" (247).

Part (e) of Rule 56 says that a party opposing a motion for summary judgment "'may not rest upon the mere allegations of denials of his pleading, but . . . must set forth specific facts showing that there is a genuine issue for trial'" (248). In other words, in order to show that there is a genuine dispute, and not just an unsubstantiated claim that a true dispute exists, the persons who want a trial must present "specific" and "material facts" to show evidence that the dispute in fact is genuine.

Part (c) says that a "material fact" does not have to be "'resolved conclusively in favor of the party asserting its existence; rather, all that is required is that sufficient evidence supporting the claimed factual dispute be shown'" (249). That is to say, in order to adequately support an attempt to force a trial, persons need present only sufficient evidence; they do not have to show "conclusively" that a dispute about a particular fact does indeed exist.

Anderson claimed that, since the articles were not printed with actual malice, there was no reason to try the case. He based his conviction upon an affidavit by Charles Bermant, the author of the two longer articles, in which Bermant said "he had spent a substantial amount of time researching and writing the articles . . . . He also stated that he had at all times believed and still believed that the facts contained in the articles were truthful and accurate" (245).

Carto claimed that the articles were in fact printed with actual malice because "Bermant had relied on several sources that respondents [Liberty Lobby and Carto] asserted were patently unreliable" (246). In general, the lobby and Carto asserted that Anderson and Bermant's failure "adequately to verify their information before publishing" (246) constituted actual malice because it showed reckless disregard for the truth.

The United States District Court for the District of Columbia ruled that, since Bermant had thoroughly researched his material and had relied on numerous sources, it would be impossible for Carto to prove actual malice. The court therefore entered the motion for summary judgment and dismissed the case.

Later, the United States Court of Appeals for the District of Columbia Circuit ruled that it was not necessary for Carto to prove actual malice by clear and convincing evidence (rather than by just a preponderance of evidence) in order to defeat the motion for a summary judgment. This court said the lower requirement of a preponderance of evidence "'would change the threshold summary judgment inquiry from a search for a minimum of facts supporting the plaintiff's case to an evaluation of the weight of those facts'" (LW 247).

SUMMARY OF THE COURT'S ANALYSIS

Justice Byron R. White writes for the Court.
Justices Thrugood Marshall, Harry A. Blackmun, Lewis F. Powell, Jr., John Paul Stevens, and Sandra Day O'Connor join.

Justice White begins his analysis with a statement describing the issue at hand. He writes, "Our inquiry is whether the Court of Appeals erred in holding that the heightened evidentiary requirements that apply to proof of actual malice in this *New York Times* case need not be considered for the purposes of a motion for summary judgment" (247). White points out that the critical words in the rule are "the requirement . . . that there be no *genuine* issue of *material* [White's emphasis] fact" (248). The question, then, is this: Does the requirement of "no genuine issue of material fact" mean that evidence of actual malice has to be shown in order to defeat a motion for summary judgment.

Whether or not the facts are material, White says, will be determined by the relevant "substantive law." He writes, "Only disputes over facts that might affect the outcome of the suit under the governing law will properly preclude the entry of summary judgment" (248). More important, however, is the requirement that the dispute about a material fact be "genuine," which White defines this way: "If the evidence is such that a reasonable jury could return a verdict for the nonmoving party" (248).

White then begins a review of previous cases related to summary judgment motions. From the review he concludes, "It is clear enough from our recent cases that at the summary judgment stage the judge's function is not himself to weigh the evidence and determine whether there is a genuine issue for trial" (248). Instead, White explains, "There is no issue for trial unless there is sufficient evidence favoring the nonmoving party for a jury to return a verdict for that party" (249). If the evidence is only "colorable," that is, if it is inconclusive, if it does not clearly support the claim that a dispute exists, then White says, "summary judgment may be granted" (249, 250).

White sums up his analysis this way:

> The inquiry performed [by the trial judge] is the threshold inquiry of determining whether there is the need for a trial--whether, in other words, there are any genuine factual issues that properly can be resolved only by a finder of fact because

> they may reasonably be resolved in favor of either party. (250)

In short, to support a request for holding a trial and to defeat a summary judgment dismissing the case, persons must convince the trial judge that a jury reasonably could decide the case either way. If the judge feels that a jury could decide only one way and that way is against those persons who want a trial, then the case must be dismissed in summary judgment.

White then compares the standard for summary judgment to the standard found in Rule 50(a) for a directed verdict. Both standards, he points out, consider whether "under the governing law, there can be but one reasonable conclusion as to the verdict" (250). "'The primary difference between the two motions,'" he continues by quoting from *Bill Johnson's Restaurants, Inc.* v. *NLRB* 461 U.S. 731 (1983), "'is procedural; summary judgment motions are usually made before trial and decided on documentary evidence, while directed verdict motions are made at trial and decided on the evidence that has been admitted'" (251). He concludes, "In essence, though, the inquiry under each is the same, whether the evidence presents a sufficient disagreement to require submission to a jury or whether it is so one-sided that one party must prevail as a matter of law" (251-252).

The next topic White addresses is the "specific issue" in this case: convincing clarity. He notes previous cases have required that actual malice must be shown with convincing clarity. As a result, he writes, "Just as the 'convincing clarity' requirement is relevant in ruling on a motion for directed verdict, it is relevant in ruling on a motion for summary judgment" (254). He then adds these words hotly disputed in Brennan's dissenting opinion, "A trial judge must bear in mind the actual quantum and quality of proof necessary to support liability under *New York Times*" (254).

In order to determine that the evidence favors one side so clearly that a reasonable jury could vote only against the party bringing the suit to court, White says, there must be a "benchmark." In libel cases, he suggests the "clear-and-convincing standard of proof" (255) is that benchmark. He explains:

> Thus, where the factual dispute concerns actual malice, clearly a material issue in a *New York Times* case, the appropriate summary question will be whether the evidence in the record could support a reasonable jury finding either that the plaintiff has shown actual malice by clear and convincing evidence or that the plaintiff has not. (255, 256)

White then takes up Carto's argument that summary judgment could seldom, if ever, be granted when "state of mind is at issue and the jury might disbelieve him [defendant who published a defamatory statement] or his witnesses as to this issue" (256). White says that Carto, in effect, is asking a judge to "return a verdict in his favor . . . by merely asserting that the jury might, and legally could, disbelieve the defendant's denial of . . . legal malice" (256). This argument is unacceptable, White says, because Rule 56 "provides that a party opposing a properly supported motion for summary judgment may not rest upon mere allegation or denials of his pleading, but must set forth specific facts showing that there is a genuine issue for trial" (256). In short, White says its takes "affirmative evidence," (257) not just a denial, to defeat a motion for summary judgment.

RULING

White writes:

> In sum, a court ruling on a motion for summary judgment must be guided by the New York Times "clear and convincing" evidence standard in determining whether a genuine issue of actual malice exists--that is, whether the evidence presented is such that a reasonable jury might find that actual malice had been shown with convincing clarity. Because the Court of Appeals did not apply the correct standard in reviewing the District Court's grant of summary judgment, we vacate its decision and remand the case for further proceedings consistent with this opinion. (257)

Justice William J. Brennan, Jr., writes a dissenting opinion.

Brennan pulls no punches in his dissent. He writes, "In my view, the Court's analysis is deeply flawed, and rests on a shaky foundation of unconnected and unsupported observations, assertions and conclusions" (257, 268). Brennan feels the Court departed from previous rulings on summary judgment and broke new ground with the assertion that a "'genuine' dispute is one which is not 'one-sided,' and one which could 'reasonably' be resolved by a 'fair-minded' jury in favor of either party" (259).

For Brennan, previous court rulings say "a jury could *infer* [Brennan's emphasis]" (260) from the evidence. He writes, "The question . . . was simply whether, as a matter of . . . law, a jury would be entitled, again as a matter of law, to infer" (263). These rulings, he writes, "Suggest that on a defendant's motion for summary judgment, a trial court must consider whether . . . a jury will be permitted to draw inferences supporting the plaintiff's legal theory" (264).

The problem with the Court's decision, for Brennan, is that "while instructing the trial judge to 'consider' heightened evidentiary standards, [it] fails to explain what that means. In other words, how does a judge assess how one-sided evidence is, or what a 'fair-minded' jury could 'reasonably' decide" (265)? In particular, Brennan is worried that a requirement calling for a judge to consider the "quantum" and the "'caliber or quality' to meet that 'quantum'" of proof will "transform what is meant to provide an expedited 'summary' procedure into a full blown paper trial on the merits" (266, 267).

He concludes:

> In my view, if a plaintiff presents evidence which either directly or by permissible inference . . . supports all of the elements he needs to prove in order to prevail on his legal

> claim, the plaintiff has made out a prima facie case and a defendant's motion for summary judgment must fail regardless of the burden of proof that the plaintiff must meet. (268)

The Court's decision, he fears, "may erode the constitutionally enshrined role of the jury, and also undermine the usefulness of summary judgment procedure" (268).

Justice William H. Rehnquist writes a dissenting opinion.
Chief Justice Warren E. Burger joins.

Rehnquist begins his dissent by asserting, "The Court . . . mistakenly decides that the 'clear and convincing evidence' standard governing finders of fact in libel cases must be applied by trial courts in deciding a motion for summary judgment in such a case" (268). He writes, "The Court has created a standard that is different from the standard traditionally applied in summary judgment motions without even hinting as to how its new standard will be applied to particular cases" (273).

Rehnquist sets up a hypothetical situation to determine if the Court's ruling would have any effect on the entering of summary judgments. From this hypothethical case, he decides that there would be little effect on cases turning on the credibility of witnesses because "credibility is exclusively for the jury" to decide (270). Nor would the Court's decision affect cases based primarily on documentary evidence because "inferences from documentary evidence" also are to be drawn by a jury (271). He concludes that the "differentiated burdens of proof" (beyond a reasonable doubt, preponderance of evidence, and clear and convincing evidence) "vague and impressionistic though they necessarily are, probably do make some difference when considered by the finder of fact, whether it be a jury or a judge in a bench trial" (272).

Nevertheless, he views the Court's action as grafting "the standard of proof applicable to a factfinder onto the law governing the procedural motion for a summary judgment," and he feels it "will do great mischief with little corresponding benefit" (272). He writes, "The primary effect of the Court's opinion today will likely be to cause the decisions of trial judges on summary judgment motions in libel cases to be more erratic and inconsistent than before" (272, 273).

SIGNIFICANCE

The setting up of a high standard of evidence (actual malice) to defeat a motion for summary judgment in a libel case involving public officials or public figures constitutes the significance of this case. The Court says that, to defeat such a motion, one must demonstrate that a reasonable jury could find there is clear and convincing evidence that false defamatory statements were published with knowledge of their falsehood or with reckless disregard for truth.

In effect, the Court established for libel cases special standards of evidence to meet the requirements of Rule 56 of the *Federal Rules of Civil*

Procedure. It said, first, that actual malice is a material fact (that is, a relevant issue) that must be considered when evaluating a motion for summary judgment. Secondly, it said that a genuine dispute about actual malice must exist in order to defeat the motion. To support the assertion of a genuine dispute, and so to force a trial, one must show that a reasonable jury would find there is clear and convincing evidence of actual malice.

Ashton v. Kentucky

Steve Ashton
v.
Kentucky

Docket No. 1966-619
384 U.S. 195, 16 L.Ed.2d 469, 86 S.Ct. 1407 (1966)
Argued April 28, 1966. Decided May 16, 1966.

BACKGROUND

This case is extremely unusual because, even though it was reviewed after *Sullivan*, the Court did not refer to the actual malice rule. Instead, it focused attention on the unacceptable broadness and vagueness of common law criminal libel.

CIRCUMSTANCES

Steve Ashton "went to Hazard, Kentucky, in 1963, where a bitter labor dispute raged, to appeal for food, clothing and aid for unemployed minors" (196). He circulated there a pamphlet in which he criticized the Hazard chief of police, the sheriff, and a coowner of the Hazard *Herald*. Among other things, he wrote the following:

> Then for a few thousand dollars Combs [the sheriff] probably bought off the jury. (197) Yet he is still the law in this county and has the support of the rich man because he will fight the pickets and the strike. The same is true of the State Police. They escort the scabs into the mines and hold the pickets at gunpoint. (197)

Ashton was later convicted of the common-law offense of criminal libel, defined by the trial judge "'as any writing calculated to create disturbances of the peace, corrupt the public morals, or lead to any act, which, when done, is indictable'" (198). The appeals court threw out the breach of peace aspect as an unconstitutional basis for criminal libel. It defined common-law criminal libel as "'the publication of a defamatory statement about another which is false, with malice'" (198).

SUMMARY OF THE COURT'S ANALYSIS

Justice William O. Douglas writes for the Court.
Chief Justice Earl Warren and Justices Tom C. Clark, Potter Stewart, Byron O. White, William J. Brennan, Jr., Hugo L. Black, John M. Harlan, and Abe Fortas join.

Agreeing with the appeals court and quoting from *Free Speech in the United States* by Chaffee, Justice Douglas says punishing a person for publishing a statement that threatens to breach the peace "'makes a man a criminal simply because his neighbors have no self-control and cannot refrain from violence'" (200).

The conviction must be overturned in the main, according to Douglas, simply because the law is nebulous and overly broad. He writes, "Since no Kentucky case had redefined the crime [British common-law criminal libel] in understandable terms, . . . the elements of the crime are so indefinite and uncertain that it could not be enforced as a penal offense in Kentucky" (198). He continues, "Vague laws in any area suffer a constitutional infirmity" (200).

Although Douglas said the appeals court ruling did constitutionally narrow down the trial judge's definition of criminal libel, the Court reverses the conviction anyway because of a ruling in *Shuttlesworth* v. *Birmingham* 382 U.S. 87, 15 L.Ed.2d 176, 86 S.Ct. 211 (1965). (Shuttlesworth, it is interesting to note, was one of the four black clergymen accused of libel by Sullivan.) In that case, the Court indicated that an appeals court cannot properly narrow down a broad unconstitutional ruling by taking out everything but the constitutional aspects. He writes, "Where an accused is tried and convicted under a broad construction of an Act which would make it unconstitutional, the conviction cannot be sustained on appeal by a limiting construction which eliminates the unconstitutional features of the Act, as the trial took place under the unconstitutional construction of the Act" (198). In short, a judge cannot make constitutional a too-broad unconstitutional law simply by interpreting it narrowly and properly within the confines of the constitution.

RULING

Douglas writes succinctly, "Reversed" (201).

SIGNIFICANCE

The Court relates this case more closely to two earlier ones [*Edwards* v. *South Carolina* 379 U.S. 536, 13 L.Ed.2d 471, 85 S.Ct. 453 (1965) and *Cox* v. *Louisiana* 372 U.S. 229, 9 L.Ed.2d 697, 83 S.Ct. 680 (1963)] focusing on a breach-of-peace conviction than it does to other libel cases. In these three, the Court directs attention to the wrongful broadness of a particular law. Like all laws, those defining libel, it would seem, must be drawn precisely and narrowly.

Beckley Newspapers Corp. v. Hanks

Beckley Newspapers Corporation
v.
C. Harold Hanks

Docket No. 1967-467
389 U.S. 81, 19 L.Ed.2d 248, 88 S.Ct. 197 (1967)
Decided November 6, 1987.

BACKGROUND

This case illustrates very nicely the reluctance of lawyers and judges to change their thinking about matters that have been relatively constant for decades, centuries, or even millennia. The notion of malice as "ill will" has been around at least since Solomon. When in 1964 the Court redefined malice to mean the publishing of a known defamatory falsehood or a reckless disregard of truth, much of the legal establishment was slow to accept this new concept. The Court seems to feel no need in this case to break new ground; instead it reaffirms the distinctive characteristics of the rather unorthodox actual malice test or rule first announced in *Sullivan*.

CIRCUMSTANCES

Three 1962 editorials in the Beckley *Post-Herald* criticized the official conduct of C. Harold Hanks, the elected Clerk of the Criminal and Circuit Courts of Raleigh County, West Virginia. Ultimately, the Court said only part of one sentence in one editorial could be considered libelous because it could have been read to suggest that Hanks put pressure on a woman to support his position on fluoridation of water supplies. This editorial reads in part as follows:

> The only conclusion to which we can come is that either Hanks and Mrs. [Elinor] Hurt have been in league toward the fanatic end, believing all the wild-eyed ravings against fluoridation despite decades of experience to disprove them, or that *perhaps his blustering threats were able to intimidate the lady* [emphasis added by the Court]. (83, 84)

Hanks, a public official, sued and was awarded $5,000 in damages by a jury even though the trial took place after the *Sullivan* case was decided. The supreme court of West Virginia refused to hear an appeal.

SUMMARY OF THE COURT'S ANALYSIS

In a *per curiam* (by the court) decision, the Court notes the only evidence Hanks presents to support a claim that the editorial was published with a reckless disregard for the truth is an admission by the president and general manager of Beckley Newspapers Corporation that the paper did not undertake a specific investigation to determine if Hanks threatened Mrs. Hurt.

In addition, the Court takes note of the fact that the trial judge said the jury could award Hanks damages "if it were shown that petitioner [the newspaper] had published the editorials 'with bad or corrupt motive,' or 'from personal spite, ill will or a desire to injure plaintiff [Hanks]'" (82). Although the Court said the instructions were "clearly impermissible" and "inadequate," it nevertheless rules the issue of instructions moot because the attorneys for the newspaper not only "failed to object to this erroneous interpretation," but also "offered instructions which were themselves inadequate" (82).

The newspaper's failure to investigate the charges, according to the Court, falls far short of the "'high degree of awareness of . . . probable falsity demanded by New York Times'" (85). The opinion reads, "It cannot be said on this record that any failure of petitioner [the newspaper] to make a prior investigation constituted proof sufficient to present a jury question whether the statements were published with reckless disregard of whether they were false or not" (84, 85).

RULING

The ruling is succinct: "The judgment is reversed, and the case remanded to the Circuit Court of West Virginia, Wyoming County, for further proceedings not inconsistent with this opinion" (85).

SIGNIFICANCE

Perhaps the greatest significance of this case is that it demonstrated to the legal world that the Court was going to stand by its new, if a bit unorthodox, rule of actual malice. In particular, two aspects of this rule should be recognized as holding vital importance. First, actual malice does not mean "ill will," but the publishing of a known defamatory falsehood or a reckless disregard of its truth. Secondly, reckless disregard of the truth of a defamatory statement means more than simply a failure to investigate the truth of what is printed. It means, as the Court first ruled in *Garrison* v. *Louisiana* (1964), a "high degree of awareness" that the statement is false.

Bose Corp. v. Consumers Union of U.S., Inc.

Bose Corporation
v.
Consumers Union of United States, Inc.

Docket No. 82-1246
466 U.S. 485, 80 L.Ed.2d 502, 104 S.Ct. 1949 (1984)
Argued November 8, 1983. Decided April 30, 1984.

BACKGROUND

Twenty years after *Sullivan*, attorneys had become expert at trying to show that journalists either knew a statement was false or had a reckless disregard for the truth. In this case, the thought processes of an engineer were used by attorneys and judges alike to show that an engineer knew a statement was false when he wrote it.

Perhaps because the notion of what actions constitute actual malice was fairly well settled by 1984, libel suits at this time began to include a focus on other issues. In this case, the other important issue is a highly technical one: Rule 52(a) of the *Federal Rules of Civil Procedure*. This rule asserts that trial judges, not appeals courts, determine facts in a case. Appellate courts are not to challenge these rulings of fact unless they are "clearly erroneous."

The rule reads this way, "Findings of fact shall not be set aside [by appeals courts] unless clearly erroneous, and due regard shall be give to the opportunity of the trial court to judge the credibility of the witnesses" (498). The *Sullivan* case, however, said the appeals courts could make an independent survey of the evidence to make sure that the defamatory statements did or did not deserve First Amendment protection. These two procedures came into conflict here when the appeals court, after an independent review of the evidence, overruled the lower court decision by refusing to apply what the trial judge determined was a fact.

CIRCUMSTANCES

Consumer Reports magazine reviewed in May 1970 "numerous brands of medium-priced loudspeakers" (487). Among the speakers was the Bose 901, which was based on a new and unusual design. The article said this about the Bose 901: "Worse, individual instruments heard through the Bose system seemed to grow to gigantic proportions and tended to wander about the room. For instance, a violin appeared to be 10 feet wide and a piano stretched from wall to wall" (488). When a request by Bose for a retraction was refused, the company sued the magazine for libel.

The district court said that Bose is a public figure, but "on three critical points . . . [it] agreed" with the company (490). It said, first, that the sentence relating the "tendency of the instruments to wander" "contained a 'false' statement of 'fact'" (490). Secondly, "it found that the statement was disparaging" (490, 491). Thirdly, it said the statement was published with actual malice.

Although agreeing that the statement was "disparaging," "the United States Court of Appeals for the First Circuit reversed" (491). In addition, "it assumed, without deciding, that the statement was one of fact, rather than opinion, and that it was false" (492). Then the court left familiar ground, asserting that Rule 52(a) notwithstanding, it would conduct an independent review "to ensure that the district court has applied properly the governing constitutional law" (492). Nevertheless, the court did concede it was "'in no position to consider the credibility of witnesses and must leave questions of demeanor to the trier of fact'" (492).

SUMMARY OF THE COURT'S ANALYSIS

Justice John Paul Stevens writes for the Court.
Justices Harry A. Blackmun, William J. Brennan, Jr., Thrugood Marshall, and Lewis F. Powell, Jr., join.

Justice Stevens says *certiorari* was granted "to consider whether the Court of Appeals erred when it refused to apply the clearly erroneous standard of Rule 52(a) to the District Court's 'finding' of actual malice" (493). To answer this question, the Court proposed looking at two items: (1) the evidence for actual malice and (2) the rationale given by the district court when it declared *Consumers Report* did in fact print an evaluation with actual malice.

Although Bose attempted to show that three statements in the article were false, the district court said only one was. According to Stevens, "The statement that instruments tended to wander 'about the room' was found false because what the listeners in the test actually perceived was an apparent movement back and forth along the wall in front of them and between the two speakers" (494).

Evidence that this false statement was published with actual malice centered upon Arnold Seligson, an engineer who "supervised the test of the Bose 901 and prepared the written report upon which the published article was based" (494). Although Seligson wrote in his report that the sound had a "tendency to wander around the room," the "editorial revision" changed the words "from 'around the room' to 'about the room'" (494). According to the Court, "Since there was no evidence that the editors were aware of the inaccuracy in the original report, the actual-malice determination rests entirely on an evaluation of Seligson's state of mind when he wrote his initial report, or when he checked the article against that report" (494).

The district court rejected as "incredible" Seligson's testimony "that the sentence, when read in context, could be understood to refer to lateral movement" (496) because lateral movement would not be the meaning given to "about the room" by the average reader. Thus, the district court concluded Seligson knew the statement was false because "at the time of the article's publication Seligson knew that the words 'individual instruments . . . tended to wander about the room' did not accurately describe the effects that he . . . had heard during the 'special listening test'" (497).

Next the Court tackles head on the conflict between "two well-settled and respected rules of law" (498), which, Stevens says, is "in some respects more apparent than real" (499). Stevens notes at the first, "Our standard of review must be faithful to both Rule 52(a) and the rule of independent reviews applied in New York Times Co. v. Sullivan" (499).

Stevens says Rule 52(a) does not "forbid" an independent examination; rather, it simply asks that the "trial judge's opportunity to observe the demeanor of the witnesses" be "given its due" (499, 500). In addition, the "constitutionally based" independent review rule "permits this opportunity to be given its due" (500). He continues, "But Rule 52(a) does not inhibit an appellate court's power to correct errors of law, including . . . a finding of fact that is predicated on a misunderstanding of the governing rule of law" (500).

"Case-by-case adjudication is of special importance," Stevens writes, "When the standard governing the decision of a particular case is provided by the constitution" (503). In cases related to First Amendment issues, Stevens says:

> The Court has regularly conducted an independent review of the record both to be sure that the speech in question actually falls within the unprotected category and to confine the perimeters of any unprotected category within acceptable narrow limits in an effort to ensure that protected expression will not be inhibited. (505)

In short, Stevens writes, "Judges . . . must exercise such review in order to preserve the precious liberties established and ordained by the Constitution" (510, 511).

The Court then begins its own independent review with this observation: "The Court of Appeals was correct in its conclusion (1) that there is a significant difference between proof of actual malice and mere proof of falsity, and (2) that such additional proof is lacking in this case" (511). It also agreed with the trial judge, however, that "Seligson's testimony that (a) he did not 'know what made me pick that particular choice of words' and (b) that the word 'about' meant what he had drawn on the board, is not credible" (512, 513). The next question, therefore, is this: Do these two facts convict Seligson of actual malice? Writes Stevens, "Seligson's testimony does not rebut an inference of actual malice . . ., but it is equally clear that it does not constitute clear and convincing evidence of actual malice" (513).

The Court's reasoning for rejecting the inference of actual malice has become well known because of its ingenuity. Seligson, Stevens said, simply made a mistake and he refused to admit it. The Court writes:

> Seligson displayed a capacity for rationalization. He made a mistake and when confronted with it, he refused to admit it and steadfastly attempted to maintain that no mistake had been made--that the inaccurate was accurate. That attempt failed, but the fact that he made the attempt does not establish that he realized the inaccuracy at the time of publication." (513)

The Court explains:

> We agree with the Court of Appeals that the difference between hearing violin sounds move around the room and hearing them wander back and forth fits easily within the breathing space that gives life to the First Amendment. We may accept all of the purely factual finding of the District Court and nevertheless hold as a matter of law that the record does not contain clear and convincing evidence that Seligson or this employer prepared the loudspeaker article with knowledge that it contained a false statement, or with reckless disregard of the truth. (513)

RULING

Stevens writes:

> We hold that the clearly-erroneous standard of Rule 52(a) of the Federal Rules of Civil Procedure does not prescribe the standard of review to be applied in reviewing a determination of actual malice in a case governed by New York Times Co. v Sullivan. Appellate judges in such a case must exercise independent judgment and determine whether the record establishes actual malice with convincing clarity.
>
> The judgment of the Court of Appeals is affirmed. (514)

Justice Byron R. White writes a dissenting opinion.

White states that determination of the "reckless disregard" for truth part of the actual malice test may not be a question of "historical fact," but "the actual-knowledge component surely is" (514). Since the district court did indeed make a factual judgment about knowledge of a false statement, the appeals court, in his opinion, erred in making a *de novo* review of the record.

Justice William H. Rehnquist writes a dissenting opinion. Justice Sandra Day O'Connor joins.

Rehnquist begins his analysis by asserting that making a decision about the presence of actual malice means "no more than findings about the mens rea [guilty mind] of an author, findings which appellate courts are simply ill-prepared to make in any context" (515). He continues, "In other contexts we have always felt perfectly at ease leaving state-of-mind determinations . . . to triers of fact with only deferential appellate review" (517).

Therefore, Rehnquist concludes, "The New York Times Rule adequately addresses the need to shield protected speech from the risk of erroneous fact finding by placing the burden of proving 'actual malice' on the party seeking to penalize expression" (519). He writes, "I cannot join the majority's sanctioning of factual second-guessing by appellate courts" (520).

Rehnquist seems to feel that the Court changed the application of Rule 52(a) when he writes:

> It is also ironic that, in the interests of protecting the First Amendment, the Court rejects the "clearly erroneous" standard of review mandated by Federal Rule of Civil Procedure 52(a) in favor of a "de novo" standard of review for the "constitutional facts" surrounding the "actual malice" determination. (515)

SIGNIFICANCE

The resolution of an apparent conflict between two highly technical legal points constitutes the significance of this case. Rule 52(a) of the *Federal Rules of Civil Procedure* says appellate courts--giving due regard to the opportunity of a trial judge to evaluate the credibility of witnesses--should not challenge a fact determined by a trial court unless the determination is "clearly erroneous." The *Sullivan* case, however, said that the Court can indeed make an independent survey of the evidence to make sure that defamatory statements do or do not deserve First Amendment protection.

The Court resolves the conflict by asserting that the "clearly erroneous" standard of the civil procedures rule does not preclude an independent review of the evidence in order to determine whether constitutional protection was properly considered. In other words, the procedural rule does not forbid an appeals court from reviewing evidence, including factual evidence, to determine if the law was correctly applied. In this case, the relevant law is the constitutional concept of actual malice.

Thus, the opinion allows appeals courts to make an independent review of the evidence to see if the facts are arrived at through proper understanding of the law. In libel law, the Court seems to have given constitutional protection here to persons who publish knowingly a false defamatory statement (i.e., who in fact lie) if in doing so they made an honest mistake. In short, factual lies made as honest mistakes are not evidence of the legal requirement necessary to prove actual malice.

The Court concludes that a false defamatory statement made as the result of an unintentional mistake is the kind of inaccuracy that fits easily within the breathing space provided by the First Amendment. In effect, it said that, although an engineer for Bose did in fact knowingly publish a falsehood, this fact does not in itself constitute sufficient lawful evidence of actual malice because the law of actual malice requires a falsehood to be published with unmistaken knowledge. Put differently, the Court said that a person who tells a lie in fact out of a mistaken belief in its falsehood does not, according to the law, knowingly publish a falsehood.

Calder v. Jones

Iain Calder and John South
v.
Shirley Jones

Docket No. 82-1401
465 U.S. 783, 79 L.Ed.2d 804, 104 S.Ct. 1482 (1984)
Argued November 8, 1983. Decided March 20, 1984.

BACKGROUND

Focusing on the distinction between employees and employers, this is the second of two cases decided the same day and devoted to a jurisdictional dispute. See *Keeton* v. *Hustler Magazine, Inc.* for background to the jurisdiction issue.

CIRCUMSTANCES

Shirley Jones, a professional television entertainer who lives and works in California, was the subject of an October 9, 1979 article in the *National Enquirer*, published in Florida, but distributed in all 50 states, with more than 600,000 copies sold in California. John South, a reporter for the newspaper, "wrote the first draft of the challenged article, and his byline appeared on it" (785). Iain Calder is president and editor of the *Enquirer*; he "reviewed and approved the initial evaluation of the subject of the article and edited it in its final form" (786).

Jones "brought suit in California Superior Court claiming she had been libeled" (784). She complained about the news story because it said she drank alcoholic beverages at work, that her drinking interfered with her work, and that her busband, against her wishes, wanted to introduce her son, Patrick Cassidy, into show business. She denied all these assertions. The newspaper responded by asking the court to "quash the service of process for lack of personal jurisdiction" (785). The superior court agreed to quash the service because of First Amendment considerations, citing "the potential 'chilling effect' on reporters and editors which would result from requiring them to appear in remote jurisdictions to answer for the content of articles upon which they worked" (786).

The California Court of Appeals reversed "on the theory that petitioners [Calder and South] intended to, and did, cause tortious injury to respondent in California" (787) and rejected the lower court's First Amendment consideration.

SUMMARY OF THE COURT'S ANALYSIS

Justice William H. Rehnquist writes for the Court.
Chief Justice Warren E. Burger and
Justices William J. Brennan, Jr., Thurgood Marshall, Lewis F. Powell, Jr.,
Harry A. Blackmun,
Byron R. White, John Paul Stevens, and
Justice Sandra Day O'Connor join.

Justice Rehnquist begins with the following well established notion, quoting in part from *Shaffer* v. *Heitner* (1977): "The Due Process Clause of the Fourteenth Amendment to the United States Constitution permits personal jurisdiction over a defendant in any State with which the defendant has 'certain minimum contacts . . . such that the maintenance of the suit does not offend 'traditional notions of fair play and substantial justice'" (788).

Rehnquist then turns to a review of the California "contacts":

> The allegedly libelous Tort concerned the California activities of a California resident. It impugned the professionalism of an entertainer whose television career was centered in California. The article was drawn from California sources and the brunt of the harm, in terms both of respondents' [Jones'] emotional distress and the injury to her professional reputation, was suffered in California. In sum, California is the focal point both of the story and of the harm suffered. (788, 789)

He concludes from this review, "Jurisdiction over petitioners [Calder and South] is therefore proper in California based on the 'effects' of their Florida conduct in California" (789).

Calder and South put forth an additional argument "that they are not responsible for the circulation of the article in California" (789), claiming, as "ordinary employees," they are not "able to control their employer's marketing activity" (789). Rehnquist says they "liken themselves to a welder employed in Florida who works on a boiler which subsequently explodes in California" (789). Their analogy, he says curtly, "does not wash" (789).

Rehnquist writes:

> [They] are not charged with mere untargeted negligence. Rather, their intentional, and allegedly tortious, actions were expressly aimed at California. Petitioner South wrote and petitioner Calder edited an article they knew would have a potentially devastating impact upon respondent [Jones]. And they knew that the brunt of that injury would be felt by respondent [Jones] in the State in which she lives and works

> and in which the National Enquirer has its largest circulation. Under the circumstances, petitioners [Calder and South] must "reasonably anticipate being haled into court there" to answer for the truth of the statements made in their article. (789, 790)

He summarizes, "An individual injured in California need not go to Florida to seek redress from persons who, though remaining in Florida, knowingly cause the injury in California" (790). Rehnquist also says they cannot be "judged according to their employer's activities," because their "contacts" must be "assessed individually" (790).

The Court also takes care to note that it disagrees with the First Amendment concerns of the district court, concerns which, it says, would "needless complicate an already imprecise inquiry" (790). The "potential chill" spoken of by the district court, says Rehnquist, is "already taken into account in the constitutional limitations" of the actual malice rule. He writes, "To reintroduce those concerns at the jurisdictional stage would be a form of double counting" (790).

RULING

Rehnquist writes, "We hold that jurisdiction over petitioners [Calder and South] in California is proper because of their intentional conduct in Florida calculated to cause injury to respondent in California. The judgment of the California Court of Appeal is affirmed" (791).

SIGNIFICANCE

The significance of this case lies in the assertion by the Court that journalists working for a newspaper published in one state can be sued for libel in another in which the newspaper is circulated if they write an article that they know will injure a resident who lives in that state. If a state is both "the focal point of the story and of the harm suffered," then that state is likely to be the site of sufficient "contacts" to qualify as a location where a libel suit can be brought against a newspaper published in another state.

Curtis Publishing Co. v. Butts

Curtis Publishing Company v. Wallace Butts
Docket No. 1976-37

Associated Press v. Edwin A. Walker
Docket No. 1967--150

388 U.S. 130, 18 L.Ed.2d 1094, 87 S.Ct. 1975 (1967)
Argued February 23, 1967. Decided June 12, 1967.
Petition to rehear Curtis v. Butts denied October 9, 1967.
389 U.S. 889, 19 L.Ed.2d 197, 88 S.Ct. 11

BACKGROUND

Not surprisingly, some libel cases were still being tried or were in the middle of an appeals process when the *Sullivan* decision was announced by the Supreme Court in 1964. Consequently, some litigants tried to force new trials, while others changed the bases of their appeals.

Butts and Walker, caught in the appeals process when the *Sullivan* ruling was handed down, attempted to change in midstream the bases of their appeals, focusing on two concepts: public officials and standards of fault. Consequently, the Court selected these two cases to draw some further distinctions about public officials and standards of fault in actual malice.

CIRCUMSTANCES

The *Curtis* case arose out of a set of very unusual, if not unbelievable, circumstances. George Burnett, an Atlanta insurance salesmen (who had been placed on probation in connection with bad check charges) claimed that, through an electronic error, he accidentally overheard a telephone conversation between Paul (Bear) Bryant, head coach of the University of Alabama football team, and Wally Butts, athletics director at the University of Georgia. The Curtis Publishing Company printed in the *Saturday Evening Post* a story based on Burnett's account of the conversation in which, he said, Bryant and Butts conspired to fix the 1962 game. Burnett named players and plays and claimed he took notes of the conversation, with specific examples of secrets divulged by Butts.

Eventually, Butts resigned his position "for health and business reasons," (137) and filed suit against Curtis seeking $5,000,000 compensatory and $5,000,000 punitive damages. Since the *Sullivan* decision had not been announced before Butts went to trial, he based his claim for damages on a fault different from actual malice. He said the *Post* "departed greatly from the standards of good investigation and reporting" (138). A jury agreed and awarded him $60,000 general and $3,000,000 punitive damages.

The *Walker* case also arose out of an interesting set of circumstances. An Associated Press reporter filed an eyewitness account of a riot at the University of Mississippi on September 30, 1962 when federal troops attempted to enforce a court order to enroll James Meredith, a black student. The report said that Walker took command of the crowd, led a charge against the marshals, and encouraged rioters to use violence.

Although a private citizen at the time, Walker had served earlier in the army as a general. He was, interestingly enough, in command of army troops "during the school segregation confrontation at Little Rock, Arkansas, in 1957" (140). Once retired, however, he began to oppose the use of federal troops as a means of enforcing desegregation orders, and he attracted a following called the "Friends of Walker." After filing suit asking for $2,000,000 in compensatory and punitive damages, he won $500,000 compensatory and $300,000 punitive damages in a trial.

SUMMARY OF THE COURT'S ANALYSIS

Justice John M. Harlan writes for the Court.
Justices Potter Stewart and Abe Fortas join.

The Court accepts these cases for review because, says Justice Harlan, it wishes "to consider the impact of . . . [*Sullivan*] on libel actions instituted by persons who are not public officials, but who are 'public figures' and involved in issues in which the public has a justified and important interest" (134). One of the first questions the Court takes up, therefore, is whether or not Butts and Walker are public figures. Arguments by the media assert that Curtis and Walker should be treated as public officials because information about them is of public concern. Harlan writes:

> We are told that the public interest in education in general, and in the conduct of the athletic affairs of educational institutions in particular, justifies constitutional protection of discussion of persons involved in it equivalent to the protection afforded discussion of public officials. (146) A similar argument is raised in the Walker case where the important public interest in being informed about the events and personalities . . . is pressed. . . . [W]e are also urged to recognize that Walker's claims to the protection of libel laws are limited since he thrust himself into the "vortex" of the controversy. (146)

The Court notes that, unlike Sullivan, Walker and Curtis cannot present arguments analogous to seditious libel prosecutions, an extremely important distinction. In *Sullivan*, the Court said an important basis for establishing a limited privilege of disseminating false defamatory statements about the official acts of public officials was that such criticism is analogous to criticism of the government (seditious libel). The question in this case, in contrast, is how "broad" is the "constitutional interest" in protecting discussion of public affairs.

Pointing out that *Sullivan* did not start a process of "unintended inexorability" (148) for applying actual malice, Harlan says the Court is reluctant to say that all information of public concern can be published with impunity. He writes, "The fact that dissemination of information and opinion on questions of public concern is ordinarily a legitimate, protected and indeed cherished activity does not mean, however, that one may in all respects carry on that activity exempt from sanctions designed to safeguard the legitimate interests of others" (150).

Harlan then gives examples of legitimate regulation, "Federal securities regulation, mail fraud statutes, and common-law actions for deceit and misrepresentation are only some examples of our understanding that the right to communicate information of public interest is not 'unconditional'" (150). Nor can the mere falsity of a defamatory statement constitute the sole grounds for regulating speech. Harlan writes, "While the truth of the underlying facts might be said to mark the line between publications which are of significant social value and those which might be suppressed without serious social harm . . . we have rejected . . . the argument that a finding a falsity alone should strip protections from the publisher" (152).
Harlan says there also must be present some form of "error."

The issue to the Court now becomes what justifies regulating communications of public interest. The answer is improper conduct. Harlan writes:

> It is the conduct element, therefore, on which we must principally focus if we are successfully to resolve the antithesis between civil libel actions and the freedom of speech and press. Impositions based on misconduct can be neutral with respect to content of the speech involved, free of historical taint, and adjusted to strike a fair balance between the interests of the community in free circulation of information and those of individuals in seeking recompense for harm done by the circulation of defamatory falsehood. (153)

In other words, the Court prefers to regulate the conduct of the communicators instead of the content of the communication. Thus, the behavior of journalists would determine whether or not the news they reported would be protected by the First Amendment. This idea raises the question of where does the Court find guidelines for regulating the conduct of news gathering. Harlan answers from general liability law. He writes, "We are prompted, therefore, to seek guidance from the rules of liability which prevail in our society with respect to compensation of persons injured by the improper performance of a legitimate activity by another" (154).

Before setting the standard of conduct, though, the Court pauses to define the nature of the persons bringing suit because certain persons can demand a higher standard of reporting than can others. Harlan writes, "And both Butts and Walker commanded a substantial amount of independent public interest at the time of the publication; both, in our opinion, would have been labeled 'public figures' under ordinary tort rules" (154). Even in non-libel cases of personal injury, then, Butts and Walker, as public figures, would have to show higher-than-ordinary levels of misconduct in order to collect damages from persons who injured them.

The Court pauses a bit longer before setting forth the required standards of conduct in order to point out why Butts and Walker are "public figures." Harlan writes:

> Butts may have attained that status by position alone and Walker by his purposeful activity amounting to a thrusting of his personality into the "vortex" of an important public controversy, but both commanded sufficient access to the means of counter argument to be able "to expose through discussion the falsehood and fallacies" of the defamatory statements. (155)

Persons who command the interest of the general public, then, are "public figures." Some are "public figures" just because of the public interest in the position they occupy while others because they seek to affect the debate on public issues. In both cases, though, they are also considered "public figures" because they are important enough to gain access to the mass media where they can respond to a statement that libels them.

Having defined a "public figure," Harlan now sets forth the standard of conduct such a person can demand from the working press. He writes:

> We consider and would hold that a "public figure" who is not a public official may also recover damages for a defamatory falsehood whose substance makes substantial danger to reputation apparent, on a showing of highly unreasonable conduct constituting an extreme departure from the standards of investigation and reporting ordinarily adhered to by responsible publishers. (155)

In short, "public figures" can win libel suits only when they can show that false defamatory statements resulted from "highly unreasonable conduct" by the journalists who reported them. This conduct is defined as extreme departure from ordinary standards of responsible publishers.

The essential question for Butts and Walker, then, is this: Did the journalists who defamed them engage in "highly unreasonable conduct?" As in the *Sullivan* case, so too here the Court undertakes a review of "the evidence and findings" (156) to see if they meet the standards just announced.

The *Butts* case, as the Court sees it, does indeed involve such misconduct. For one thing, the "story was in no sense 'hot news,'" (157) thus giving the editors time to check out the facts, an activity they gave little attention to. Harlan writes simply, "Elementary precautions were . . . ignored" (157). For example, the *Post* did not even look at Burnett's notes. In addition, a man named "John Carmichael who was supposed to have been with Burnett when the phone call was overhead was not interviewed" (157). Nor did anyone view the films of the game to see if Burnett's information was accurate, and the writer assigned to the story was not expert in football. The Court also takes note of the *Post*'s purposeful efforts to institute a series of "'sophisticated muckraking'" (158) articles in an attempt to change its image as a means to counter declining sales.

Walker's situation is viewed much differently. Here the news "required immediate dissemination" (158). The reporter at the scene "gave every indication of being trustworthy and competent" (158). Moreover, the events described "would not have seemed unreasonable to one familiar with General Walker's prior publicized statements on the underlying controversy" (159). Harlan concludes, "Considering the necessity for rapid dissemination, nothing in this series of events gives the slightest hint of a severe departure from accepted publishing standards" (159). Therefore, the Court refuses damages to Walker.

The next issue taken up by the Court is whether or not a higher level of misconduct is required for punitive damages than for compensatory awards. Curtis argues "that an unlimited punitive award against a magazine publisher constitutes an effective prior restraint by giving the jury the power to destroy the publisher's business" (159). It also contends that "a higher degree of fault is necessary to sustain a punitive imposition than a compensatory award" (160).

The Courts rejects both arguments. First, it says that appeals courts can protect the media from unreasonably high punitive damage awards granted by juries. Secondly, it says the requirement of showing "ill will" to win punitive damages is sufficient protection. Writes Harlan, "We would hold, therefore, that misconduct sufficient to justify the award of compensatory damages also justifies the imposition of a punitive award" (161).

RULING

The judgment against Butts is upheld, but the judgment against Walker is reversed and his case is sent back for "further proceedings not inconsistent with the opinions that have been filed herein" (162).

Chief Justice Earl Warren writes a concurring opinion.

Warren objects to what he feels is the Court's new standard of conduct required of journalists reporting on public figures involved in matters of public interest. He says the public official standard announced in *Sullivan* (actual malice) should also apply to public figure cases. He notes, for example, "Surely as a class these 'public figures' have as ready access as 'public officials' to mass media of communication, both to influence policy and to counter criticism of their views and activities" (164).

In support of his position, Warren asserts that the conduct of editors and reporters for the *Post* constitutes actual malice. He says the journalists were "slipshod and sketchy" (160). He writes, "Suffice it to say that little investigative effort was expended initially, and no additional inquiries were made" (160). To Warren this was a "reckless course" of action (170).

Justice Hugo L. Black concurs with Walker and dissents from Butts. Justice William O. Douglas joins both.

Black reaffirms his objection to the low level of protection accorded by the actual malice requirement. He writes:

> These cases illustrate, I think, the accuracy of my prior predications that the New York Times constitutional rule concerning libel is wholly inadequate to save the press from being destroyed by libel judgments. (171)
>
> If this precedent is followed, it means that we must in all libel cases hereafter weigh the facts and hold that all papers and magazines guilty of gross writing or reporting are constitutionally liable, while they are not if the quality of the reporting is approved by a majority of us. (171)
>
> [This] is a flat violation of the Seventh Amendment. (171)

He concludes by repeating his position first stated in *Sullivan*, "I think it is time for the Court to . . . adopt the rule to the effect that the First Amendment was intended to leave the press free from the harassment of libel judgments" (172).

Justice William J. Brennan, Jr., concurs with Walker and dissents from Butts. Justice Byron R. White joins both.

Although Brennan agrees with the Court that the "evidence unmistakably would support a judgment for Butts under the New York Times standard," he nevertheless would order a new trial so that the charge to the jury conforms to the *Sullivan* rule. In particular, Brennan objects to the trial judge equating "actual malice" to "ill will" instead of knowledge of falsity or serious concern for truth. Thus, Brennan and White also seem to be saying that the actual malice requirement should apply to public figures as well as to public officials.

SIGNIFICANCE

Without question the most significant contribution of this case is the creation of the public figure category. The impact of the Court's newly announced standard of conduct for public figures (highly unreasonable conduct constituting an extreme departure from the standards of investigation and reporting ordinarily adhered to by responsible publishers) is muted somewhat, however, because only three justices accepted this idea. Two rejected any standard short of absolutely no media liability in libel, and four preferred the actual malice standard. (Actual malice eventually did indeed become a requirement for public officials.)

No less important than the new conduct standard is the Court's development of definitions of public figures. In general, the Court said that public figures are persons who command the interest of the general public.

In addition, some persons become public figures just because of the public interest in the position they occupy. Others because they seek to affect the debate on public issues. The Court adopts an idea from Goldberg's concurring opinion in *Sullivan* when it says that, in either case, persons are considered public figures if they are important enough to gain access to the mass media where they can respond to a statement that libels them. (For refined definitions of various forms of public figures see *Gertz*, 1971.)

As part of its analysis, the Court noted that the right to communicate information of public interest is not unconditional. The conditions, however, are related to conduct, not subject matter. In other words, government can regulate the conduct of the communicators, but not the content of the communication. The guidelines for regulating the conduct of news gathering are patterned on the conduct requirements found in general liability law.

Finally, conduct sufficient to justify the award of compensatory damages was ruled sufficient to justify the imposition of a punitive award. It is not necessary, the court said, to show a higher fault in order to collect punitive damages. Seven years later in *Gertz v. Welch* (1974), however, the Court ruled that, in certain instances, a libel plaintiff would have to show the very high fault of actual malice in order to collect punitive damages even when only a lower fault is required to win a compensatory award. (See also Harlan's and Marshall's dissent in *Rosenbloom* v. *Metromedia*, 1971.)

Dun & Bradstreet v. Greenmoss Builders

Dun & Bradstreet, Inc.
v.
Greenmoss Builders, Inc.

Docket No. 83-18
472 U.S. 749, 86 L.Ed.2d 593, 105 S.Ct. 2939 (1985)
Argued March 31, 1984. Reargued October 3, 1984.
Decided June 26, 1985.

BACKGROUND

In a concurring opinion to this case, Justice Byron R. White writes, "New York Times Co. v Sullivan was the first major step in what proved to be a seemingly irreversible process of constitutionalizing the entire law of libel and slander" (766). He adds, "This judgement overturning 200 years of libel law was deemed necessary to implement the First Amendment interest in 'uninhibited, robust, and wide-open' debate on public issues" (766).

Adding to this cursory historical survey in his dissent, Justice William J. Brennan, Jr., writes, "Our First Amendment libel decisions in the last two decades have in large measure been an effort to explore the full ramifications of the New York Times Co. v Sullivan principles" (777). He continues, "Our cases since New York Times Co. v Sullivan have proceeded from the general premise that all libel law implicates First Amendment values to the extent it deters true speech that would otherwise be protected by the First Amendment" (778).

One of the basic distinctions drawn in that watershed decision focuses on the level of fault that needs to be shown in differing circumstances. The fault of actual malice was designed to be the highest level, and the court required in *Sullivan* that it must be demonstrated with "clear and convincing" evidence by falsely defamed public officials. Later, in *Curtis*, the Court determined that public figures would also have to show actual malice. Still later, in *Gertz*, the Court ruled that requirements to show lower levels of fault could be set by the states for defamed private persons. If those persons want punitive damages, however, then they too would have to show actual malice.

The question raised by this case is whether or not private persons involved in purely private matters, as contrasted to private persons involved in public matters, have to show actual malice in order to win punitive damages.

altogether by asking the Court to create a special privilege exempting the news media from damages when private persons in private situations are libeled. It refused to do so.

CIRCUMSTANCES

On July 16, 1976, Dun & Bradstreet, a credit agency, sent to five subscribers a false report saying that Greenmoss had filed a voluntary petition for bankruptcy. It turns out that "a 14-year-old high school student paid to review Vermont bankruptcy pleadings, had inadvertently attributed to . . . [Greenmoss] a bankruptcy petition filed by one of . . . [its] employees" (751). No one at the agency attempted to verify the information before it was sent out and received by Greenmoss's banker and four other subscribers.

Dun & Bradstreet sent out a correction August 3. Greenmoss was dissatisfied with the correction and upset at the refusal of the agency to name the subscribers who received the false report. He sued for damages and won "$50,000 in compensatory or presumed damages and $300,000 in punitive damages" (752). *Dun & Bradstreet* asked for a new trial, claiming the judge's instructions wrongly permitted the jury to award punitive damages without finding the report was published with actual malice. The judge granted a new trial, although he said he was not sure this form of the actual malice rule would apply to nonmedia defendants.

The Vermont Supreme Court reversed saying that Dun & Bradstreet and other such firms are not "'the type of media worthy of First Amendment protection as contemplated by New York Times . . . and its progeny'" (753). The United States Supreme Court affirmed, but for different reasons.

SUMMARY OF THE COURT'S ANALYSIS

Justice Lewis F. Powell, Jr., writes for the Court.
Justices William H. Rehnquist and Sandra Day O'Connor join.

Justice Powell points out that the central question to be addressed here is whether or not *Gertz* is in fact relevant to this situation. He notes that the Court held in *Gertz*, "The First Amendment restricted the damages that a private individual could obtain from a publisher for a libel that involved a matter of *public concern* [emphasis added]" (751). "The question presented in this case," he continues, "Is whether this rule of Gertz applies when the false and defamatory statements do not involve matter of public concern" (751).

Powell begins a review of *Gertz* by asserting, "We have never considered whether the Gertz balance [requiring defamed private persons to show actual malice in order to collect punitive damages] obtains when the defamatory statements involve no issue of public concern" (757). The Court then finds that one side of the balance here is the same as in *Gertz*: the state's interest in an "individual's right to the protection of his own good name" (757). Contrarily, the Court finds the other side of the balance not to be the same, "The First Amendment interest, on the other hand, is less important than the one weighed in *Gertz*" (758).

"Not all speech is of equal First Amendment importance," (758) Powell writes, quoting in part from *First National Bank of Boston* v. *Bellotti* 435 U.S. 765, 55 L.Ed.2d 707, 98 S.Ct. 1497 (1978) "[and] speech on '"matters of public concern" is 'at the heart of the First Amendment's protection'"(758, 759). He adds, "In contrast, speech on matters of purely private concern is of less First Amendment concern" (759). While the Court feels "such speech is not totally unprotected . . . its protections are less stringent" (760). Consequently, Powell writes, "We hold that the state interest adequately supports awards of presumed and punitive damages--even absent a showing of 'actual malice'" (761). Thus, the Court feels that *Gertz* does not necessarily apply when the falsely defamed private person is involved in a purely private situation.

Consequently, the issue now facing the Court, Powell writes, is whether or not the "credit report involved a matter of public concern" (761). The Court concludes it did not. Powell writes, "It [the report] was speech solely in the individual interest of the speaker and its specific business audience" (762).

Such speech, Powell writes, "warrants no special protection" (762) for a number of reasons. For one thing, "Since the credit report was made available to only five subscribers, who . . . could not disseminate it further, it cannot be said that the report involves any 'strong interest in the free flow of commercial information'" (762). He terms these forms of commercial speech "hardy and unlikely to be deterred by incidental state regulations" (262). He writes, "It is solely motivated by the desire for profit, which, we have noted, is a force less likely to be deterred than others" (762). He concludes, "Thus, any incremental 'chilling' effect of libel suits would be of decreased significance" (763).

RULING

Powell writes:

> The trial court's conclusion that the instructions did not satisfy Gertz was correct, and the Vermont Supreme Court's determination that Gertz was inapplicable was necessary to its decision that the trial court erred in granting the motion for a new trial.
>
> We conclude that permitting recovery of presumed and punitive damages in defamation cases absent a showing of "actual malice" does not violate the First Amendment when the defamatory statements do not involve matters of public concern. Accordingly, we affirm the judgment of the Vermont Supreme Court. (763)

Chief Justice Warren E. Burger writes a concurring opinion.

Burger agrees "that Gertz is limited to circumstances in which the alleged defamatory expression concerns a matter of general importance and that the expression in question here relates to a matter of essentially private concern" (764). He adds, however, "I continue to believe . . . that Gertz was ill-conceived, and therefore . . . should be overruled" (764).

Justice Byron R. White writes a concurring opinion.

White's concurrence reflects two decades of difficulties the Court experienced in attempting to apply First Amendment protection in varying degrees to various forms of speech. He writes:

> I joined the judgment and opinion in New York Times. But I have come to have increasing doubts about the soundness of the Court's approach and about some of the assumptions underlying it. (766)
>
> I remain convinced that Gertz was erroneously decided. I have also become convinced that the Court struck an improvident balance in the New York Times case between the public's interest in being fully informed about public officials and public affairs and the competing interest of those who have been defamed in vindicating their reputation. (767)

He then goes on to point out what he feels are the shortcomings of the *New York Times* decision, and he asserts that, in both *Sullivan* and *Gertz*, "the Court engaged in severe overkill" (771). "As I see it, " he writes, "The Court undervalued the reputational interest at stake" (772).

White proposes as an alternative to the actual malice rule a limit on recoverable damages. He writes, "The necessary breathing room for speakers can be ensured by limitations on recoverable damages" (771).

He does agree with the Court, however, in rejecting a special privilege for the media. He writes, "The First Amendment gives no more protection to the press in defamation suits than it does to others exercising their freedom of speech. None of our cases affords such a distinction; to the contrary, the Court has rejected it at every turn" (773).

He also agrees that *Gertz* should not be applied to the set of circumstances found in this case. He writes, "First, I am unreconciled to the Gertz holding and believe that it should be overruled. Second, . . . the defamatory publication in this case does not deal with a matter of public importance" (774).

Justice William J. Brennan, Jr.,
writes a dissenting opinion.
Justices Thurgood Marshall, Harry A. Blackmun, and
John Paul Stevens join.

Writes Brennan, "The four who join this opinion would reverse the judgment of the Vermont Supreme Court" (775). Although Brennan concedes that the form of speech at issue in this case is not "central" to the First Amendment, it "nonetheless, requires restraints on presumed and punitive awards" (775).

He returns to the *Sullivan* case, where he discovers the manifestation of a "general proscription against unnecessarily broad content-based regulation" that "permeates First Amendment jurisprudence" (778). He concludes, "States must therefore use finer instruments to ensure adequate space for protected expression" (778). *Gertz*, he feels, used properly fine distinctions requiring different levels of fault for different forms of speech in differing circumstances.

For Brennan the issue in this case is simple: "The only question presented is whether a jury award of presumed and punitive damages based on less than a showing of actual malice is constitutionally permissible" (781). First, he agrees with the Court that a distinction between media and nonmedia defendants "is irreconcilable with the . . . First Amendment" (781) in part because it would create "definitional questions" and in part because, given new technologies, it "would be born an anachronism" (782). Besides, the First Amendment, he writes, "Also protects the rights of listeners" (783).

Moving to the central issue, Brennan says the plurality opinion presents "an impoverished definition of 'matters of public concern' that is irreconcilable with the First Amendment" (786). The Court, he feels, does not give enough importance to "the realm of matters of economic concern" (787). He uses support from *Thornhill* v. *Alabama*, 310 U.S. 88, 84 L.Ed. 1093, 60 S.Ct. 763 (1940) when he writes, "The choices we make when we step into the voting booth may well be the products of what we have learned from the myriad of daily economic and social phenomenon that surround us" (788).

Brennan continues to give reasons for supporting the importance of economic speech when he writes, "An announcement of the bankruptcy of a local company is information of potentially great concern to residents of the community where the company is located" (789). He adds, "And knowledge about solvency and the effects and prevalence of bankruptcy certainly would inform citizen opinions about questions of economic regulation" (789). Moreover, he notes, bankruptcy law "requires invocation of judicial mechanisms to effectuate it and makes the fact of the bankruptcy a matter of public record" (789).

"Even if the subject matter of credit reporting were properly considered . . . as purely a matter of private discourse," Brennan writes as he moves to a new tact, "This speech would fall well within the range of valuable expression for which the First Amendment demands protection" (790). Private credit reports, Brennan insists, "bear few of the earmarks of commercial speech that might be entitled to somewhat less rigorous protection" (791). Those forms of commercial speech are "pure advertising--an offer to buy or sell goods and services or encouraging such buying and selling" (792). "Credit reports," he emphasizes, "Are not commercial advertisements for a good or service" (792).

He sums up his opposition this way, "Any further interest in deterring potential defamation through case-by-case judicial imposition of presumed and punitive damages awards on less than a showing of actual malice simply exacts too high a toll on First Amendment values" (796).

SIGNIFICANCE

After *Sullivan*, the Court at various times focused its decisions on the nature of the persons libeled and at other times on the nature of the issues involved. At first, court observers felt the primary distinction related to the differences between the public and private conduct of a public person. In later cases, however, the Court just about eliminated those differences by asserting that it would be very difficult to find any activity that is not relevant to the public responsibilities of a public person.

Without doubt the significance of this case rests in the distinction drawn between speech about a private person involved in private matters and speech about a private person involved in public matters. This distinction further refines elements of earlier distinctions drawn in *Gertz* between the levels of fault required to be shown by private persons seeking presumed, compensatory, or actual damages, and those seeking punitive damages. According to *Gertz* all defamed persons, public or private, are required to show actual malice in order to collect punitive damages. In contrast, this case allows private persons involved in private matters to collect punitive damages for showing a lesser fault.

This ruling, therefore, combines two areas of conflict initiated with the *Sullivan* decision. On the one hand, distinctions between the levels of fault to be shown by libel plaintiffs were based in some post-*Sullivan* cases on the nature of the persons defamed, that is, on the basis of whether or not the person defamed is considered public or private. On the other hand, these same distinctions were based in other post-*Sullivan* cases on the nature of the controversy giving rise to the defamation, that is, on the basis of whether the subject matter of the activities engaged in is public or private.

Here the Court combines the two areas (persons and the subject matter of the activities) with primary attention focused on the private person; it reaffirms its original distinction between public and private persons and then proceeds to draw a new distinction between private persons involved in activities of private concern and private persons involved in activities of public concern.

In addition, although the plurality opinion did not address the request for a special privilege for media defendants, five members of the Court reaffirmed a long-standing position that the media have no special First Amendment rights not accorded to the general public.

Garrison v. Louisiana

Jim Garrison
v.
State of Louisiana

Docket No. 1964-04
379 U.S. 64, 13 L.Ed.2d 125, 85 S.Ct. 209 (1964)
Argued October 19, 1964. Decided November 23, 1964.

BACKGROUND

Although Garrison was brought to trial before the *Sullivan* case, his appeal was argued in front of the high court afterwards. Consequently, his case represents the first opportunity the Court took after *New York Times* v. *Sullivan* (1964) to clarify what it meant by the term "actual malice" when used in reference to libel. Since Garrison was charged with criminal libel, the Court is able to rule on whether or not actual malice was applicable to other than civil libel cases. This, then, is the first in a long series of cases clarifying the ramifications of the actual malice rule.

CIRCUMSTANCES

A controversial figure who attacked the Warren report on the Kennedy assassination, Jim Garrison was the district attorney of Orleans Parish, Louisiana. Not entirely happy with the pace of justice meted out by the eight judges of his parish's criminal district court, he called a press conference where he issued a statement attacking their judicial conduct. His charges included the following: "A large backlog of pending criminal cases [can be attributed to] the inefficiency, laziness, and excessive vacations of the judges. [B],y refusing to authorize disbursements to cover the expenses of undercover investigations of vice in New Orleans, the judges had hampered his efforts to enforce the vice laws" (66). Following the conference, Garrison was tried before a judge from another parish and convicted of criminal libel. The Supreme Court of Louisiana upheld his conviction.

SUMMARY OF THE COURT'S ANALYSIS

Justice William J. Brennan, Jr., writes for the Court.
Chief Justice Earl Warren and Justices Tom C. Clark, John M. Harlan, Potter Stewart, and Byron R. White join.

Justice William J. Brennan, Jr., begins the Court's analysis by writing, "At the outset, we must decide whether, in view of the differing [from civil libel] history and purpose of criminal libel, the New York Times rule also limits state power to impose criminal sanctions for criticism of the official conduct of public officials. We hold that it does" (67).

Brennan then reviews quickly the history of criminal libel and its notion of malice as "ill will" or "evil intent."
He writes, quoting in part from an article in the *Columbia Law Review*:

> Debate on public issues will not be uninhibited if the speaker must run the risk that it will be proved in court that he spoke out of hatred; even if he did speak out of hatred, utterances honestly believed contribute to the free interchange of ideas and the ascertainment of truth. Under a rule like the Louisiana rule, permitting a finding of malice based on an intent to inflict harm, rather than a intent to inflict harm through falsehood, "it becomes a hazardous matter to speak out against a popular politician." (73)

For the Court, the essential question is not whether the defamation is false or was uttered out of hatred; it is whether or not the defamation was spoken with knowledge that the accusation was false. Brennan then pens these oft-quoted words, "Only those false statements made with the high degree of awareness of their probable falsity demanded by New York Times may be the subject of either civil or criminal sanctions" (74).

To show what is and what is not protected by the First Amendment, Brennan draws a distinction using some famous words from *Chaplinsky* v. *New Hampshire* (1942), the well-known "fighting words" case:

> Calculated falsehood falls into that class of utterances which "are no essential part of any exposition of ideas, and are of such slight social value as a step to truth that any benefit that may be derived from them is clearly outweighed by the social interest in order and morality." (75)

Brennan takes up next the claim by the Louisiana Supreme Court that Garrison's words "constituted an attack upon the personal integrity of the judges rather than on official conduct" (76). He concedes, "Of course any criticism of the manner in which a public official performs his duties will tend to affect his private, as well as his public, reputation" (77). But, using words that also achieve notice in many future cases, he writes, "Anything which might touch on an official's fitness for office is relevant" (77).

The final issue given attention by the Court is the trial judge's usage of a "reasonable-belief standard" as the test of the level of fault necessary to constitute actual malice. Brennan selects these words from that judge's opinion, "'It is inconceivable to me that the Defendant could have had a reasonable belief, which could be defined as an honest belief, that not one but all eight judges of the Criminal District Court were guilty of what he charged them with in the defamatory statement'" (78). To the judge, Brennan responds, "The reasonable-belief standard applied by the trial judge is not the same as the reckless-disregard-of-truth standard" (79). He characterizes the judge's standard as "mere negligence," which is not a high enough level of fault to constitute actual malice.

RULING

Brennan writes, "Where criticism of public officials is concerned, we see no merit in the argument that criminal libel statutes serve interests distinct from those secured by civil libel laws, and therefore should not be subject to the same limitations. (67) Reversed" (79).

Justice Hugo L. Black writes a concurring opinion.
Justice William O. Douglas joins.

Black first reaffirms his dissent in *Sullivan*. He then adds the following to that dissent: "I believe that the Court is mistaken if it thinks that requiring proof that statements were "malicious" or "defamatory" will really create any substantial hurdle to block public officials from punishing those who criticize the way they conduct their office" (79).

Justice William O. Douglas writes a concurring opinion.
Justice Hugo L. Black joins.

Douglas also objects to the actual malice test as a means to protect words critical of government officials. He notes, "The Bill of Rights is constantly watered down through judicial 'balancing' of what the Constitution says and what judges think is needed for a well-ordered society" (81, 82).

Justice Arthur J. Goldberg writes a concurring opinion.

Goldberg reaffirms his position in *Sullivan* "'that the Constitution accords citizens and press an unconditional freedom to criticize official conduct'" (88). He adds, "In my view, if the rule that libel on government has no place in our Constitution is to have real meaning, then libel . . . on the official conduct of the governors likewise can have no place in our Constitution" (88).

SIGNIFICANCE

Certainly, this case is significant because it applied the actual malice rule to criminal as well as civil libel.

It is also important, however, for skeletal ideas that were fleshed out later in other Court rulings. One idea is the notion that nearly any action by a public official is relevant to an evaluation of official conduct; thus, almost any words criticizing these actions are likewise relevant and so protected by the actual malice rule.

A second idea is that reckless disregard of the truth does not mean negligence nor an intent to inflict harm. Rather, it means either that writers intend to inflict harm through falsehood or that writers have a high degree of awareness of probable falsity.

Gertz v. Welch

Elmer Gertz
v.
Robert Welch, Inc.

Docket No. 72-617
418 U.S. 323, 41 L.Ed. 2d 789, 94 S.Ct. 2997 (1974)
Argued November 14, 1973. Decided June 25, 1974.

BACKGROUND

Because the opinion in *Rosenbloom* was so fractured, some members of the Court were eager to find another case that would produce a majority--as contrasted to a plurality--opinion. It remained badly fractured in *Gertz*, however, with six separate opinions issued. Four of them were dissenting opinions. In point of fact, Blackmun concurred solely for the purpose of producing a majority vote. Thus, a bare majority of the Court did seem ready to arrest its movement toward extending protection of the First Amendment to an ever-widening class of speech.

In *Sullivan* the Court used the notion of actual malice (knowledge that a published defamatory statement is false or reckless disregard of the statement's truth) to give some constitutional protection to criticism of the official actions of public officials. In *Curtis* that protection was granted to speech about public figures and in *Rosenbloom* to speech about private persons involved in matters of public interest. In this case, the Court backs away from using public interest as a criterion for requiring a showing of actual malice. It also came to grips with the punitive damages issue.

CIRCUMSTANCES

Strangely enough, the seeds of this case were sown when a Chicago policeman named Richard Nuccio shot and killed a youth named Ronald Nelson in 1968. After the policeman was convicted for second-degree murder, Nelson's family retained Elmer Gertz to sue Nuccio for damages.

Robert Welch produced a monthly magazine called *American Opinion* for the John Birch Society. According to Justice Powell, "Early in the 1960's the magazine began to warn of a nationwide conspiracy to discredit local law enforcement agencies and create in their stead a national police force capable of supporting a Communist dictatorship" (325). As part of this effort, an article, entitled "Frame-Up" by Alan Stang, containing serious inaccuracies about Gertz's work for Nelson was published. The managing editor admitted he "made no effort to verify or substantiate the charges" (327). Instead, he "stated he had relied on the author's reputation and on his prior experience with the accuracy and authenticity of the author's contributions to American Opinion" (328).

The magazine falsely said, among other things, that Gertz had a criminal record, and he was a Leninist, a Communist-fronter, and a member of the Marxist League for Industrial Democracy.

The jury awarded Gertz $50,000, but the judge took it away, saying that Gertz had to meet the actual malice test because the subject matter of the defamation was of public interest. The court of appeals agreed that Gertz was required, but failed, to meet the *Times* test.

SUMMARY OF THE COURT'S ANALYSIS

Justice Lewis F. Powell, Jr., writes for the Court.
Justices Harry A. Blackmun, Potter Stewart,
Thurgood Marshall, and William H. Rehnquist join.

Powell opens the analysis for the Court with these words: "The principal issue in this case is whether a newspaper or broadcaster that publishes defamatory falsehoods about an individual who is neither a public official nor a public figure may claim a constitutional privilege against liability for the injury inflicted by those statements" (332). He then gives a fairly extensive review of the opinions issued in *Rosenbloom* (1971).

Following the review, Powell notes that, although all the justices feel "there is no such thing as a false idea," they also agree "there is no constitutional value in false statements of fact" (339, 340). He points out that problems arise because "erroneous statement of fact . . . is nevertheless inevitable in free debate" and "punishment of error runs the risk of inducing a cautious and restrictive exercise of . . . [free] speech" (340).

He says holding the media to a standard of "strict liability" (i.e., awarding damages whenever they falsely defamed someone, even if they committed no fault) would "lead to intolerable self-censorship" (340). In other words, if the press had to verify exactly the truth of every single word printed, then journalists may not print very important and valuable truthful information simply because they could not prove its truth. Thus, Powell, says, "The First Amendment requires that we protect some falsehood in order to protect speech that matters" (341). In short, the media need some "breathing space" (342).

At the same time, the state has a legitimate interest in compensating persons "for harm inflicted on them by defamatory falsehood" (341). Moreover, Powell writes, "The state interest in compensating injury to the reputation of private individuals requires that a different rule should obtain with respect to them" (343). One reason for the different rule, according the Court, is that private persons are not as able as public persons to use "self-help."

Powell asserts there is also a more important normative reason. He writes, "An individual who decides to seek governmental office must accept certain necessary consequences of that involvement in public affairs. He runs the risk of closer public scrutiny" (344).

Picking up concepts first mentioned in *Curtis*, the Court then proceeds to describe three types of public figures: an involuntary public figure, a voluntary public figure for all purposes, and a voluntary public figure for limited purposes. Powell writes:

> Hypothetically, it may be possible for someone to become a public figure through no purposeful action of its own, but the instances of truly involuntary public figures must be exceedingly rare. (345) Some occupy positions of such persuasive power and influence that they are deemed public figures for all purposes. (345) More commonly, those classed as public figures have thrust themselves to the forefront of particular public controversies in order to influence the resolution of the issues involved. (345)

All three types share some common characteristics. Powell writes, "Those who attain this status have assumed roles of especial prominence in the affairs of society" (345). Because of this prominence, "the communications media are entitled to act on the assumption that public officials and public figures have voluntarily exposed themselves to increased risk of injury from defamatory falsehood concerning them. No such assumption is justified with respect to a private individual" (345). The Court then concludes that private persons are "more vulnerable to injury" and "more deserving of recovery" (345).

In an effort to give the media breathing space and at the same time to protect the reputations of private persons, the Court says the states may develop their own rules for the conduct of a journalist as long as they do not hold reporters and editors liable for printing defamatory falsehoods without some sort of fault.

The Court then institutes one more safeguard for the media because the "state interest extends no further than compensations for actual injury" (349). Writes Powell, "We hold that the States may not permit recovery of presumed or punitive damages, at least when liability is not based on a showing of knowledge of falsity or reckless disregard for the truth" (349). The Court is saying here that the states may award actual damages for any standard of fault they chose to impose upon the media, but punitive damages can be awarded only if the media disseminate a defamatory falsehood with actual malice.

The reasons given by the Court for this additional protection of requiring actual malice in order to award punitive damages are varied. First, traditional libel theory asserts that injury does not have to be proved in libel; it can be presumed--hence presumed damages. The Court's problem with this idea is "the largely uncontrolled discretion of juries to award damages where there is no loss" (349). Powell also notes, "The doctrine of presumed damages invites juries to punish unpopular opinion rather than to compensate individuals for injury" (349). He adds a third reason: "More to the point, the States have no substantial interest in . . . damages far in excess of any actual injury" (349).

Before ending discussion of damages, Powell pauses long enough to give some examples of actual damages, which he says, are not limited to "out-of-pocket expenses" (350). He writes, "The more customary types of actual harm inflicted by defamatory falsehood include impairment of reputation and standing in the community, personal humiliation, and mental anguish and suffering. Of course . . . all awards must be supported by competent evidence" (350).

Finally, the Court gives some guidance about how to determine whether or not a person is a public figure. Powell writes:

> We would not lightly assume that a citizen's participation in community and professional affairs rendered him a public figure for all purposes. Absent any *clear evidence* [emphasis added] of general fame or notoriety in the community, and pervasive involvement in the affairs of society, an individual should not be deemed a public personality for all aspects of his life. (352) [We should look] . . . to the nature and extent of an individual's participation in the particular controversy giving rise to the defamation. (352).

On the basis of this criterion, the Court rules that Gertz is not a public figure. Writes Powell, "He plainly did not thrust himself into the vortex of this public issue, nor did he engage the public's attention in an attempt to influence its outcome" (352).

RULING

Powell writes:

> We hold that, so long as they do not impose liability without fault, the States may define for themselves the appropriate standard of liability for a publisher or broadcaster of defamatory falsehood injurious to a private individual. (347) Because the jury was allowed to impose liability without fault and was permitted to presume damages without proof of injury, a new trial is necessary. We reverse. (353)

Justice Harry A. Blackmun writes a concurring opinion.

Blackmun says he prefers his position outlined in *Rosenbloom* (that a showing of actual malice should be required by all falsely defamed persons engaged in matters of public interest), but joins the Court's opinion here because a majority is needed to produce "a definitive ruling" (354).

Justice William O. Douglas writes a dissenting opinion.

Douglas reaffirms his long-standing absolutist position on media libel: "In my view the First and Fourteenth Amendments prohibit the imposition of damages upon the respondent [media] for this discussion of public affairs" (360).

Justice William J. Brennan, Jr., writes a dissenting opinion.

Brennan agrees that Gertz is not a public figure, but he objects to the Court allowing the states to lower the standard of fault for private persons falsely defamed when engaged in activities of general interest to the public. In short, he also continues to hold to his position in *Rosenbloom*.

The dangers of a lower standard, such as reasonable care, are succinctly described by Brennan this way:

> Under a reasonable-care regime, publishers and broadcasters will have to make pre-publication judgments about juror assessment of such diverse considerations as the size, operating procedures, and financial condition of the newsgathering system, as well as the relative costs and benefits of instituting less frequent and more costly reporting at a higher level of accuracy. (366)

Brennan is also fearful that limiting the recovery of damages to actual injury when showing a fault lower than actual malice "will not provide the necessary elbowroom for First Amendment expression" (367). He says it will "inevitably allow a jury bent on punishing views a formidable weapon for doing so" (367).

Justice Byron R. White writes a dissenting opinion.

White writes a long, impassioned dissent, based for the most part, on his belief that the Court in this case wrongly departed from the time-tested standards of traditional libel litigation.

In the main, he supports the long-established common-law notion that "given a false circulation, general damage to reputation was presumed and could be awarded by the jury, along with any special damages such as pecuniary loss and emotional distress" (372).

White objects to the shift in the burden of proof. Before, the media had to prove the truth of their statements; now the person defamed must prove that even a false statement was circulated as a result of some fault by the media.

He also objects to the additional burden of showing actual damages because he says it is extremely difficult to prove damage to reputation. He writes, "Damage to reputation is recurringly difficult to prove and . . . requiring actual proof would repeatedly destroy any chance for adequate compensation" (394). This statement stands in stark contrast to Brennan's assertion that the Court's description of actual damages is so broad that juries can award large damages for vaguely defined injuries like "humiliation."

Finally, White objects to discarding the old notion of malice as "ill will." He writes, "It is difficult to understand what is constitutionally wrong with assessing punitive damages to deter a publisher from departing from those standards of care ordinarily followed in the publishing industry, particularly if common-law malice is also shown" (396). He terms the Court's position "a classic example of judicial overkill" (397).

SIGNIFICANCE

This ruling overturned the public interest standard of *Rosenbloom* and returned to the distinction between public and private persons first articulated in *Sullivan*. In other words, the criterion for determining who would be required to show actual malice focuses no longer on the public's interest in the matter giving rise to the defamation, but once again on the nature of the person defamed.

In addition, building on concepts first mentioned in *Curtis* (1967), the Court classified public figures into three types and provided some guidelines for defining each type. The involuntary public figure who engages in no purposeful action is a hypothetical possibility, but would be rare. Voluntary public figures, in contrast, are persons who "assume special prominence in the resolution of public questions" (351).

There are two types of voluntary public figures. First, a public figure for "all purposes and in all contexts" is one who achieves "pervasive fame or notoriety" (351). Second, a limited public figure is a person who "voluntarily injects himself or is drawn into a particular public controversy and thereby becomes a public figure for a limited range of issues" (351).

The final significance of this ruling is that it allows the states to set their own level of fault for media performance related to defamation of private persons. Moreover, defamed private persons showing no more error than this state-determined fault can be compensated only for actual damages. Only if actual malice can be demonstrated may punitive damages also be assessed.

In addition to out-of-pocket expenses, actual damages, said the Court, could consist of impairment of reputation and standing in the community, personal humiliation, and mental anguish and suffering.

Greenbelt Coop. Pub. Asso. v. Bresler

Greenbelt Cooperative Publishing Association, Inc.
v.
Charles S. Bresler

Docket No. 1970-413
398 U.S. 6, 26 L.Ed.2d 6, 90 S.Ct. 1537 (1970)
Argued February 24 and 25, 1970. Decided May 18, 1970.

BACKGROUND

A full four years after the Court defined actual malice, lower courts and attorneys were still using the old notion of malice as "ill will." Another legal issue central to this case is how to determine the meanings of words. Further, there is this question: If words are capable of more than one meaning, which meaning is used to determine if the remarks are defamatory? The Court at times sided with the media when words were used ambiguously and at other times with the defamed persons.

CIRCUMSTANCES

Charles S. Bresler was a "prominent local real estate developer and builder in Greenbelt," (7) Maryland. He also happened to be in the autumn of 1965 "a member of the Maryland House of Delegates from a neighboring district" (7). He was negotiating two deals with the Greenbelt City Council. On the one hand, he was seeking a zoning variance so he could build high-density houses on some land he owned in the city. On the other hand, "the city was attempting to acquired another tract of land owned by Bresler for the construction of a new high school" (7).

Members of the community attended the city council meetings to express their opinions about what some of them saw as a conflict of interest. Not surprisingly, some citizens accused Bresler of trying to "blackmail" the city into granting him the zoning variance in order to get a good price on the land for the high school. The Greenbelt *News Review* printed these charges in two news stories. Bresler sued, saying the word falsely defamed him, and was awarded $5,000 in compensatory damages and $12,500 in punitive damages. The Maryland Court of Appeals affirmed the judgment.

SUMMARY OF THE COURT'S ANALYSIS

Justice Potter Stewart writes for the court.
Chief Justice Warren E. Burger, and
Justices John M. Harlan, William J. Brennan, Jr., Thurgood Marshall, and
Harry A. Blackmun join.

Justice Stewart takes note that "Bresler's counsel conceded in his opening statement to the jury that Bresler was a public figure in the community" (8). For the most part, this concession was based on Bresler's work for the city and on his involvement in a public controversy.

The question of actual malice thus becomes central to this case. The trial judge allowed the jury to chose between two meanings of malice: one as "spite, hostility or deliberate intention to harm" and the other as reckless disregard of the truth. Moreover, the judge said the jury could determine malice from the "language" of the published words. Writes Stewart succinctly, "This was error of constitutional magnitude" (10). Because the jury was thus free to select an unconstitutional definition of malice, he concludes, "The erroneous instructions to the jury would, therefore, alone be enough to require the reversal of the judgment before us" (11).

Nevertheless, the Court decides to review the facts of the case "to make certain that those principles have been constitutionally applied" (11). The first issue addressed is the accuracy of the news reports, which, Stewart notes, were not challenged. He writes, "In this sense, therefore, it cannot even be claimed that the petitioners [Greenbelt] were guilty of any 'departure from the standards of investigation and reporting ordinarily adhered to by responsible publishers'" (12). This departure test was the public figure standard announced by the Court in the *Curtis* case.

Bresler claims that the newspaper printed the word "blackmail" with actual malice because the journalists there knew a charge of criminal blackmail was false. The Court rejects Bresler's argument that readers would understand the word "blackmail" as meaning a charge of criminal action. Stewart writes:

> It is simply impossible to believe that a reader who reached the word "blackmail" in either article would not have understood . . . it was Bresler's public and wholly legal negotiating proposals that were being criticized. No reader could have thought that either the speakers at the meetings or the newspaper articles reporting their words were charging Bresler with the commission of a criminal offense. [T]he word was no more than rhetorical hyperbole. (14)

RULING

Stewart writes:

> To permit the infliction of financial liability upon the petitioners [Greenbelt] for publishing these two news articles

> would subvert the most fundamental meaning of a free press, protected by the First and Fourteenth Amendments. Accordingly, we reverse the judgment and remand the case to the Court of Appeals of Maryland for further proceedings not inconsistent with this opinion. (14, 15)

Justice Bryon R. White writes a concurring opinion.

White agrees the trial judge gave unconstitutional instructions to the jury. He disagrees with the Court's analysis of the term blackmail.

White thinks that the jury not only could have interpreted the words to impute criminal actions to Bresler, but also did just that when it brought back a "general verdict" against the newspaper. What would be the consequences of the jury determining that the words do indeed impute criminal actions?

Well, White reasons that the newspaper could argue it "should not be liable if it had no intention of charging a crime and had a good-faith, nonreckless belief that it was not doing so" (22). This argument, however, is insufficient for him. He feels the actual malice protection should not be granted to ambiguous words because the purpose of this rule is to avoid self-censorship of legitimate news. The protection of ambiguous language, White asserts, would not reduce the tendency of the media to engage in self-censorship of legitimate news.

White states, "I see no reason why the members of a skilled calling should not be held to the standard of their craft and assume the risk of being misunderstood--if they are--by the ordinary reader of their publications" (23). He concludes, "If one assumes that the jury found that the crime of blackmail was charged, 'malice' is conceded, since the defendants admittedly knew such a charge was false" (23).

Justice Hugo L. Black writes a concurring opinion.
Justice William O. Douglas joins.

Black and Douglas once again concur for the reasons set forth in *New York Times* v. *Sullivan* (1964).

SIGNIFICANCE

This case precludes the notion of malice as "ill will" when public figures, as well public officials, are falsely defamed. According to White, "The constitutional prohibition in this respect is no different whether the plaintiff be considered a 'public official' or a 'public figure.'"

Nevertheless, the Court did take care to point out the newspaper's accuracy in its news stories, and so from this it would appear that accurate reporting is at least a partial defense in cases involving libel of public figures.

Harte-Hanks Communications, Inc. v. Connaughton

Harte-Hanks Communications, Inc.,
v.
Daniel Connaughton

Docket No. 88-10; 57 LW 4847
491 U.S. ---, 105 L.Ed.2d 562, 109 S.Ct. 2678 (1989)
Argued March 20, 1989. Decided June 22, 1989.

BACKGROUND

This case in another in a series refining the meaning of actual malice first announced in *New York Times* v. *Sullivan* (1964). Actual malice was defined by the court there as knowingly publishing false defamatory statements or publishing them with reckless disregard for their truth. Although from the very first the Court said that actual malice is more than merely failing to investigate the truth of a defamatory accusation, here it concedes that purposely failing to make such investigations can indeed constitute reckless disregard of the truth.

In addition, the Court's 1964 notion of actual malice has since then often conflicted with traditional notions of court procedures. One of those conflicts first came to a head in *Bose Corp*. v. *Consumers Union of U.S., Inc.*(1984). In *Bose* the Court attempted to resolve a conflict between two highly technical legal points. On the one hand, Rule 52(a) of the *Federal Rules of Civil Procedure* says that appellate courts--giving due regard to the opportunity of a trial judge or a jury to evaluate the credibility of witnesses--should not challenge a fact determined by a trial court unless the determination is "clearly erroneous." The *New York Times* v. *Sullivan* case, on the other hand, said the Court should make an independent survey of the evidence to make sure that the defamatory statements do or do not deserve First Amendment protection. The resolution in *Bose* said Rule 52 applies to matters of fact, but the *New York Times v. Sullivan* requirement refers to matters of law based on facts.

Similarly, here the Court says that determining whether the facts are sufficient to support the existence of actual malice is a matter of law and so a matter open to the independent evaluation of the appellate courts.

CIRCUMSTANCES

An extremely confusing set of circumstances surrounds the origin of this libel case. The Court reviews many of the events causing this confusing, but, in some ways, that review tends to hide the forest with too many trees. Here follows a brief summary of these events.

The arrest on bribery charges of the Director of Court Services for Hamilton, Ohio, started this case in motion because Hamilton Judge James Dolan was at that time running for re-election. Alice Thompson, a member of the grand jury looking into the bribery charges, accused Dolan's opponent, Daniel Connaughton, of using "dirty tricks" and bribery to influence the jury's investigation. Her story was printed by the Hamilton *Journal News*, which supported Dolan. Connaughton, in turn, sued the newspaper for libel, saying the journalists knew the story was false when they published it.

In defense, the *Journal News* asked for a summary judgment, claiming, in part, that the doctrine of neutral reportage, which has been accepted to some degree in Ohio, protected the media from such libel suits. The district court, however, rejected the newspaper's argument because the doctrine was valid only if a "responsible, prominent organization" issued the libelous statement. In this court's opinion, a grand jury witness making accusations does not qualify.

Connaughton's appeal focused for the most part on three questions the district court asked the libel jury to answer. Here are the questions:

> 1. Do you unanimously find by a preponderance of the evidence that the publication in question was defamatory toward the plaintiff?
> 2. Do you unanimously find by a preponderance of the evidence that the publication in evidence was false?
> 3. Do you unanimously find by clear and convincing proof that the publication in question was published with actual malice? (105 L.Ed.2d 572)

The jury answered yes to all three questions, and Connaughton was awarded $5,000 in compensatory damages and $195,000 in punitive damages.

Looking at what it called the "core issue" of witness credibility, the court of appeals affirmed the decision. In short, the appeals court, following Rule 52, said the jury's findings of fact were not "clearly erroneous" (105 L.Ed.2d 573).

Connaughton appealed again, saying that the court of appeals itself erred twice. First, he said that the court did not apply the actual malice standard of *New York Times* v. *Sullivan* (1964), but wrongly used the lower standard of *Curtis Publishing* v. *Butts* (1967), which required showing only "highly unreasonable conduct constituting an extreme departure from the standards of investigation and reporting ordinarily adhered to by responsible publishers" (388 *U.S.* at 155). Secondly, he said the appeals court failed to make an independent review of the evidence, a review required by *New York Times* v. *Sullivan*.

SUMMARY OF THE COURT'S ANALYSIS

Justice John Paul Stevens writes for the Court.
Chief Justice William H. Rehnquist, and Justices William J. Brennan, Jr., Thurgood Marshall, Harry A. Blackmun, Sandra Day O'Connor, and Anthony M. Kennedy join.

Justice Stevens agrees with Connaughton's assertion that actual malice is the standard to be used here, not extreme departure from the standards of investigation and reporting ordinarily adhered to by responsible publishers. He also notes that certain statements by the appeals court, "when read in isolation," appear to indicate that this lower court did indeed apply wrongly the extreme departure standard. "When read as a whole," though, these statements about extreme departure, Stevens writes, "Were merely supportive of the court's ultimate conclusion" (105 L.Ed.2d 577). Thus, for Stevens, evidence concerning the newspaper's motives in publishing the defamation and evidence relating to the standard of care (both aspects of the extreme departure standard) are also evidence relevant to actual malice. Moreover, the appeals court did not depend upon only these two kinds of evidence for its finding of actual malice. Therefore, since Stevens feels that the court did conduct a proper review, he dismisses Connaughton's first basis for appeal.

The main issue, as Stevens sees it, is whether or not the appeals court conducted a truly independent review of the evidence as it is required by both *New York Times* v. *Sullivan* (1964) and *Bose Corp.* v. *Consumers Union of U.S., Inc.* (1984). To resolve this question, Stevens reviews at great length the events leading up to Connaughton's lawsuit, quoting long passages from the trial transcript. Eventually, he concludes that the evidence shows the newspaper accurately reported both Thompson's allegations and Connaughton's statements issued in his defense. In addition, he concludes that, although the evidence could support a finding that either one was telling the truth, the jury concluded "Connaughton was telling the truth and Thompson's charges were false" (105 L.Ed.2d 585).

Still, the mere fact that the jury believed Thompson lied is not in itself sufficient evidence to say that the newspaper published her charges knowing they were false. Nevertheless, other items, when added to the jury's finding, do provide enough support, Stevens says.

One other item is the failure by the *Journal News* to interview Patsy Stephens, one of six witnesses to conversations between Thompson and Connaughton. Of this failure, Stevens writes, "It is utterly bewildering in light of the fact that the Journal News committed substantial resources to investigating Thompson's claims, yet chose not to interview the one witness who was most likely to confirm Thompson's account of the events" (105 L.Ed.2d 585).

In addition, Stevens writes, "The newspaper's decision not to listen to tapes of the Stephens interview in Connaughton's home also supports the finding of actual malice" (105 L.Ed.2d 585, 586). He notes, "Much of what Thompson had said about the interview could easily have been verified or disproven by listening to the tapes" (105 L.Ed.2d 586).

A third damaging item is an October 30 editorial that Stevens said indicated the newspaper was going to print the allegations on November 1 regardless of the outcome of its investigation into these events.

The fourth and last piece of evidence is the discrepancies in the testimonies of the journalists at the *Journal News*. These discrepancies, Stevens says, "may have given the jury the impression that the failure to conduct a complete investigation involved a deliberate effort to avoid the truth" (105 L.Ed.2d 587).

Stevens then notes that the question of how much evidence is enough to show actual malice is a question of law. The law says that to answer this question the reviewing court "must consider the factual record in full" (105 L.Ed.2d 589). So, while the Court agrees that there is sufficient factual evidence for the jury to issue of a finding of actual malice, it must also determine whether or not the appeals courts undertook an adequately independent review of those facts, a review like the one just undertaken above by Stevens.

In essence, Stevens concludes that, although the appeals court's review is different from the Court's, it is in fact independent. The appeals court concluded that the jury "may" or "could have" drawn certain valid conclusions about evidence supporting a charge of actual malice, whereas the Court concludes "that the jury *must* [emphasis Steven's] have" come to these same conclusions (105 L.Ed.2d 590).

In the end, Stevens says both courts agree that the newspaper's "purposeful avoidance of the truth" is not just extreme departure from the standards of investigation and reporting ordinarily adhered to by responsible publishers, but is indeed actual malice.

RULING

Stevens writes, "The evidence . . ., when reviewed in its entirely, is 'unmistakably' sufficient to support a finding of actual malice. The judgment of the Court of Appeals is accordingly affirmed" (105 L.Ed.2d 592).

Justice Byron R. White writes a concurring opinion.
Chief Justice William H. Rehnquist joins.

White writes to highlight a highly technical distinction in law by pointing out relevant implications resting in the differences between the two parts of the actual malice rule. The knowledge-of-falsity part, he says, is a question of fact and so can be reviewed only under the "clearly erroneous standard" of federal court Rule 52. The reckless-disregard-of-the-truth part, however, is not a question of fact, and so the trial court's conclusions about this part are to be reviewed independently by the appellate court. He is of the opinion that the Court correctly conducted the second type of review.

From this two-paragraph opinion, it appears that White is saying the jury's finding that the newspaper avoided the truth constitutes a finding that those journalists recklessly disregarded truth. Since determining reckless disregard of the truth is a judgment of law, not fact, the evidence presented to the jury is to be reviewed independently by the appellate court.

Justice Harry A. Blackmun writes a concurring opinion.

Justice Blackmun says he writes to stress two points: "First, the case reaches us in an odd posture" (105 L.Ed.2d 593). In other words, for reasons Blackmun does not understand, the newspaper, in the appeal process, unwisely gave up the defense of neutral reportage. He writes, "Were this Court to adopt the neutral reportage theory, the facts of this case arguably might fit within it" (105 L.Ed.2d 593).

Secondly, he asserts that "the form and content of the story are relevant . . . to the question of actual malice" (105 L.Ed.2d 593). He gives as an example of form the reporting of allegations not as facts but as allegations. He writes, "Because I am convinced that the majority has considered the article's content and form in the course of its . . . review . . ., I conclude that the result the majority reaches is proper even when the contents of the story are given due weight, I concur" (105 L.Ed.2d 594).

Justice Anthony M. Kennedy writes a concurring opinion.

Kennedy writes, "I join the opinion of the Court, for in my view it is not inconsistent with the analysis set out in Justice Scalia's separate concurrence" (105 L.Ed.2d 594).

Justice Antonin Scalia writes a concurring opinion.

Justice Scalia says he agrees with the Court's analysis of the requirement for showing actual malice. He disagrees, however, with the Court's assertion that the appellate courts must undertake an independent review of the factual evidence when ruling on the question of actual malice.

Drawing a fine distinction, he focuses on the obligations of the trial judge and the appellate courts to review the conclusions of a jury in this matter. The distinction, as Scalia sees it, is as follows. On the one hand, there is the assertion that the courts must make their own independent evaluation of the facts supporting the existence of actual malice. On the other hand is the assertion that the courts must assume "*all of the facts that could reasonably be found in favor of the plaintiff were found in favor of the plaintiff* [emphasis Scalia's]" (105 L.Ed.2d 595). On the basis of this assumption, the appellate courts, Scalia asserts, must offer only an independent evaluation that these facts are indeed sufficient to support the existence of actual malice.

In other words, one view asserts that the courts are required to evaluate the truth of the evidence to see what evidence is factual and what is not. The other view asserts that, assuming the jury correctly determined the facts, the courts are to evaluate whether these facts are sufficient to support the existence of actual malice.

Here the Court accepts what the jury said are the facts of the case and then makes an independent evaluation concluding that these facts are sufficient to support the existence of actual malice. Scalia's problem with the Court's procedure is that the only facts considered are those related to the three questions posed by the trial judge. Scalia says the Court should have assumed "the jury made all the supportive findings it reasonable could have made" (105 L.Ed.2d 597).

SIGNIFICANCE

It appears that one aspect of this case carries significance for journalists and another for attorneys. The significance for journalists is that giving the appearance of purposely avoiding an investigation into a story can be interpreted constitutionally by a jury to constitute adequate evidence of reckless disregard for the truth. Although the Court specifically and emphatically rejected the notion of extreme departure from the standards of investigation and reporting ordinarily adhered to by responsible publishers, a notion first asserted by the three justices who formed the plurality opinion in *Curtis Publishing* v. *Butts* (1967), it also said that purposely avoiding an investigation is a much more wrong than merely failing to investigate.

The significance for attorneys is the Court's affirmation of its review procedures first announced in *Bose Corp*. v. *Consumers Union of U.S., Inc.* (1984). This affirmation is summarized pointedly in Justice Scalia's concurring opinion. He notes that the appellate courts are to make an independent evaluation not of the facts determined by the jury, but of the value of those facts for establishing sufficient evidence to assert that the journalists involved published with actual malice.

Henry v. Collins

Henry v. Collins
Docket No. 1965-89

Henry v. Pearson
Docket No. 1965-90

380 U.S. 356, 13 L.Ed.2d 892, 85 S.Ct. 992 (1965)
Announced March 29, 1965.

BACKGROUND

Like Garrison, this case went to trial before the *Sullivan* decision was handed down by the Court. Not surprisingly, therefore, the trial judge's instructions to the jury were based on the traditional understanding of malice as "ill will" or an intent to inflict harm.

CIRCUMSTANCES

Henry issued a statement claiming that his arrest on charges of disturbing the peace was the result of "a diabolical plot" designed by the county attorney and the chief of police. They sued him for libel.

SUMMARY OF THE COURT'S ANALYSIS

In a *per curiam* (by the court) opinion, the Court asserts the jury was wrongly instructed by the trail judge when he said, "'Malice does not necessarily mean hatred or ill will, but that malice may consist merely of culpable recklessness or a willful and wanton disregard of the rights and interests of the person defamed'" (356). The Court responds, "The jury might well have [wrongly] understood these instructions to allow recovery on a showing of intent to inflict harm, rather than intent to inflict harm through falsehood" (357). The Court then quotes the actual malice definition from *Sullivan*.

criticism against respondents' [public officials'] performance of their public duties" (357).

SIGNIFICANCE

Although the Court also asserted in *Garrison* v. *Louisiana* (1964) that actual malice does not mean "ill will," this case is the first opinion since *Sullivan* (1964) devoted precisely to this one point. Thus, the Court appears to be instructing the lower courts that the 12-month-old actual malice term is different in at least one critical way from the centuries-old traditional notion of malice: It does not focus on intent to harm.

Herbert v. Lando

Anthony Herbert
v.
Barry Lando

Docket No. 77-1105
441 U.S. 153, 60 L.Ed.2d 115, 99 S.Ct. 1635 (1979)
Argued October 31, 1978. Decided April 18, 1979.

BACKGROUND

In some ways the context for libel suits changed in the 1970s from the civil rights struggles to the controversy over the Vietnam War. Accusations about the conduct of the war and about the participation of various military and political leaders spawned a number of libel suits. Herbert's suit was one of the early ones.

Since *Sullivan* (1964), the Court had been attempting to clarify the actual malice definition. By the time Herbert's case found its way to the top of the ladder, the problems of how to prove reckless disregard of truth were becoming important. Public officials and figures reasoned that, if they could not prove journalists knew that certain statements were false when written or broadcast, then maybe it would be possible to prove journalists demonstrated reckless disregard for the truth.

Lawyers soon concluded that it was often difficult, if not impossible, to show reckless disregard for the truth on the basis of objective evidence, like the news story itself. Therefore, they looked at two other forms of evidence: (1) the journalists' state of mind (attitude toward the value of the truth of the news being gathered); and (2) the editorial process itself of gathering, editing, and refining a news story before it is disseminated.

The state-of-mind issue can be described roughly as an attempt to find out what thoughts are going through the minds of journalists when they write news stories. The purpose of such an inquiry is to show that journalists don't care very much about the truthfulness of the information they are working with. Since a defamed public official, in order to meet the actual malice requirement, may wish to show that journalists don't care very much about the truth, that official may wish to ask questions about their attitude toward the truth of information included in a news story.

Some lawyers felt that reckless disregard of the truth could also be established by inquiring into the process of putting a news story together. Thus, in order to show reckless disregard for the truth, a defamed public official may attempt to find out what was written or said in the news room about a news story before it was disseminated.

In an effort to combat attempts to get into reporters' state of mind, the media proposed a limited evidentiary privilege for the editorial process. This proposal asserted a First Amendment privilege protecting the news media from being forced to turn over to a court information about the editorial process. The Court, however, did not support this privilege.

CIRCUMSTANCES

Anthony Herbert, an army officer in Vietnam gained media attention when, in 1969 and 1970, he "accused his superior officers of covering up reports of atrocities and other war crimes" (155). On February 4, 1973, CBS aired a Sixty Minutes show (produced and edited by Barry Lando) devoted to his accusations; "Lando later published a related article in Atlantic Monthly Magazine" (156).

Herbert sued saying the program and article "falsely and maliciously portrayed him as a liar and a person who had made up war-crimes charges to explain his relief from command" (156). When his lawyers asked in the discovery process for certain information from Lando, the producer refused to give it, claiming a constitutional privilege against revealing aspects of the editorial process. The district court rejected the privilege, but the appeals court reversed.

SUMMARY OF THE COURT'S ANALYSIS

Justice Byron R. White writes for the Court.
Chief Justice Warren E. Burger and
Justices Harry A. Blackmun, William H. Rehnquist, and
John Paul Stevens join.

White begins the analysis by rejecting the idea of a special editorial privilege for the media. He writes:

> Nor did these [post-*Sullivan*] cases suggest any First Amendment restriction on the sources from which the plaintiff could obtain the necessary evidence to prove the critical elements of his cause of action. On the contrary, New York Times and its progeny made it essential to proving liability that the plaintiff focus on the conduct and state of mind of the defendant. (160)
>
> In the first place, it is plain enough that the suggested privilege for the editorial process would constitute a substantial interference with the ability of a defamation plaintiff to establish the ingredients of malice [i.e., reckless disregard for the truth] as required by New York Times. (170)

First, White says that a defamed public official, in an attempt to show reckless disregard for the truth, not only may--but indeed must--inquire about journalists' state of mind. He points out that state-of-mind evidence is older than the First Amendment, commonly used to show the attitude (such as ill will) or intent (such as desire to inflict injury) of a person who defamed another.

Nor, adds White, are the media protected from questions about the editorial process. He then states reasons for rejecting this privilege. One is that the "outer boundaries of the editorial privilege now urged are difficult to perceive" (170). White says it would be difficult to know exactly what actions, thoughts, conversations, documents, and the like would be covered by the editorial process.

After rejecting the notion of a First Amendment editorial privilege, the Court analyzes the arguments for asserting its existence: "The reason given for claiming the privilege is that requiring disclosure of editorial conversations and of a reporter's conclusions about the veracity of the material he has gathered will have an intolerable chilling effect on the editorial process and editorial decision making" (171).

To this argument, the Court responds by saying, "Those effects are precisely what New York Times . . . held to be consistent with the First Amendment" (171). In other words, White is saying that the actual malice test was designed, among other reasons, precisely because it would discourage "the publication of erroneous information known to be false or probably false" (172). He notes, "Spreading false information in and of itself carries no First Amendment credentials" (171). The Court asserts that the result of allowing questions about the editorial process is, "Only knowing or reckless error will be discouraged" (173).

Another proposed problem with allowing questions about the editorial process is "that frank discussion among reporters and editors will be dampened and sound editorial judgment endangered" (173). To this argument the Court suggests that journalists, as a consequence, have "even more reason to resort to prepublication precautions, such as a frank interchange of act and opinion" (174).

Nevertheless, the Court does feel that "editorial discussions or exchanges" do have "constitutional protection from casual inquiry" (174). The editorial process should not be subjected to questions "merely to satisfy curiosity or to serve some general end such as the public interest" (174).

In general, however, the Court feels that "evidentiary privileges [the right to refuse to reveal evidence sought by one party in a lawsuit] are not favored" (174). White notes that even "the President, for example, does not have an absolute privilege against disclosure of materials subpoenaed for a judicial proceeding" (175).

In addition, the Court asserts that an editorial or evidentiary privilege "would not cure the problems" of mushrooming litigating costs, much of it due to pretrial discovery" (176). The Court's answer to the high costs of libel suits is a change in the *Federal Rules of Civil Procedure*. In the meantime, the media will have to rely on the district judge to prevent abuse of pretrial discovery into the editorial process. In particular, the Court encourages district judges take care to apply "firmly" "the requirement of Rule 26(b)(1) that the material sought in discovery be 'relevant'"(178).

RULING

White writes, "We concluded that the present construction of the First Amendment should not be modified by creating the evidentiary privilege which the respondents now urge" (175). Thus, "the judgment of the Court of Appeals is reversed" (177).

Justice Lewis F. Powell, Jr., writes a concurring opinion.

Powell agrees with the Court that the First Amendment "should not be expanded to create an evidentiary privilege" (178). Still, he is concerned about the widespread abuse of pretrial discovery because "discovery techniques and tactics have become a highly developed litigation art--one not infrequently exploited to the disadvantage of justice" (179).

Therefore, Powell wishes to underscore the Court's cautionary note that "the initial inquiry in enforcement of any discovery request is one of relevance" (179).

Justice William J. Brennan, Jr., writes a dissenting opinion.

Brennan agrees that there should be no editorial privilege to "shield" journalists' "mental processes" (181). Yet, he does feel that there is a qualified First Amendment privilege for "predecisional communication among editors" (181). This privilege gives way, however--as Brennan sees it--whenever "a public-figure plaintiff is able to demonstrate to the prima facie satisfaction of a trial judge that the publication in question constitutes defamatory falsehood" (181). In other words, the privilege is limited to only those instances in which a trial judge reasonably believes that the media have not disseminated a false defamatory statement.

The appeals court divided the information sought by Herbert--but refused by Lando, claiming he was shielded by an editorial privilege--into five categories. Brennan devotes a few pages to an analysis of how to consider the value of these five categories.

He begins by saying, "The editorial privilege claimed by respondents must be carefully analyzed to determine whether its creation would significantly further . . . social values" (188). He goes on, "But it is clear that disclosure of the editorial process of the press will . . . discourage participants in that editorial process" (191). He concludes, "Our inquiry, therefore, becomes the independent First Amendment [social] values served by the editorial process and the extent to which exposure of that process would impair these First Amendment values" (192).

First, Brennan asserts that this exposure will not stop journalists from thinking; thus, inquiry into state of mind is permissible. The prepublication editorial processes are another matter. He writes, "The possibility of future libel judgments will dampen full and candid discussion among editors of proposed publications" (194). He continues:

> Those editors who have doubts might remain silent; those who would prefer to follow other investigative leads might be restrained; those who would otherwise counsel caution might

> hold their tongues. In short, in the absence of such an editorial privilege the accuracy, thoroughness, and profundity of consequent publications might well be diminished.
>
> Such a diminution would affect First Amendment [social] values. (194)

He concludes, "To the extent the accuracy, effectiveness, and thoroughness of such coverage is undermined, the social values protected by the First Amendment suffer abridgment. I find compelling these justifications for the existence of an editorial privilege" (195).

For Brennan, though, the privilege is clearly limited. He writes,

> In my judgment the existence of a privilege protecting the editorial process must . . . be determined with reference to the circumstances of a particular case.
>
> If . . . a public-figure plaintiff is able to establish to the prima facie satisfaction of a trial judge, that the publication at issue constitutes defamatory falsehood, the claim of damaged reputation becomes specific and demonstrable, and the editorial privilege must yield. (197)

In short, editorial privilege is waived when a trial judge believes journalists have circulated a false defamatory statement.

At the end of his analysis, Brennan returns to the five categories designed by the appeals court. He writes, "Four of the five categories concern respondents' mental processes, and thus would not be covered by an editorial privilege" (198). The fifth category consists of conversations between Lando and Mike Wallace. These, Brennan feels, "would seem to be protected by a proper editorial privilege" (198).

Justice Potter Stewart writes a dissenting opinion.

Stewart asserts straightforwardly that "inquiry into the broad 'editorial process' is simply not relevant" (199) in this case. While for Stewart the old notion of actual malice (ill will) does indeed raise the question of why someone falsely defamed another, the *Sullivan* definition of actual malice, in contrast, does not raise the issue of why. He writes, "A publisher's motivation in a case such as this is irrelevant, there is clearly no occasion for inquiry into the editorial process as conceptualized in this case" (201).

Justice Thurgood Marshall writes a dissenting opinion.

Marshall begins by noting that the present case points out two conflicting values. He writes, "Libel actions . . . [create] incentives for the press to exercise considered judgment before publishing material that compromises personal integrity. Against these objectives must be balanced society's interest in promoting unfettered debate on matters of public importance" (202). For Marshall, the actual malice notion seems to strike an appropriate balance between these two issues; he feels "it must be reassessed in light of the procedural realities under which libel actions are conducted" (204).

Marshall writes:

> The potential for abuse of liberal discovery procedures is of particular concern in the defamation context. [S]elf-perceived victims of defamation are animated by something more than a rational calculus of their chances of recovery. (204) [P]retrial maneuvers may be fashioned more with an eye to deterrence or retaliation than to unearthing germane material. [T]he societal consequences attending such abuse are of special magnitude. Faced with the prospect of escalating attorney's fees, diversion of time from journalistic endeavors, and exposure of potentially sensitive information, editors may well make publication judgments that reflect less the risk of liability than the expense of vindication. (205)

Marshall proposes a remedy to this problem he has just outlined. He writes, "I would require that district courts superintend pretrial disclosure . . . so as to protect the press from unnecessarily protracted or tangential inquiry. [D]iscovery requests should be measured against a strict standard of relevance" (206). Not satisfied with strict enforcement of a relevancy standard, however, Marshall goes on to assert, "I believe some additional protection in the form of an evidentiary privilege is warranted" (206).

Like the Court, Marshall divides the discovery requests into those "concerning the state of mind of an individual journalist, principally his conclusions" and "communications between journalists" (206). "With respect to state-of-mind," he writes, "It is unclear how journalists faced with the possibility of such questions can be 'chilled in the very process of thought'" (207). He adds, "Editors must continue to think, and to form opinions and conclusions about the veracity of their sources and the accuracy of their information" (207). He therefore sees no privilege for state-of-mind inquiry.

Nevertheless, Marshall sees "external evidence" standing "on a different footing" (208). He writes:

> Journalists cannot stop forming tentative hypotheses, but they can cease articulating them openly. [E]ditors and reporters may well prove reluctant to air their reservations or to explore other means of presenting information and comments. The threat of unchecked discovery may well stifle the collegial discussion essential to sound editorial dynamics. (209)

Marshall would grant an editorial privilege from this kind of discovery attempt because "there are a variety of other means to establish deliberate or reckless disregard for the truth" (210). Among those means, Marshall notes these: "Inherent implausibility, obvious reasons to doubt the veracity or accuracy of information, and concessions or inconsistent statements by the defendant" (210).

SIGNIFICANCE

Attempts to find ways for demonstrating journalists' reckless disregard for the truth and efforts to establish an editorial privilege against such attempts make this case significant.

Herbert attempted to show Lando's reckless disregard for the truth in two ways: (1) By inquiring into Lando's state of mind before and during production of the show; and (2) asking about various preproduction actions, such as conversations with Mike Wallace. Lando tried to defend against these attempts by asserting the existence of a First Amendment editorial privilege protecting journalists from revealing information that is part of the editorial process. He claimed that, without such protection, the news-gathering process would be threatened.

The Court rejected both attempts. It noted first that state-of-mind inquiries are an ancient legal tradition. It also said that actual malice was designed for the specific purpose of discouraging that part of the editorial process that may tend to result in the publication of false defamatory information.

In addition, the Court said the rules of civil procedure require a trial judge to protect the media from requests for irrelevant information.

The media found in the dissenting opinions some hope for relief from extended and thus expensive discovery attempts. At least two of the justices proposed a constitutional privilege for the editorial process. All of the dissenters joined the Court, however, in rejecting the claim of a First Amendment privilege against answering state-of-mind questions.

Hustler Magazine v. Falwell

Hustler Magazine and Larry C. Flynt
v.
Jerry Falwell

Docket No. 86-1278; 56 Law Week 4180
485 U.S. ---, 99 L.Ed.2d 41, 108 S.Ct. 876 (1988)
Argued December 2, 1987. Decided February 24, 1988.

BACKGROUND

It is particularly difficult to win a libel suit when the defamatory statement at issue is avowedly an opinion, not a fact. The Court is fond of saying that there is no such thing as a false idea. So, in addition to asking for damages for injury to reputation, Jerry Falwell also asked for emotional damages for injury suffered as a result of deliberately outrageous speech. Falwell reasoned that, since actual malice is a rule of libel law, a claim for damages from emotional distress may not have to show that the statements were published with knowledge that they were false or with reckless disregard for the truth. His argument was an ingenious attempt to get around the actual malice burden of libel litigation, but it failed.

CIRCUMSTANCES

Hustler magazine printed what it called an "ad parody" of Campari liqueur. The Campari advertisements typically included interviews of various celebrities who talked about their "first times," a deliberate double entendre. The *Hustler* parody featured an alleged interview with Jerry Falwell (a nationally known minister active in public affairs), in which he reveals that his "'first time' was during a drunken incestuous rendezvous with his mother in an outhouse" (99 L. Ed.2d 47). The advertisement also portrayed Falwell "and his mother as drunk and immoral, and suggests that . . . [he] is a hypocrite who preaches only when he is drunk" (LW 4180). A disclaimer, at the bottom of the page in small print reads, "'ad parody--not to be taken seriously'" (99 L. Ed.2d 47).

Falwell sued. The United States District Court for the Western District of Virginia issued a directed verdict against Falwell's invasion-of-privacy claim, and the jury turned in a verdict against his libel claim. "The jury ruled for . . . [Falwell] on the intentionally infliction of emotional distress claim, however," (99 L. Ed.2d 47) and awarded him $100,000 in compensatory damages and $50,000 in punitive damages. The United States Court of Appeals for the Fourth Circuit affirmed the jury's judgment, saying Falwell did not have to show actual malice in order to recover for emotional distress.

SUMMARY OF THE COURT'S ANALYSIS

Chief Justice William H. Rehnquist writes for the Court.
Justices William J. Brennan, Jr., Thurgood Marshall, Harry A. Blackmun, John Paul Stevens, Sandra Day O'Connor, and Antonin Scalia join.

Justice Rehnquist notes, "This case presents us with a novel question involving the First Amendment limitations upon a State's authority to protect its citizens from the intentional infliction of emotional distress" (99 L. Ed.2d 48). In essence, Falwell was asking for damages from emotional distress caused by an intentionally outrageous opinion. Rehnquist writes:

> [Falwell] would have us find that a State's interest in protecting public figures from emotional distress is sufficient to deny First Amendment protection to speech that is patently offensive and is intended to inflict emotional injury, even when that speech could not reasonable have been interpreted as stating actual facts about the public figure involved. (99 L. Ed.2d 48)

Rehnquist says Falwell is arguing "that a different standard [from actual malice] should apply" when the damage is not "reputational" but "severe emotional distress suffered by the person who is the subject of an offensive publication" (99 L. Ed.2d 50). According to Rehnquist, the ingredients Falwell asserts justify removing the speech from constitutional protection are "the utterance was intended to inflict emotional distress, was outrageous, and did in fact inflict serious emotional distress" (99 L. Ed.2d 50). The key to Falwell's argument, as Rehnquist sees it, is "the intent to cause injury" (99 L. Ed.2d 50). "The State's interest in preventing emotional harm," Rehnquist says Falwell is arguing, "simply outweighs whatever interest a speaker may have in speech of this type" (99 L. Ed.2d 50).

"Generally speaking, the law does not regard the intent to inflict emotional distress" (99 L. Ed.2d 50) as a serious offense, Rehnquist writes. He asserts that, although bad motives may be an important consideration in other forms of injury, the First Amendment "prohibits" their consideration "in the area of public debate about public figures" (99 L. Ed.2d 50). If this were not so, Rehnquist writes, "There can be little doubt that political cartoonists and satirists would be subjected to damages awards without any showing that their work falsely defamed its subject" (99 L. Ed.2d 50).

The chief justice notes, though, that Falwell also claims "the caricature in question here was so 'outrageous' as to distinguish it from more traditional political cartoons" (99 L. Ed.2d 51). He admits, "The caricature of respondent [Falwell] and his mother published in Hustler is at best a distant cousin of the political cartoon . . ., and a rather poor relation at that" (99 L. Ed.2d 51). The problem is that the Court sees no way to lay "down a principled standard to separate the one from the other" (99 L. Ed.2d 51). Outrageousness cannot be that standard, according to the Court, because "in the area of political and social discourse [it] has an inherent subjectiveness about it which would allow a jury to impose liability on the basis of the juror's tastes or views, or perhaps on the basis of their dislike of a particular expression" (99 L. Ed.2d 52).

RULING

Rehnquist writes:

> We conclude that public figures and public officials may not recover for the tort of intentional infliction of emotional distress by reason of publications such as the one here at issue without showing in addition that the publication contains a false statement of fact which was made with "actual malice." (99 L. Ed.2d 52) [S]uch a standard is necessary to give adequate "breathing space" to the freedoms protected by the First Amendment. (99 L. Ed.2d 53)
> The judgment of the Court of Appeals is accordingly *reversed*. (99 L. Ed.2d 53)

Justice Byron R. White concurs without writing an opinion.

SIGNIFICANCE

In order to collect damages for outrageous speech intentionally designed to inflict severe emotional distress, one must show actual malice, which means, in part, that the speech itself must be shown to be factual. If the speech is opinion, then it cannot be false because there is no such thing as a false idea.

Hutchinson v. Proxmire

Ronald R. Hutchinson
v.
William Proxmire and Morton Schwartz

Docket No. 78-680
443 U.S. 111, 61 L.Ed.2d 411, 99 S.Ct. 2675 (1979)
Argued April 17, 1979. Decided June 26, 1979.

BACKGROUND

Although the Court continues to refine the definitions of public and private persons, it also begins in the late 1970s to look at libel issues unrelated to the actual malice concept promulgated in *Sullivan*. Here, one of those other issues is the limits of the privilege granted members of Congress what is known as the speech or debate clause of the Constitution. That clause is found in Article I, Section 6. The relevant words are these, "The senators and representatives shall . . . in all cases, except treason, felony, and breach of peace, be privileged . . . for any speech or debate in either house."

CIRCUMSTANCES

In March 1975, Senator William Proxmire from Wisconsin "initiated the 'Golden Fleece of the Month Award' to publicize what he perceived to be the most egregious examples of wasteful governmental spending" (114). His second award, in April 1975, went to three government agencies (including the National Science Foundation and NASA) "for spending almost half a million dollars during the preceding seven years to fund Hutchinson's research" (114). The director of research at the Kalamazoo, Michigan, State Mental Hospital, Ronald R. Hutchinson "sought an objective measure of aggression, concentrating upon the behavior pattern of certain animals such as the clenching of jaws when they were exposed to various aggravating stressful stimuli" (115).

The award was based upon research by Proxmire's legislative assistant, Morton Schwartz. Schwartz wrote a speech for Proxmire to give in the Senate; "the text was then incorporated into an advance press release" (116). Among other things, the speech said, "The good doctor has made a fortune from his monkeys and in the process made a monkey out of the American Taxpayer" (116). It goes on, "In view of the transparent worthlessness of Hutchinson's study of jaw-grinding and biting by angry or hard-drinking monkeys, it is time we put a stop to the bite Hutchinson and the bureaucrats who fund him have been taking of the taxpayer" (116).

Hutchinson sued claiming he "'suffered a lose of respect in his profession, has suffered injury to his feelings, and has been humiliated, held up to public scorn, suffered extreme mental anguish and physical illness and pain to his person'" (118).

The United States District Court in Wisconsin dismissed the case in a summary judgment saying that the press release fell within the "informing function" of the speech or debate clause. The appeals court upheld the dismissal for similar reasons.

SUMMARY OF THE COURT'S ANALYSIS

Chief Justice Warren E. Burger writes for the Court. Justices Byron R. White, Thurgood Marshall, Harry A. Blackmun, Lewis F. Powell, Jr., William H. Rehnquist, John Paul Stevens, and Potter Stewart join.

Justice Burger begins by focusing attention on these three issues:

> (1) Whether a Member of Congress is protected by the Speech or Debate Clause . . . for allegedly defamatory statements made by the Member in press releases and newsletters;
> (2) whether petitioner Hutchinson is either a "public figure" or a "public official";
> (3) whether respondents [Proxmire and Schwartz] were entitled to summary judgment. (113)

The first issue, Burger writes, "Involves the scope of the Speech or Debate Clause" (122). Proxmire argues that "press releases and newsletters are necessary for Members of Congress to communicate with other Members" (124). He also argues "that an essential part of the duties of a member of Congress is to inform constituents, as well as other Members, of the issues being considered" (124).

Burger notes that, although the Court in five decisions from 1881 to 1973 has "given the Clause a practical rather than a strictly literal reading . . . the gloss . . . has not, however, departed from the objective of protecting only legislative activities" (124, 125). He adds:

> Whatever imprecision there may be in the term "legislative activities," it is clear that nothing in the history or in the explicit language of the Clause suggests any intention to create an absolute privilege from liability or suit for defamatory statements made outside the Chamber. (127) Indeed, the precedents abundantly support the conclusion that a Member may be held liable for republishing defamatory statements originally made in either House. (127, 128)

In addition, Burger is not inclined to extend the privilege of the clause to newsletters and press releases because neither "was 'essential to the deliberations of the Senate' and neither was part of the deliberative process" (130). He does concede, however, the Court "may assume that a Member's published statements exert some influence on other votes in the Congress and therefore have a relationship to the legislative and deliberative process" (131). But, in *Johnson*, 383 U.S. 169, 15 L.Ed.2d 681, 86 S.Ct. 749 (1966), the Court drew a distinction between what is "only 'related to the due functioning of the legislative process'" and what is central enough to be "entitled to immunity" (131).

Proxmire argues that press releases are privileged because they are "part of the 'informing function' of Congress" (131). But Burger says there exist two notions of this function. There is a narrow "Wilsonian sense that . . . Congressional efforts to inform itself though committee hearings are part of the legislative function" (132, 133). The broader sense "relied upon by respondents [Proxmire and Schwartz], perceives it to be the duty of Members to tell the public about their activities" (133). Since information falling in this broader sense "is not part of the legislative function or the deliberations that make up the legislative process," the Court says it "is not protected by the Speech or Debate Clause" (133). Burger writes, "Newsletters and press releases . . . are primarily means of informing those outside the legislative forum; they represent the views and will of a single Member" (133).

Turning to the second issue, Burger notes first that no one involved asserts that Hutchinson "attained such prominence that he is a public figure for all purposes" (134). But Proxmire argues that Hutchinson "is a public figure for the limited purpose of comment on his receipt of federal funds for research projects" (134). Burger writes:

> That conclusion was based upon two factors; first, Hutchinson's successful application for federal funds and the reports in the local newspapers of the federal funds; second, Hutchinson's access to the media, as demonstrated by the fact that some newspapers and wire services reported his response to the announcement of the Golden Fleece Award. (124)

The main problem with these two arguments, according to the Court, is that neither "demonstrates that Hutchinson was a public figure prior to the controversy" (133, 134). Burger notes that Hutchinson did not voluntarily thrust himself into a public controversy, pointing out that Proxmire failed to identify a "particular controversy" other than a general concern over "public expenditures" (134). According to the Court, such a general concern wrongly focuses on the subject matter test rejected in *Gertz* (1974). Burger adds, "Moreover, Hutchinson at no time assumed any role of public prominence in the broad question of concern about expenditures" (135).

Finally, the Court finds that Hutchinson's access to the media is too limited to qualify him as a public figure. Burger writes, "He did not have the regular and continuing access to the media that is one of the accouterments of having become a public figure" (136).

RULING

Burger writes, "We therefore reverse the judgement of the Court of Appeals and remand the case to the Court of Appeals for further proceedings consistent with this opinion" (136).

Justice William J. Brennan, Jr., writes a dissenting opinion.

Brennan feels newsletters and press releases do not "fall outside the protection of the speech or debate immunity" (136). He writes, "In my view, public criticism . by legislators of unnecessary governmental expenditures, whatever its form, is a legislative act shielded by the Speech or Debate Clause" (136).

SIGNIFICANCE

This case is significant for two reasons. First, it did not broaden the scope of the speech or debate clause to include information "not essential to the deliberations" of Congress. This definition excludes press releases sent to the media and newsletters sent to constituents. Secondly, to qualify as public figures, persons must have "regular and continuing access to the media," and they must voluntarily enter a "particular controversy" of interest to the public with the intention of influencing others.

Keeton v. Hustler Magazine, Inc.

Kathy Keeton
v.
Hustler Magazine, Inc.,

Docket No. 82-485
465 U.S. 770, 79 L.Ed.2d 790, 104 S.Ct. 1473 (1984)
Argued November 8, 1983. Decided March 20, 1984.

BACKGROUND

This is the first of two cases decided the same day and focusing on a jurisdictional dispute. Beginning with a famous case in 1945, *International Shoe Co.* v. *Washington*, the Court established a rule of "minimum contacts" to analyze the notion of jurisdiction mentioned in the Fourteenth Amendment. The relevant section of this amendment is the first one; it reads as follows:

> All persons born or naturalized in the United States, and subject to the jurisdiction therefore, are citizens of the United States and of the state wherein they reside. No state shall make or enforce any law which shall abridge the privileges or immunities of citizens of the United States; nor shall any state deprive any person of life, liberty, or property, without due process of law; nor deny to any persons within its jurisdiction the equal protection of the laws.

In the main, the rule of minimum contacts says that a state has jurisdiction over nonresidents only when they have certain "minimum contacts" with that state so that the filing there of a lawsuit against them does not violate traditional notions of justice and fair play.

Thus, when the plaintiff and defendant are residents of different states, then the question of jurisdiction often comes down to the frequency and nature of contacts among the litigants and the state in which suit is filed. In a libel suit, the persons defamed try to show that the offending publication has the required "minimum contacts" with the state in which they filed their suit; whereas the journalists connected with the publication, if they do not want to try the case in that state, try to show it does not.

CIRCUMSTANCES

Kathy Keeton, the associate publisher for *Penthouse* magazine and a resident of New York State, claimed she had been defamed in five separate issues of *Hustler* magazine published between September 1975 and May 1976. The common-law wife of Robert C. Guccione, *Penthouse* publisher, she was accused by a *Hustler* magazine cartoon, printed in the May 1976 issue, of being infected by Guccione with a venereal disease.

She filed suit in New Hampshire (even though less than 1 percent of all *Hustler* sales--10,000 copies--are sold there) because it is the only state in which the statute of limitations (six years) had not run out. New Hampshire also had a "long arm" statute that allowed nonresidents to sue other nonresidents in its courts. In addition, Keeton took advantage of "the single publication rule," which allowed her to sue in one state for the damages she suffered in all 49 others. *Restatement of Torts* defines the rule this way:

> As to any single publication, (a) only one action for damages can be maintained; (b) all damages suffered in all jurisdictions can be recovered in the one action; and (c) a judgment for or against the plaintiff upon the merits of any action for damages bars any other action for damages between the same parties in all jurisdictions. [577A (4) (1977)]

Keeton's only connection with New Hampshire is that the magazine she works for circulates there. *Hustler* magazine is an Ohio corporation, but its principal place of business is California. It sold about 10,000 to 15,000 copies a year in New Hampshire during the time of the litigation.

The district court dismissed the case, saying her "lack of contacts with New Hampshire rendered the State's interest in redressing the tort of libel to petitioner [Keeton] too attenuated for an assertion of personal jurisdiction over petitioner [*Hustler* magazine]" (773). The court of appeals affirmed, saying that such jurisdiction would be unfair because New Hampshire has a minimal interest "in applying its unusual statute of limitations to, and awarding damages for, injuries to a nonresident occurring outside the State, particularly since petitioner suffered such a small proportion of her total claimed injury within the State" (773).

SUMMARY OF THE COURT'S ANALYSIS

Justice William H. Rehnquist writes for the Court.
Chief Justice Warren E. Burger and Justices Byron R. White,
Thurgood Marshall, Harry A. Blackmun, Lewis F. Powell, Jr.,
John Paul Stevens, and Sandra Day O'Connor join.

Justice Rehnquist states that the appeals court erred in saying the suit could not be filed in New Hampshire. He writes, "Respondent's regular circulation of magazines in the forum State is sufficient to support an assertion of jurisdiction in a libel action based on the contents of the magazine" (773, 774). He adds, "Such regular monthly sales of thousands of magazines cannot by any stretch of the imagination be characterized as random, isolated, or fortuitous" (774). In addition, Rehnquist takes note of New Hampshire's long-arm statute, which "authorizes service of process on nonresidents whenever permitted by the Due Process Clause" (774).

The Court then deals with the fairness requirement of the "minimum contacts rule," which, Rehnquist says, "depends to some extent on whether respondent's [*Hustler* magazine's] activities are such as to give that State [New Hampshire] a legitimate interest in holding respondent [*Hustler*] answerable on a claim related to those activities" (776). The first point in support of the fairness requirement is that Keeton was injured at least in part in New Hampshire, and New Hampshire does have "a significant interest in redressing injuries that actually occur within the State" (776). Secondly, since false statements harm readers as well as defamed persons, "New Hampshire may rightly employ its libel laws to discourage the deception of its citizens" (776). Thirdly, even though Keeton is a nonresident, "the reputation of the libel victim may suffer harm even in a State in which he has hitherto been anonymous" (777).

Rehnquist notes in addition: "New Hampshire also has a substantial interest in cooperating with other States, through the 'single publication rule' to provide a forum for efficiently litigating all issues and damages claims arising out of a libel in a unitary proceeding" (777). The rule, he says, reduces the number of libel suits and protects defendants from the harassment of multiple suits.

Next Rehnquist notes that the appeals court erred by asserting that there was something unfair in filing in New Hampshire just because the statute of limitations had run out in every other state. He replies that the statute of limitations is irrelevant to the fairness requirement. The statute of limitations issue is relevant, he asserts, only after jurisdiction has been established.

The Court then takes note of the appeals court's objection to Keeton's minimal contacts with New Hampshire, saying that her contacts--while not completely irrelevant--are not essential in meeting the fairness requirement. It is the defendant's contacts that count.

Rehnquist sums up the analysis this way:

> Where, as in this case, respondent Hustler Magazine, Inc., has continuously and deliberately exploited the New Hampshire market, it must reasonably anticipate being haled into court there in a libel action based on the contents of its magazine. (781)
>
> And, since respondent [*Hustler* magazine] can be charged with knowledge of the "single publication rule," it must anticipate that such a suit will seek nationwide damages. Respondent [*Hustler* magazine] produces a national publication aimed at a nationwide audience. There is no unfairness in calling it to answer for the contents of that publication wherever a substantial number of copies are regularly sold and distributed. (781)

RULING

Rehnquist writes, "The judgment of the Court of Appeals is reversed, and the case is remanded for proceedings consistent with this opinion" (781).

Justice William J. Brennan, Jr., writes a concurring opinion.

Brennan writes to emphasize his feelings that the regular circulation of the magazine by itself meets the fairness requirement. He adds, "The State's interest in enforcing its substantive libel laws or its unique statue of limitations . . . should be relevant only to the extent that they bear upon the liberty interests of the respondent that are protected by the Fourteenth Amendment" (782).

SIGNIFICANCE

This ruling seems to imply that publishers who circulate on a regular basis copies of their newspaper or magazine in a given state should expect to be held responsible in that state for defamatory statements.

The Court pointed out in a footnote, however, that just because a state has jurisdiction over a magazine as a corporation does not mean that it also has jurisdiction over its employees or other persons related in some way to the magazine. The Court writes, "But jurisdiction over an employee does not automatically follow from jurisdiction over the corporation which employs him; nor does jurisdiction over a parent corporation automatically establish jurisdiction over a wholly owned subsidiary" (781).

Letter Carriers v. Austin

Old Dominion Branch No. 496, National Association of Letter Carriers, AFL-CIO v. Henry M. Austin

Docket No. 72-1180
418 U.S. 264, 41 L.Ed.2d 745, 94 S.Ct. 2770 (1974)
Argued November 14, 1973. Decided June 25, 1974.

BACKGROUND

In *Linn* v. *Plant Guard Workers* (1966), the Court ruled that defamatory statements made in the course of a labor dispute governed by the National Labor Relations Board (NLRB) are protected by the actual malice test announced two years earlier in *Sullivan*. The reason the Court gave for extending the test into labor law is a desire to give some protection to words spoken in the heat of a conflict, so that one side could not use a libel suit to gain an unfair economic advantage over the other. The Court also said it wanted to allow both sides to use their fullest written and spoken powers of persuasion.

Executive Order 11491 established for certain federal employees a legal system for labor-management relations essentially similar to that provided employees in the private sector by the National Labor Relations Act (291). One large question facing the court in this case, therefore, is whether the *Linn* ruling regarding the NLRB also applies to public sector unions covered by the executive order.

CIRCUMSTANCES

During the spring of 1970, the Old Dominion Branch was engaged in what the Court called "an ongoing effort to organize the remainder of the letter carriers" (267) in the Richmond, Virginia, area. All but 15 of the 435 carriers were members. Henry M. Austin and two other carriers, L. D. Brown and Roy P. Ziegengeist, were among the 15.

The union's monthly newsletter contained a column called "List of Scabs," which included the names of these three men. In addition, one issue printed a definition of a scab commonly attributed to author Jack London. Among other things, this definition says the following:

> The scab sells his birthright, country, his wife, his children and his fellowmen for an unfulfilled promise from his employer.
>
> Esau was a traitor to himself; Judas was a traitor to his God; Benedict Arnold was a traitor to his country; a SCAB is a traitor to his God, his country, his family and his class. (268)

Austin and the two others objected to being called a traitor and sued for libel. The union asked for dismissal of the case on the ground that the newsletter was protected by the *Linn* decision. Instead, the three carriers were awarded a total of $165,000; $10,000 each in compensatory damages and $45,000 in punitive. The Supreme Court of Virginia affirmed.

SUMMARY OF THE COURT'S ANALYSIS

Justice Thurgood Marshall writes for the Court.
Justices William J. Brennan, Jr., Potter Stewart, Byron R. White, and Harry A. Blackmun join.

Justice Marshall notes that the reason the protection of actual malice was given in *Linn* to words spoken in a labor dispute is that such words can be coercive, and not simply defamatory. Since the concern about using libel cases to gain an unfair economic advantage in order to win labor disputes is true of public as well as private collective bargaining situations, the Court finds that the actual malice rule should also be extended to public union conflicts.

Marshall writes, quoting in part from *Linn*, "Vigorous exercise of this right 'to persuade other employees to join' must not be stifled by the threat of liability for overenthusiastic use of rhetoric or the innocent mistake of fact (277)." He continues, "[E]pithets such as 'scab,' 'unfair,' and 'liar' are commonplace in these struggles'" (278). Austin argues that this protection is forfeited, however, because it is to be granted only in a labor dispute, and no dispute existed. To this argument, Marshall responds:

> But whether Linn's partial pre-emption [actual malice] of state libel law remedies is applicable obviously cannot depend on some abstract notion of what constitutes a "labor dispute"; rather, application of Linn must turn on whether the defamatory publication is made in a context where the policies of the federal labor laws leading to protection for freedom of speech are significantly implicated. (279)

The Court concludes, "Accordingly, we think that any publication made during the course of union organizing efforts, which is arguably relevant to that organizational activity, is entitled to the protection of Linn" (279).

If the actual malice test is to be considered, the Court reasons, then it must be defined. Marshall says the trial judge wrongly defined it as "'hatred, personal spite, ill will, or desire to injure'" (281). He writes, "It is therefore clear that the libel judgment in this case must be reversed because of the court's erroneous instructions" (282).

The Court does not rest its inquiry here, however. Marshall writes, "We have the obligation . . . to review the facts to insure that the speech involved is not protected under federal law" (282). The first point he makes in this review is that the "epithet 'scab' was protected under federal law" because "naming the appellees [Hanks and the two other carriers] as scabs was literally and factually true" (283). He explains:

> To be sure, the word is most often used as an insult or epithet. But Linn recognized that federal law gives a union license to use intemperate, abusive, or insulting language without fear of restraint or penalty if it believes such rhetoric to be an effective means to make its point. (283).

Austin objected to the word scab in large part, however, because the Jack London definition said a scab was, among other things, a traitor. Austin argued he was not a traitor, and the union knew it when they printed the charge. The Court responds this way:

> We cannot agree. We believe that publication of Jack London's rhetoric is equally entitled to the protection of the federal labor laws. (283)
>
> The definition's use of words like "traitor" cannot be construed as representations of fact. (284) . . . [J]ack London's "definition of a scab" is merely rhetorical hyperbole, a lusty and imaginative expression of the contempt felt by union members towards those who refuse to join. (286)

Finally, the Court does take care to note that words can be "taken out of context and used in such a way as to convey a false representation of fact" (286). Is such cases, the Court warns, "The use of this writing . . . could be actionable" (186).

RULING

Marshall writes, "The publication is protected under the federal labor laws. Accordingly, the judgments appealed from must be reversed" (287).

Justice William O. Douglas writes a concurring opinion.

Douglas agrees with the reversal of judgment, but he takes issue with the majority opinion on another matter. He writes:

> Since I do not think that discussion is free in the constitutional sense when it subjects the speaker to the penalty of libel judgments, in my view the ability of Congress or the Executive to formulate any labor policy penalizing

> those who might 'say naughty things during labor disputes' is precisely nil. (289)

Justice Lewis F. Powell, Jr, writes a dissenting opinion.
Chief Justice Warren E. Burger and Justice William H. Rehnquist join.

These three justices dissent first from the Court's characterization of the present situation as a labor dispute because it represents an "on going organizational campaign" (294). Powell writes:

> Certainly, there was no dispute between labor and management. There was also no conflict between competing labor organizations and no effort, either organized or otherwise, to encourage defection from appellant union. There was, in short, no dispute of any sort save the union's attempt to coerce appellees by scurrilous and defamatory statements to do what they had an admitted legal right not to do. Thus, the union, *by its own coercive conduct* [emphasis in the original], created a 'dispute'. (295)

The three justices also dissent from the Court's interpretation of the definition of scab. Powell writes, "The plain meaning and import of this publication was that appellees [Austin and the two other carriers] lacked character, that they had 'rotten principles,' and that they were traitors to their God, their country, their families, and their friends" (296).
In addition, the dissenters say the majority "failed to distinguish between defamatory references to an anonymous group . . . and a . . . named individual" (297). "Here," Powell writes, "The union did not merely voice its opinion of 'scabs' generally; it identified these appellees by name and specifically impugned their character" (297).

SIGNIFICANCE

Although ostensibly concerned with the authority over libel suits of the National Labor Relations Act (NLRA), as amended in 1964, this case and its progenitor (*Linn*) focus for the most part on the role of libel suits arising out of labor disputes. Over the objections of unions, which said that the NLRA precluded these suits, the Court in *Linn* allowed the filing of libel suits, but only upon proof of actual malice. Thus, the union's protection from libel suits arising over defamatory words spoken in the heat of a labor dispute was reduced in 1966 only to words the union could prove were not spoken with actual malice, that is, with knowledge they were false or with reckless disregard of whether they were true.

Since the NLRA covered only the private sector, the question arising here is whether or not the Court's ruling in *Linn* applies also to unions in the public sector. The Court rules that it does, thus granting the reduced protection of actual malice to unions in the public sector. Moreover, the Court also takes pains yet once again to reaffirm its definition of actual malice as excluding the notion of "ill will."

Two other issues should be noted in passing. First, there was disagreement in the Court over the definition of a labor dispute. This disagreement is important because the actual malice protection is limited to only those instances in which an actual dispute does, in fact, exist. The Court refused to create a specific definition of labor dispute, saying, instead, that a general context of labor unrest is sufficient to invoke the protection. Three dissenters, however, said the only dispute that existed was the one created by the union's libelous statements, implying, it appears, that the union invoked the protection of actual malice simply by issuing defamatory statements that elicited a libel suit.

The other issue centers upon the distinction between a fact and an opinion. Although the majority and the dissenters disagree agree over whether or not the words used by the union were fact or opinion, both sides agree that only a fact and not an opinion can be used to demonstrate actual malice. The importance of establishing factual statement becomes, interestingly enough, central in *Hustler Magazine* v. *Falwell* (1988).

Linn v. United Plant Guard Workers

William C. Linn
v.
United Plant Guard Workers of American, Local 114

Docket No. 1966-45
383 U.S. 53, 15 L.Ed.2d 582, 86 S.Ct. 657 (1966)
Argued November 18, 1965. Decided February 21, 1966.

BACKGROUND

The court in this case uses the actual malice concept fashioned in 1964 to relate labor law to libel law. Two conflicts take center stage. The first consists on one side of the state interest in protecting the good name and reputation of its citizens and on the other of the federal government's interest in resolving peaceably labor disputes. The second conflict focuses on lines of authority drawn between the courts and the National Labor Relations Board.

Together these two conflicts raise the central issue of whether parties in a labor dispute are allowed by federal law to file in state courts libel suits based on words spoken while a labor dispute is taking place.

CIRCUMSTANCES

During a campaign to organize Detroit employes of the Pinkertons National Detective Agency, Inc., union organizer Leo J. Doyle was charged by William C. Linn, a Pinkerton assistant general manager, with distributing libelous leaflets. Among the statements Linn found objectionable are these: "The Pinkerton manegers [*sic*] were *lying* [emphasis in original] to us--all the time the contract was in effect. No doubt the Saginaw men will file criminal charges. Somebody may go to Jail" (56).

Saying he was one of the managers referred to in the leaflet, Linn asserted not only that the references to him were false, defamatory, and libelous *per se*, but also that Doyle and the other union organizers knew they were false.

The district court, though, feeling that the National Labor Relations Board had jurisdiction over a charge of libel arising out of a labor dispute because such a charge could constitute an unfair labor practice, dismissed Linn's complaint. The court of appeals affirmed the dismissal.

The Court, however, said that courts do have jurisdiction over libel suits arising out of labor disputes "if the complainant pleads and proves that the statements were made with malice and" (55) did indeed injure the plaintiff. It therefore reversed the two lower courts' decisions.

SUMMARY OF THE COURT'S ANALYSIS

Justice Tom C. Clark writes for the Court.
Justices John M. Harlan, William J. Brennan, Jr., Potter Stewart, and Byron R. White join.

Justice Clark begins the analysis with a statement of the main point at issue, outlining the question of whether or not federal law allows the filing in state court of a libel suit arising out of a labor dispute:

> The case before us presents the question whether, and to what extent, the National Labor Relations Act, as amended . . . (1964 ed.), bars the maintenance of a civil action for libel instituted under state law by an official of an employer subject to the Act, seeking damages for defamatory statements published during a union organization campaign by the union and its officers. (55)

This question, Clark continues, involves "the extent to which the National Labor Relations Act, as amended, supersedes state law with respect to libels published during labor disputes" (56). He notes that, on the one hand, there exists "the federal interest in uniform regulation of labor relations" and, on the other, "the traditional concern and responsibility of the State to protect its citizens against defamatory attacks" (56). The task of the Court, then, according to Clark, is "to determine whether libel actions in such circumstances might interfere with the national labor policy" (58).

Dissatisfied with the "failure of Congress to furnish precise guidance in either the language of the Act or its legislative history," Clark says the Court must find its own solution to the question of whether or not libel is "pre-empt" from the jurisdiction of the labor board. Case law guidance rests, he says, "primarily" in *San Diego Building Trades Council* v. *Garmon*, 359 U.S. 236 (1959). Clark notes that the *Garmon* case presented two bases for exemption. The first occurs when "'the activity regulated was a merely peripheral concern of the Labor Management Relations Act'" (59). The second occurs when "'the regulated conduct touched interests so deeply rooted in local feeling and responsibility that . . . we could not infer that Congress had deprived the States of power to act" (59).

The main point to consider when applying these two bases, says Clark, is this: "Although the Board tolerates intemperate, abusive and inaccurate statements made by the union during attempts to organize employees, it does not interpret the Act as giving either party license to injure the other intentionally by circulating defamatory or insulting material know to be false" (61).

So, in regard to the first basis, the Court says "exercise of state jurisdiction" can be considered legitimately related to a "'merely peripheral'" concern of the act as long as this authority is "limited to redressing libel issued with knowledge of its falsity, or with reckless disregard of whether it was true or false" (61). In other words, the Court is asserting that, where actual malice can be demonstrated, the state courts do have jurisdiction over libel litigation arising out of a labor dispute. The Court also justifies intrusion by the states according to the second basis when it writes, "We similarly conclude that a State's concern with redressing malicious libel is 'so deeply rooted in local feeling and responsibility' that it fits within the exception specifically carved out by Garmon" (62). In summary, Clark states, "The most repulsive speech enjoys immunity provided it falls short of a deliberate or reckless untruth" (63).

The Court than takes care to point out, "The malicious publication of libelous statements does not in and of itself constitute an unfair labor practice" (63) because "Judicial condemnation of the alleged attack on Linn's character would reflect no judgment upon the objectives of the union" (64).

Next, Clark takes up the argument "that such suits might be used as weapons of economic coercion" (64). In an attempt to preclude this tactic, the Court limits "the availability of state remedies for libel to those instances in which the complainant can show that the defamatory statements were circulated with malice and caused him harm" (64, 65). In addition, the Court states, "We therefore hold that a complainant may not recover [merely] upon proof of such harm, which may include general injury to reputation, consequent mental suffering, alienation of associates, specific items of pecuniary loss, or whatever form of harm would be recognized by state tort law" (65). Clark continues, "The defamed party must establish that he has suffered some sort of compensable harm as a prerequisite to the recovery of additional punitive damages" (66).

In reply to the argument that giving states jurisdiction over libel suits arising out of labor disputes would "cause employers and unions to spurn appropriate administrative sanctions for contemporaneous violations of the Act," the Court responds simply, "We disagree" (66). The reason given by the Court is this, "The Board would not be ignored since its sanctions alone can adjust the equilibrium disturbed by an unfair labor practice" (66). In other words, the Court is asserting that only the penalties of the board are related to the labor dispute itself. Libel suits are personal and so will not affect unfairly the balance of power between the two sides as it exists outside libel matters.

RULING

Hedging its bets, the Court writes:

> We believe that under the rules laid down here it [known defamation] can be appropriately redressed without curtailment of state libel remedies beyond the actual needs of national labor policy. However, if experience shows that a greater curtailment, even a total one, should be necessary to

prevent impairment of that policy, the Court will be free to reconsider today's holding.

Reversed and remanded. (67)

Justice Hugo L. Black writes a dissenting opinion.

Black states his objection to the ruling in no uncertain terms. He writes, "The new Court-made law tosses a monkey wrench into the collective bargaining machinery Congress set up to try to settle labor disputes, and at the same time exalts the law of libel to an even higher level of importance in the regulation of the day-to-day life in this country" (67). He continues, "The objective of the National Labor Relations Act was to bring about agreements by collective bargaining, not to add fuel to the fire by encouraging libel suits with their inevitable irritations and dispute-prolonging tendencies" (68).

"Because libel suits in my judgment are inconsistent with both the Constitution of the United States and the policies of the Act," writes Black, "I dissent from the holding of the Court reversing the judgment below" (69).

Justice Abe Fortes writes a dissenting opinion.
Chief Justice Earl Warren and Justice William O. Douglas join.

Fortes focuses his dissent on the process for resolving labor disputes. He writes:

> In my judgment, the structure provided by Congress for the handling of labor-management controversies precludes any court from entertaining a libel suit between parties to a labor dispute or their agents where the allegedly defamatory statement is confined to matters which are part of the fabric of the dispute (69, 70).

He terms the court's limitations on damages "cold comfort" and asserts that the protection afforded by the requirement of demonstrating actual malice is "dubious" because malice is "largely subjective." Fortes feels that the outcome of a libel suit is "apt to reflect immediate community attitudes towards unionization" (71).

In his view, the Court's decision "marks the first departure from what has become a well-established rule that only where the public's compelling interest in preventing violence or the threat of violence is involved the exclusiveness of the federal structure for resolving labor disputes be breached" (72). "The majority's opinion," writes Fortes, "Fails to make clear why the participant's interest in protecting his reputation from the sting of words uttered as part of a labor dispute is a compelling concern which this Court must allow the States to protect, while his interest in preserving his economic well-being from illegal picketing is not" (72).

SIGNIFICANCE

The Court used its newly fashioned concept of actual malice to justify granting state courts the authority in certain instances to try libel suits arising out of labor disputes. Heretofore, it was felt that the National Labor Relations Board held, with few explicit exception, sole authority to resolve labor conflicts. Now the Court is saying that, if a false defamatory statement was issued during a labor dispute either with knowledge that the statement was false or with a reckless disregard of its falsity, then that statement does not deserve First Amendment protection. Consequently, it can become the basis of a libel suit in a state court. The Court's ruling here is also relevant to *St. Amant* v. *Thompson*, 390 U.S. 727 (1968), which is related to a union controversy.

Ocala Star-Banner Co. v. Damron

Ocala Star-Banner Company
v.
Leonard Damron

Docket No. 1971-118
401 U.S. 295, 28 L.Ed.2d 57, 91 S.Ct. 628 (1971)
Argued December 17, 1970. Decided February 24, 1971.

BACKGROUND

This case is the third in a series of three decided on the same day in an attempt to clarify yet more precisely the *Sullivan* decision. In particular, this case focuses on only one of the issues addressed earlier in *Patriot Co.* v. *Roy* (1971). That issue is defining what government can or cannot say about the qualifications of a public official.

CIRCUMSTANCES

On April 18, 1966, the Ocala *Star-Banner*, a small daily newspaper in rural central Florida near Orlando, ran a news story wrongly stating that Leonard Damron, mayor of Crystal River and candidate for county tax assessor, "had been charged in a federal court with perjury" (296). In fact, his brother James was the person so charged.

An area editor, who had been working at the paper for little longer than a month, accepted the story over the telephone from a reporter who correctly identified James as the Damron brother accused of perjury. During the libel trial, the editor explained that, because he had never heard of James, he "inadvertently changed the name "to Leonard as a result of 'a mental aberration'" (297). The jury awarded Leonard Damron $22,000 in compensatory damages.

SUMMARY OF THE COURT'S ANALYSIS

Justice Potter Stewart writes for the Court.
Chief Justice Warren E. Burger and Justices Harry A. Blackmun, William J. Brennan, Jr., John M. Harlan, Thurgood Marshall, and Byron R. White join.

Justice Stewart asserts Leonard Damron was, as mayor, "without question a 'public official'" (299). In addition, Stewart says that Damron was also to be considered a public official "in his status as a candidate for the office of county tax assessor" (299).

Damron claimed, however, that the libel was directed toward his "purely 'private'" activities (300) and so was not relevant to his fitness for public office. The Court responds, quoting in part from the same-day decision of *Patriot Co.* v. *Roy*, "A charge of criminal misconduct against an official or a candidate, no matter how remote in time or place, is always 'relevant to his fitness for office' for purposes of applying the New York Times rule of knowing falsehood or reckless disregard of the truth" (300).

The Court's statement here is a specific application of its words in *Garrison* v. *Louisiana* (1964): "Anything which might touch on an official's fitness for office is relevant" (Garrison at 11). In short, the Court is saying that the word "anything" used in Garrison does indeed include such things as "a charge of criminal conduct . . . no matter how remote in time or place" (300).

RULING

Stewart writes:

> And under any test we can conceive, the charge that a local mayor and candidate for a county elective post has been indicted for perjury in a civil rights suit is relevant to his fitness for office. The First Amendment and Fourteenth Amendment require reversal of the judgment. The case is remanded for further proceedings not inconsistent with this opinion. (301)

Justice Byron R. White writes a concurring opinion.

White notes, "Inevitably, New York Times v. Sullivan . . . will result in extending constitutional protection to lies and falsehoods which, though neither knowing nor reckless, do severe damage to personal reputation" (301). He continues, "The sole basis for protecting publishers who spread false information is that otherwise the truth would too often be suppressed. That innocent falsehoods are sometimes protected only to ensure access to the truth has been noted before" (301). [White refers here to *NAACP* v. *Button* 371 U.S. 425, 9 L.Ed.2d 405, 83 S. Ct. 328 (1963), which is quoted in *Sullivan*.]

Justice Hugo L. Black writes a concurring opinion.
Justice William O. Douglas joins.

Black and Douglas note once again that they concur for reasons they set forth in the *Sullivan* case.

SIGNIFICANCE

This case gives specific application to the Court's earlier ruling in *Garrison* v. *Louisiana* (1964) that anything touching on a candidate's fitness for office is relevant to that person's qualifications. In particular, the Court said that a charge of criminal misconduct against public officials or candidates for public office, no matter how remote in time or place, is always relevant to questions about their fitness for office. Such a charge is not an attack on these persons' private lives. In order to win damages, therefore, these persons must show that the charge was printed with actual malice. That is, they must show that the journalists knew the charge was false when it was published or that it was printed with reckless disregard for the truth.

Patriot Co. v. Roy

Monitor Patriot Co.
v.
Roselle A. Roy

Docket No. 1971-62
401 U.S. 265, 28 L.Ed.2d 35, 91 S.Ct. 621 (1971)
Argued December 17, 1970. Decided February 24, 1971.

BACKGROUND

This case is the first in a series of three decided on the same day in an attempt to clarify yet more precisely the *Sullivan* decision. In particular, this case expands on parts of *Garrison* v. *Louisiana* (1964), where distinctions between the private and public actions of a public official were first addressed during the post-*Sullivan* era. The Court's attention focuses on three main issues: (1) Who is a public figure; (2) what is the difference between the public and private actions of a public official; and (3) what is the level of fault that a candidate for public office must demonstrate in order to win a libel suit.

CIRCUMSTANCES

The *Monitor*, a daily newspaper in Concord, New Hampshire, published a column characterizing Alphonse Roy, a candidate for the U.S. Senate, as "'a former small-time bootlegger'" (266). Roy sued the Monitor Patriot Co., publishers of the *Monitor*, and the North American Newspaper Alliance (NANA), distributor of the column entitled "D.C. Merry-Go-Round."

SUMMARY OF THE COURT'S ANALYSIS

Justice Potter Stewart writes for the Court.
Chief Justice Warren E. Burger and Justices John M. Harlan, William J. Brennan, Jr., Byron R. White, Thurgood Marshall, and Harry A. Blackmun join.

Justice Potter Stewart, writing for the Court, notes early in the opinion, "The defendants also alleged that they had published in good faith, without malice, with a reasonable belief in the probable truth of the charge, and on a lawful occasion" (268).

Stewart then proceeds to discuss the instructions given to the jury by the trial judge, who did correctly point out that Roy is a public official. The judge told the jury it could distinguish between public and private conduct by considering these points:

> "Is it more probable than otherwise that the publication that the plaintiff [Roy] was a former small-time bootlegger was a public affair on a par with official conduct of public officials?" (268. 269)
>
> "That is, anything which might touch on Alphonse Roy's fitness for the office of United States Senator would come within the concept of official conduct." (269)

In other words, the trial judge was asking the jury to decide whether a charge of being a "former samll-time bootlegger" is relevant to Roy's official duties or if, instead, the charge is related purely to Roy's private life.

Next Stewart comments on the relevance of *Sullivan* to this case. He writes, "The approach of New York Times was to identify a class of persons--there public officials--and a type of activity--there official conduct--and to require as to defamation concerning them a particularly high standard of liability--knowing falsehood or reckless disregard of the truth" (270, 271). From this he notes, "The New York Times itself was intended to apply to candidates" (271).

A jury awarded Roy $10,000 from the newspaper and $10,000 from the NANA based on a belief that the bootlegger charge was in the "private sector" (272) and not a part of Roy's official conduct. The Court asserts, however, "The syllogistic manipulation of distinctions between 'private sectors' and 'public sectors' . . . is of little utility in resolving questions of First Amendment protection" (273).

Stewart explains in more detail, saying that the Court here has been lead "to reformulate the 'official conduct' rule of New York Times in terms of 'anything which might touch upon an official's fitness for office'" (274) [see *Garrison* (1964)]:

> The New York Times rule is not rendered inapplicable merely because an official's private reputation, as well as his public reputation, is harmed. (273) . . . [A]nything which might touch on an official's fitness for office is relevant. (273)
>
> The principal activity of a candidate in our political system . . . consists in putting before the voters every conceivable aspect of his public and private life that he thinks may lead the electorate to gain a good impression of him. (274) And the candidate who vaunts his spotless record and sterling integrity cannot convincingly cry "Foul!" when an opponent or an industrious reporter attempts to demonstrate the contrary. (274)

Stewart then takes up in more detail the problems caused by the trial judge's instructions. Allowing a jury to decide if it is "more probable than otherwise" that a particular activity is relevant to the duties of a public official in effect, says Stewart, substitutes a lower standard of fault than actual malice. It substitutes for knowing falsity or recklessness the notion of reasonableness determined by a mere "'preponderance of the evidence'" (275). Stewart objects to this lower standard of fault because it does not adequately protect political speech. He writes, "It is simply inconsistent with this commitment [to robust political debate] to permit the imposition of liability for political speech that 'more probably than otherwise' in the opinion of the jury 'would not touch upon or be relevant' to a candidate's fitness for office" (276).

Stewart admits that "some uncertainty as to what publications are and what are not protected" is "perhaps unavoidable," (276) but he sees "a major difference" "between liability based on a standard of care [like actual malice], and liability based on a judgement of relevance" (276). He writes, "A standard of "relevance" . . . holds a real danger of becoming an instrument for the suppression of those 'vehement, caustic, and sometimes unpleasantly sharp attacks' . . . which must be protected if the guarantees of the First and Fourteenth Amendments are to prevail" (276, 277). A standard of care, in contrast, "'can be neutral with respect to the content of the speech involved'" (276).

RULING

Stewart writes:

> We therefore hold as a matter of constitutional law that a charge of criminal conduct, no matter how remote in time or place, can never be irrelevant to an official's or a candidate's fitness for office for purposes of application of the "knowing falsehood or reckless disregard" rule of New York Times Co. v Sullivan. (277)

Justice Hugo L. Black writes a concurring opinion.
Justice William O. Douglas joins.

Black and Douglas concur for reasons set out in the *Sullivan* case.

SIGNIFICANCE

Certainly, the greatest significance of this case is the Court's refusal to draw fine distinctions between the public and private activities of a public official. According to this ruling, there is precious little private activity that is not relevant to the duties of a public official. The Court said anything that might touch on an official's fitness for office is relevant to an evaluation of his official conduct.

The Court also touched on two other issues that are important to its continuing efforts to elucidate the ramifications of the *Sullivan* decision.

For one thing, Stewart noted that the distinction between when, in a libel case, actual malice will have to be shown and when it will not is based on two sets of factors: (1) "a class of persons," and (2) "a type of activity" (270, 271). Although seen here as compatible criteria, these two sets of factors are seen later by the Court to contain important differences. Indeed, later decisions focus on the very problem of determining which set of factors triggers the actual malice requirement. See especially *Curtis Publishing* v. *Butts* (1967), *Gertz* v. *Welch* (1974), *Ocala Star-Banner Co.* v. *Damron* (1971), *Rosenbloom* v. *Metromedia* (1971), and *Time*, Inc. v. *Firestone* (1976).

Another issue that later becomes extremely important is Stewart's observation that, although adequate for private liability requirements, a "reasonable man" standard is not adequate protection for political speech about public officials. The level of care needed to be taken by speakers also takes center stage in a number of later libel cases. See especially *Gertz*, *Firestone*, and *Bose*.

Although the Court did not reach back to this case in order to support its decisions on these two issues, it is worthwhile to note here the Court's embryonic thoughts on these issues.

Finally, note should be taken of Stewart's distinction between a standard of care and a standard of relevance. He said that allowing a jury to decide if it is more probable than otherwise that a particular activity is relevant to the duties of a public official, in effect, substitutes a lower standard of fault than the standard of care required to show actual malice. A standard of relevance is lower than the actual malice standard of care because showing relevance requires presenting only a preponderance of the evidence, whereas showing actual malice requires clear and convincing evidence of knowing falsity or reckless disregard of the truth.

Philadelphia Newspapers, Inc. v. Hepps

Philadelphia Newspapers, Inc.
v.
Maurice S. Hepps

Docket No. 84-1491
475 U.S. 767, 89 L.Ed.2d 783, 106 S.Ct. 1558 (1986)
Argued December 3, 1985. Decided April 21, 1986.

BACKGROUND

Although the Court, by 1982, had spent nearly two decades refining its attempt to "constitutionalize" libel law, it had never been faced with this one truly fundamental question: Who has the burden of proof? Pennsylvania libel laws, like those in most other states, were based on libel common law inherited from Britain. One assumption of that common law is that all persons, unless proven otherwise, have good names and so defamatory statements about them are presumed false. The burden of proof, therefore, rests upon defamers to show that their defamatory statement are true.

When this case came to trial, a judge ruled the Pennsylvania law unconstitutional, saying that defamed persons suing a media defendant for speech of public concern have the burden of showing that the statements about them are false.

There is one other consideration arising out of the fact that this case originated in Pennsylvania, which has a shield law. Like most state shield laws, Pennsylvania's permits employees of the media to refuse to identify the sources of their news stories. This protection means that defamed persons may find it very difficult to obtain evidence from the media. Thus, an additional question is posed: is it fair to place the burden of proving falsity on defamed persons who file libel suits in states having shield laws?

CIRCUMSTANCES

The Philadelphia *Inquirer* published a series of news stories between May 1975 and May 1976 saying, in general, that Maurice Hepps had connections to organized crime and that he had used these connections to influence the course of governmental affairs in Pennsylvania. Hepps was "the principal stockholder of General Programming, Inc., a corporation that franchises a chain of stores--known at the relevant time as 'Thrifty' stores--selling beer, soft drinks, and snacks" (769).

The articles also charged that former state senator Frank Mazzei, a convicted felon, used political influence to allow the Thrifty chain, in which he owned an interest, to continue to do business even though it was operating in violation of state law.

Hepps sued the *Inquirer* for libel. After the trial, the judge "concluded that Pennsylvania's statute giving the defendant the burden of proving the truth of the statements violated the Federal Constitution" (770). He refused, however, to give the jury any special instructions about the impact of the shield law.

The Pennsylvania Supreme Court said that "a showing of fault [as required in *Gertz*] did not require a showing of falsity," and so "to place the burden of showing truth on the defendant did not unconstitutionally inhibit free debate" (771). The court then ordered a new trial.

SUMMARY OF THE COURT'S ANALYSIS

Justice Sandra Day O'Connor writes for the Court.
Justices William J. Brennan, Jr., Thurgood Marshall, Harry A. Blackmun, and Lewis F. Powell, Jr., join.

Justice O'Connor begins her analysis with a review of the Court's decisions on libel since the *Sullivan* case in 1964. At the end of that review, she writes, "One can discern in these decisions two forces that may reshape the common-law landscape to conform to the First Amendment. The first is whether the plaintiff is a public official or figure, or is instead a private figure. The second is whether the speech at issue is one of public concern" (775). In short, the Court said that in past decisions a "common law rule was superseded by a constitutional rule" (776). She continues, "We believe that the common law's rule on falsity--that the defendant must bear the burden of proving truth--must similarly fall here to a constitutional requirement that the plaintiff bear the burden of showing falsity, as well as fault, before recovering damages" (776).

Justice O'Connor explains, "To ensure that true speech on matters of public concern is not deterred, we hold that the common-law presumption that defamatory speech is false cannot stand when a plaintiff seeks damages against a media defendant for speech of public concern" (776, 777). Putting the burden on proving true speech, she adds, would deter such speech "because of the fear that liability will unjustifiably result," causing a "'chilling' effect . . . antithetical to the First Amendment's protection of true speech on matters of public concern" (777). Proving falsity "adds only marginally to the burdens that the plaintiff must already bear," Justice O'Connor writes, because "evidence offered by plaintiffs on the publisher's fault . . . will generally encompass evidence of falsity" (778).

Moving to the shield law issue, Justice O'Connor writes, "We recognize that the plaintiff's burden in this case is weightier because of Pennsylvania's 'shield' law" (779). After considering the effects of the law, though, she writes, "We are unconvinced that the State's shield law requires a different constitutional standard than would prevail in the absence of such a law" (779).

RULING

Justice O'Connor writes, "The judgment of the Pennsylvania Supreme Court is reversed, and the case is remanded for further proceedings not inconsistent with this opinion" (779).

Justice Harry A. Blackmun writes a concurring opinion.

Blackmun writes, "I believe that where allegedly defamatory speech is of public concern, the First Amendment requires that the plaintiff, whether public official, public figure, or private individual, prove the statements at issue to be false" (779, 780). He also takes care to comment on an issue not addressed by the Court when he writes, "While the Court reserves the question whether the rule it announces applies to non-media defendants . . . I adhere to my view that such a distinction is 'irreconcilable with the . . . First Amendment'" (780).

Justice John Paul Stevens writes a dissenting opinion.
Chief Justice Warren E. Burger and Justices Byron R. White and William H. Rehnquist join.

Writing a rather caustic dissent, Justice Stevens asserts in his first paragraph, "The only litigants--and the only publishers--who will benefit from today's decision are those who act negligently or maliciously" (780). He continues, "By attaching no weight to the state's interest in protecting the private individual's good name, the Court has reached a pernicious result" (781).

Stevens feels that, if libelers are found to be at fault in some way, then they lose any constitutional protection that would relieve them of proving the truth of their statements. He writes, "The antecedent fault determination makes irresistible the inference that a significant portion of this speech is beyond the constitutional pale" (783).

"The Court today seems to believe that the character assassin has a constitutional license to defame," (785) Stevens writes. He continues:

> I simply do not understand, however, why a character assassin should be given an absolute license to defame by means of statements that can be neither verified nor disproven. The danger of deliberate defamation by reference to unprovable facts is not a merely speculative or hypothetical concern. . . . [A]host of factors--make it impossible for an honorable person to disprove malicious gossip about his past conduct, his relatives, his friends, or his business associates. (785-786)

Because the Court "grossly undervalues the strong state interest in redressing injuries to private reputations," (787) Stevens feels it has made a fundamental error. He writes, "[The Court exhibits a] . . . mistaken belief that doubt regarding the veracity of a defamatory statement must invariably be resolved in favor of constitutional protection of the statement and against vindication of the reputation of the private individual" (787). He concedes that "government or its agents must at a minimum shoulder the burden of proving that speech is false and must do so with sufficient reliability that we can be confident that true speech is not suppressed" (787).

For private persons, though, Stevens says "a different calculus is appropriate" because they are "'more vulnerable to injury'" and "'more deserving of recovery'" (788). They are more vulnerable because "they lack 'access to the channels of effective communication . . . to counteract false statements'" and are more deserving because they have not voluntarily thrust "'themselves to the forefront of particular public controversies in order to influence the resolution of the issues involved'" (789).

He concludes:

> In my view, as along as publishers are protected by the requirement that the plaintiff has the burden of proving fault, there can be little, if any basis, for a concern that a significant amount of true speech will be deterred unless the private person victimized by malicious gossip can also carry the burden of proving falsity. (790)

SIGNIFICANCE

Placing on private persons defamed by the media when addressing matters of public concern the burden of proving defamatory statements about them are false makes this decision significant. Before this case, it was common for states to use the common-law assumption that statements about presumed upright persons were, *ipso facto*, presumed false and so defamers had to prove that their accusations were true.

It is important to note that the court limited the burden to (1) private persons (2) who are engaged in matters of public concern (3) who had been defamed by the media. The Court also pointed out that the existence of a shield law does not alter the nature of the burden, even though the shield law may make it a bit more difficult to obtain evidence from the media to prove defamatory statements are false.

It should also be noted that the Court did not address the question whether the burden of proving falsity is required of persons suing nonmedia defendants.

Rosenblatt v. Baer

Alfred D. Rosenblatt
v.
Frank P. Baer

Docket No. 1966-38
383 U.S. 75, 15 L.Ed.2d 597, 86 S.Ct. 669 (1966)
Argued October 20, 1965. Decided February 21, 1966.

BACKGROUND

The Court takes advantage of the questions posed in this case to define more precisely what is a public official. In fact, when agreeing to hear the case, it specifically asked both parties "to brief and argue . . . whether respondent (Baer) was a 'public official' under New York Times and under our decision in Garrison" (77).

CIRCUMSTANCES

Alfred D. Rosenblatt contributed an unpaid opinion column to the Laconia, New Hampshire, *Evening Citizen*. One of his favorite targets was the recreation area administered by the Belknap County Commissioners, who employed Frank P. Baer to manage the facility. "During the 50's," according to the Court, "A public controversy developed over the way respondent [Baer] and the Commissioners operated the Area; some protested that respondent [Baer] and the Commissioners had not developed the Area's full potential, either as a resort for local residents or as a tourist attraction that might contribute to the county's taxes" (77, 78). Then in 1959, the New Hampshire legislature passed a law "transferring control of the Area to a special five-man commission" (78). In January 1960, Rosenblatt decided to run a column giving his assessment of the new situation. He writes:

> "This year, a year without snow till very late . . .; the difference in cash income simply fantastic, almost unbelievable."
>
> "What happened to all the money last year? and every other year? [*sic*] What magic has Dana Beane [Chairmperson of the new commission] and rest of

commission . . . wrought to make such tremendous difference in net cash results?" (78, 79)

Baer sued and was awarded $31,500, an award the Supreme Court of New Hampshire supported.

SUMMARY OF THE COURT'S ANALYSIS

Justice William J. Brennan, Jr., writes for the Court. Chief Justice Earl Warren and Justices Tom C. Clark, Potter Stewart, and Byron O. White join.

The first question tackled by the Court is whether the column simply applauds the new managers or also criticizes the old ones. Witnesses, the Court concludes, testified both ways.

Moving on, Brennan notes that Baer said he should recover on two theories, the first of which focuses on his identification. According to the Court, Baer claimed, "That the jury could award him damages if it found that the column cast suspicion indiscriminately on the small number of persons who composed the former management group, whether or not it found that the imputation of misconduct was specifically made of and concerning him" (79, 80).

The question of identification is addressed specifically in the *Sullivan* case. The problem seen by the Court in both cases is that "in the absence of sufficient evidence that the attack focused on the plaintiff, an otherwise impersonal attack on governmental operations cannot be utilized to establish a libel of those administering the operations" (80). Thus, the Court took care in *Sullivan* to note that criticism of the conduct of a public official is not defined as a personal attack on a person when it is in reality an attack on the government. Brennan writes, "There must be evidence showing that the attack was read as specifically directed at the plaintiff. [Otherwise, the courts would] . . . invite the specter of prosecutions for libel on government, which the Constitution does not tolerate in any form" (81).

Since Rosenblatt printed (1) "no explicit charge of peculation" (2) "made specifically of and concerning" Baer, the Court asserts the trial judge was wrong in letting the jury determine (1) whether the column included any defamatory content and (2) whether it applied to Baer.

Baer's second theory is that at least some of the witnesses who read the column felt it referred to him specifically because he was "'the man in charge'" (81). If the readers did in fact feel the column referred to Baer, then the question for the Court becomes whether or not he is a public official.

In this regard, the first thing to take note of, says Brennan, is that a public official is not determined by definitions the states have developed "for local administrations purposes" (84). Moreover, *Sullivan* provides little guidance, he notes, because the Court did not have to face the question of "how far down into the lower ranks of government employees the 'public official' designation would extend for purposes of this rule" (85).

So, in order to tune more finely this definition, Brennan suggests that it would be helpful to look at the Court's two reasons for inventing it in the first place. He writes, "There is, first, a strong interest in debate on public issues, and, second, a strong interest in debate about those persons who are in a position significantly to influence the resolution of those issues" (85). He concludes, "It is clear, therefore, that the 'public official' designation applies at the very least to those among the hierarchy of government employees who have, or appear to the public to have, substantial responsibility for or control over the conduct of governmental affairs" (85). With no little irony, the Court then declares Baer a public official. It does so by asserting that Baer's evidence showing readers thought of him as the "man in charge" is also evidence that he is a public official.

RULING

Brennan writes:

> A theory that the column casts indiscriminate suspicion on the members of the group responsible for the conduct of this governmental operation is tantamount to a demand for recovery based on libel of government, and therefore is constitutionally insufficient. Since the trial judge's instructions were erroneous in this respect, the judgement must be reversed." (83)

Justice Tom C. Clark concurs without writing a separate opinion.

Justice William O. Douglas writes a concurring opinion.

Douglas finds the problem of drawing a line between who is and who is not a public official extremely difficult, if not impossible, to solve. He writes, "I see no way to draw lines that exclude the night watchman, the file clerk, the typist, or, for that matter, anyone on the public payroll" (89). Harkening back to his dissent in *Sullivan*, he asserts, "The question is whether a public *issue* [emphasis his], not a public official, is involved" (91).

Justice Potter Stewart writes a concurring opinion.

Stewart begins by noting that the constitution does not allow seditious libel laws, that is, laws forbidding defamation of the government. The actual malice rule, therefore, should be applied only if a state unconstitutionally passes a law of defamation that is really a seditious libel law. In other words, this rule should be used only to limit or to qualify unconstitutional seditious libel laws. Stewart opposes using the rule in other instances because it can "deprive a defamed public official of any hope for legal redress without proof that the lie was a knowing one, or uttered in reckless disregard of the truth" (93).

His reason for limiting the usage of the rule is often quoted in later cases by other justices. He writes, "The right of a man to the protection of his own reputation from unjustified invasion and wrongful hurt reflects no more than our basic concept of the essential dignity and worth of every human being--a concept at the root of any decent system of ordered liberty" (92).

Justice Hugo L. Black writes a concurring opinion.
Justice William O. Douglas joins.

Black drives directly to the point. He writes, "I think the publication here, discussing the way an agent of government does his governmental job, is the very kind that the First Amendment was adopted primarily to protect. (94) And the right to criticize a public agent engaged in public activities cannot safely, and should not depend upon whether or not that agent is arbitrarily labeled a 'public official'" (95). He repeats his belief stated in *Sullivan* that the First Amendment protects all speech related to "public affairs" (95).

Finally, he says, in any case, a jury, not a judge, should determine all facts in a case, including whether or not a defendant is a public official.

Justice John M. Harlan writes a dissenting opinion.

Harlan says the Court is wrong when it claims the jury was allowed "to convert an 'impersonal' into a 'personal' libel" (98). He explains:

> It seems manifest that in instructing the jury as to a "small group," the trial judge was not allowing the plaintiff to transform impersonal governmental criticism into an individual cause of action, but was simply referring to this traditional tort doctrine that more than one person can be libeled by the same statement. (100)

Harlan is saying that libel law often allows persons not identified by name or other telling characteristics to sue for damages if they are members of a defamed group small enough in number so that those outside the group would believe the defamation refers to each individual member.

He concurs with all other aspects of the ruling.

Justice Abe Fortas writes a dissenting opinion.

Since this case was tried before the *Sullivan* decision was announced, Fortas feels that the facts are not "shaped" to fit the actual malice rule. Thus, Fortas says it does little good to review facts not relevant to the very rule upon which the Court's decision is based.

SIGNIFICANCE

A singular refinement of the definition of a public official makes this case significant. The Court asserted that public officials are "government employees who have, or appear to the public to have, substantial responsibility for or control over the conduct of governmental affairs."

In addition, the Court also noted that trial courts should take care to see that defamation of a public official's conduct is not made into personal defamation of the person's private life. Criticism of a public official's conduct constitutes an action very similar to defamation of the government, a form of speech protected by the First Amendment.

The concurring opinions also make this case important in that they emphasize the need to protect speech related to public issues, not just speech directed at a public officials. Eventually, in *Rosenbloom* v. *Metromedia* (1971), the Court adopts 6this position, but only for a brief period.

Rosenbloom v. Metromedia

George A. Rosenbloom
v.
Metromedia, Inc.

Docket No. 1971-66
403 U.S. 29, 29 L.Ed.2d 296, 91 S.Ct. 1811 (1971)
Argued December 7 and 8, 1970. Decided June 7, 1971.

BACKGROUND

The Supreme Court began a process of refining and clarifying the nature of First Amendment limitations upon state libel laws when it ruled in the *Sullivan* case that these laws were subject to the limitations of the First Amendment. Most legal scholars suggest that, at first, this process resulted in continual enlargement of constitutional protections for the media mainly because the court continually expanded the class of persons who had to demonstrate the media defamed with actual malice. These scholars also say the Court reached in this case its farthermost limit and then began to contract the protection in future decisions.

It is not surprising that *Rosenbloom* marks a reversal of direction because the decision itself is so fractured. Only two persons joined the author of the Court's opinion, and four separate opinions--half concurring--were written. A close reading of the case reveals that members of the Court were re-examining the theoretical framework upon which they built in *Sullivan* a distinction between libeled public and private persons. The framework was built on two pillars. One is the nature of the person defamed (a conduct standard); the other is the nature of the circumstances giving rise to the defamation (a subject matter standard).

By devoting so much attention to theory, this case, more than any other since the actual malice test was devised, shows that, from 1964 to 1971, the Court had been doing more than fine tuning a general rule for guiding the resolution of a wide variety of libel cases. It had, in fact, been attempting to explore the philosophical ramifications of asserting that the First Amendment imposes limitations upon state libel laws.

In addition to presenting a new theoretical approach to actual malice, however, this case also demonstrates the hazards of a lawsuit. Rosenbloom had built his case using the Court's previously articulated concepts of public persons, concepts carefully refined by the Court itself for the seven years since *Sullivan*. Even though Rosenbloom defines himself correctly as a private figure, the Court extends the notion of a class of persons who must bare the burden of proving actual malice to falsely defamed persons caught in matters of public importance. This extension includes Rosenbloom. Then, three years after *Rosenbloom*--in Gertz (1974)--the Court, in effect, retreats to its pre-*Rosenbloom* distinction between public and private figures, a distinction that, ironically, excludes Rosenbloom.

CIRCUMSTANCES

George A. Rosenbloom distributed what the Court called "nudist magazines" in the Philadelphia area. In 1963, the Special Investigations Squad of the Philadelphia Police Department began to crack down on persons felt to be breaking the city's obscenity laws. Rosenbloom was arrested October 1 along with several newsstand operators and again on October 4 after police seized materials from a rented barn he used as a warehouse.

Following the second arrest, a Captain Clarence Ferguson, who was in charge of the operation, telephoned radio station WIP with information about Rosenbloom's arrest. WIP's news story on the arrest included this passage that Rosenbloom said was libelous: "Capt. Ferguson says he believes they have hit the supply of a main distributor of obscene material in Philadelphia" (33). The last six of the eight broadcasts of this story inserted the word "reportedly" in front of the word "obscene."

WIP also broadcast a series of news stories when Rosenbloom, claiming the materials seized were not in fact obscene, sued the city and police. Part of the news story about this suit contains these words: "'The girlie-book peddlers say the police crackdown and continued reference to their borderline literature as smut or filth is hurting their business'" (34).

After Rosenbloom was cleared in state court of criminal obscenity charges, he filed a libel suit against WIP, claiming that the characterization of his books as "obscene" is libel *per se* (on the face of it). He also claimed that stories about the trial defamed him when they described him and others as "smut distributors" and "girlie-book peddlers."

WIP pled truth and privilege as defenses. News director Paul Rust said the primary source of information about the first broadcasts was Captain Ferguson, and Ferguson testified that "WIP had accurately broadcast what he told" (37) them. Nevertheless, evidence of any attempt by WIP to investigate the lawsuit was described by the Court as "sparse" (37). The news director admitted that "half-hour deadlines required" the station to "rely on wire-service copy and oral reports from previously reliable sources" (37).

The jury awarded Rosenbloom $25,000 in general and $750,000 in punitive damages. The court of appeals (third circuit) reversed the judgment on the bases that: (1) "the broadcasts concerned matters of public interest and (2) they were involved in 'hot news' prepared under deadline pressure" (40).

SUMMARY OF THE COURT'S ANALYSIS

Justice William J.Brennan, Jr., writes for the Court.
Chief Justice Warren E. Burger and Justice Harry A. Blackmun join.

Brennan points out the Court accepts this case for review because it presents a question of whether "the New York Times' knowing-or-reckless-falsity standard applied in a state civil libel action brought by . . . a private individual for a defamatory falsehood . . . about the individual's involvement in an event of public or general interest" (31, 32).

Early in the analysis Brennan notes an admission by Rosenbloom:

> Petitioner [Rosenbloom] concedes that the police campaign to enforce the obscenity laws was an issue of public interest, and, therefore that the constitutional guarantees for freedom of speech and press imposed limits upon Pennsylvania's power to apply its libel laws to compel respondent [Metromedia] to compensate him in damages for alleged defamatory falsehoods about his involvement. (40)

This passage leads to a breaking down of the Court's former distinctions between public and private persons when matters of public interest are at issue. Brennan writes, "Later [after *Sullivan* (1964)] decisions have disclosed the artificiality, in terms of the public's interest, of a simple distinction between 'public' and 'private' individuals or institutions" (41).

For Brennan these distinctions were irrelevant to the actual malice requirement. The important point is the public's interest in the defamatory subject matter. He writes:

> Self-governance in the United States presupposes far more than knowledge and debate about the strictly official activities of various levels of government. . . . [I]n private hands [are] vast areas of economic and social power that vitally affect the nature and quality of life in the Nation. Our efforts to live and work together in a free society . . . necessarily encompass far more than politics in a narrow sense. (41)

After narrowing the distinction between public and private persons, Brennan begins to broaden the area of public interest for citizens. He writes:

> If a matter is a subject of public or general interest, it cannot suddenly become less so merely because a private individual is involved, or because in some sense the individual did not "voluntarily" choose to be involved. (43) We honor the commitment to robust debate on public issues, which is embodied in the First Amendment by extending constitutional protection to all discussion and communication involving matters of public or general concern, without regard to whether the persons involved are famous or

> anonymous. (43, 44) We think the time has come forthrightly to announce that the determinant whether the First Amendment applies to state libel actions is whether the utterance involved concerns an issue of public or general concern. (44)

In short, the Court is asserting that the *New York Times* test of actual malice is relevant to a libel case whenever the defamatory subject matter is of public interest or concern even if the person defamed is private and not a public figure or official.

Rosenbloom argues that the standard of fault for the media in the defamation of a private person should be "reasonable care." In other words, he says that he should win his suit against Metromedia if WIP radio did not take "reasonable care" when investigating and reporting information that later turned out to be false and defamatory. He supports his argument with two reasons. First, he says that "the private individual, unlike the public figure, does not have access to the media to counter the defamatory material" (45). Secondly, the private person "has not assumed the risk of defamation by thrusting himself into the public arena" (45).

The Court summarily dismisses Rosenbloom's arguments. Brennan writes, "Drawing a distinction between 'public' and 'private' figures makes no sense in terms of the First Amendment guarantees" (45, 46). He says the actual malice test was devised "to encourage ventilation of public issues, not because the public official has any less interest in protecting his reputation than an individual in private life" (46).

In regard to the ability of public figures to command access to counter argument in the media, the Court asserts, "If the States fear that private citizens will not be able to respond adequately to publicity involving them, the solution lies in the direction of ensuring their ability to respond, rather than in stifling public discussion of matters of public concern" (47). Brennan then calls the idea that public figures "voluntarily" expose themselves to publicity while private persons avoid it "at best, a legal fiction" (48). He continues, "In any event, such a distinction could easily produce the paradoxical result of dampening discussions of issues of public or general concern because they happen to involve private citizens (48).

Rosenbloom's other argument is that the Court should give proper emphasis to the values of "preventing and redressing attacks upon reputation" (45). Brennan sees two interests in these values: a "desire to preserve a certain privacy . . . from unwarranted intrusion" and a desire to preserve a "public good name and reputation" (48). Privacy, Brennan says, "is not involved in this case . . . since . . . the individual is involved in matters of public or general concern" (48).

Rosenbloom's good name is a relevant issue says the Court, but "Pennsylvania libel law recognizes that society's interest in protecting an individual's reputation often yields to other important social goals" (49, 50). Thus, Brennan asserts Rosenbloom's interest in protecting his good name is not enough "to obtain damage judgements on the basis of . . . [a failure] to use reasonable care" (50).

The problem with reasonable care as a standard of fault in a libel case concerned with matters of general interest to the public, says Brennan, is that "the vagueness of the negligence standard would create a strong impetus toward self-censorship, which the First Amendment cannot tolerate" (50). He mentions here a theme the Court is fond of using in libel cases: "The negligence standard gives insufficient breathing space to First Amendment values" (52).

Since the Court states that Rosenbloom must meet the actual malice test in order to prevail, the next question to consider is whether or not WIP knew the charges (by police that the material is obscene) were false or recklessly disregarded their truth. Although some dissenting members object to a review of the evidence, Brennan writes, "The simple fact is that First Amendment questions of 'constitutional fact' compel this Court's de novo review" (54). He concludes:

> Our independent analysis of the record leads us to agree with the Court of Appeals that none of the proofs . . . satisfies the constitutional standard [actual malice] with the convincing clarity necessary to raise a jury question whether the defamatory falsehoods were broadcast with knowledge that they were false or with reckless disregard of whether they were false or not. (55)

Rosenbloom does make an effort to show that WIP may have recognized that the charges of obscenity were false. He argues that, if someone from WIP had asked him about his side of the story, then that person would have learned that the charges were false. The Court rejects this contention. Brennan answers with a well-known quotation from *St. Amant* v. *Thompson* (1968), "'There must be sufficient evidence to permit the conclusion that the defendant in fact entertained serious doubts as to the truth of his publication'" (56).

RULING

The Court affirms the judgment of the court of appeals and takes away the damages awarded by the district court. Brennan writes:

> We thus hold that a libel action, as here, by a private individual against a licensed radio station for a defamatory falsehood in a newscast relating his involvement in an event of public or general concern may be sustained only upon clear and convincing proof that the defamatory falsehood was published with knowledge that it was false or with reckless disregard of whether it was false or not. (52)

In short, just like public officials and public figures, private persons caught up in matters of public interest have to show that the media disseminated false defamatory statements with actual malice in order to win a libel case. Such a private person, that is, must show that journalists knew they ewere disseminating a falsehood or had a reckless disregard for the truth of it.

Justice Hugo L. Black writes a concurring opinion.

Black once again states his absolutist position on libel by the media. He writes, "In my view, the First Amendment does not permit the recovery of libel judgments against the news media even when statements are broadcast with knowledge they are false" (57).

Justice Byron R. White writes a concurring opinion.

White begins his argument by saying that free speech is not an end in itself, but rather a means to the end of effective self government. He writes, "My interest is not in protecting the treasuries of communicators but in implementing the First Amendment by insuring that effective communication which is essential to the continued functioning of our free society" (60).

As he sees it, all that WIP did was to publicize incidentally the actions of Rosenbloom when it broadcast a news story about the official actions of public officials (the police). He asserts that, if the media disseminate a news story without actual malice, then they have a privilege to include information about private citizens caught up in the story. His notion of this privilege means these citizens cannot, in such cases, collect damages for false defamation of their character.

Justice John M. Harlan writes a dissenting opinion.

Harlan's first objection to the plurality's ruling is that he feels it would require the Court "to scrutinize carefully every jury verdict in every libel case, in order to ascertain whether the final judgment leaves fully protected whatever First Amendment values transcend the legitimate State interest in protecting the particular plaintiff who prevailed" (63). Although the Court denies that its ruling necessarily requires a case-by-case analysis, Harlan still asserts that "a general rule" is needed "in order to preserve a measure of order and predictability in the law . . . and to avoid subjecting the press to judicial second-guessing of the newsworthiness of each item they print" (63).

He then proposes what he feels are three important concepts that should be part of libel proceedings. He writes:

> I . . . think that, when dealing with private libel, the States should be free to define for themselves the applicable standard of care so long as they do not impose liability without fault; that a showing of actual malice should be requisite to recovery for libel; and that it is impermissible . . . to fail to confine the amount of jury verdicts. (64)

In short, Harlan says the states should be allowed to continue to set the rules when a private person is libeled; that defamed persons should not be able to collect money unless they can show that they actually were damaged in some way; and that financial damages should have a reasonable cap put on them.

Harlan also feels the distinction between public and private persons is indeed legitimate and so the States can constitutionally impose a "duty of reasonable care" upon journalists who defame private persons (70).

If no cap is placed on punitive damages, then, according to Harlan, the "specter of being forced to pay out substantial punitive damage awards is likely to induce self-censorship" (72). At the same time, the "specter" of self-censorship does not justify setting an "arbitrary limitation on the amount of actual damages recoverable" (72). Harlan proposes a number of steps the states can take to resolve the problem of damages.

First, he feels the First Amendment limits "the imposition of punitive damages to those situations where actual malice is proved" (73). The "rationale" for punitive damages is to provide a "deterrent" (73). But deterrence does not justify "punitive damages that bear no discernible relationship to the actual harm cause by the publication at issue" (75). So, he concludes:

> Where the compensatory scheme seeks to achieve deterrence as a subsidiary by-product, the desired deterrence, if not precisely measured by actual damages, would be informed by that touchstone.(75)
>
> A careful and properly instructed jury should ordinarily be able to arrive at damage awards that are self-validating. (76) The defendant's resources, the actual harm suffered by the plaintiff and the publication's potential for actual harm are all susceptible of more or less objective measurement. (76)

In sum, Harlan fells that libel laws exist only to compensate persons for some injury suffered. Punitive damages, in contrast, are necessary to deter the media from injuring (by falsely defaming) private persons, but these damages are to be limited by having some relationship to the actual damage suffered by the persons libeled. Since the directions given to the *Rosenbloom* jury did not include these concepts, he would send the case back to the district court for a trial based on them.

Justice Thurgood Marshall writes a dissenting opinion.
Justice Potter Stewart joins.

Marshall begins his opinion on a high philosophical plane when he writes, quoting in part from *Rosenblatt*:

> The protection of the reputation of such anonymous persons "from unjustified invasion and wrongful hurt reflects no more than our basic concept of the essential dignity and worth of every human being--a concept at the root of any decent system of order." But the concept of a citizenry informed by a free and unfettered press is also basic to our system of ordered liberty. Hence these two essential and fundamental values conflict. (78)

He objects to the Court's resolution of these conflicts in part because it requires "a determination that the event was of legitimate public interest" (79). He continues, "Courts will be required to somehow pass on the legitimacy of interest in a particular event or subject" (79).

In what is to Marshall a paradoxical contrast, the Court's resolution "threatens society's interest in protecting private individuals . . . since all human events are arguably within the area of 'public or general concern'" (79). He continues, "Moreover, such an approach will require this Court to engage in a constant and continuing supervision of defamation litigation throughout the country" (81). He feels there is a general rule that will eliminate the necessity of a case-by-case balancing of the values of a free press against those of private reputation.

To Marshall and Stewart, the root of the problem is the notion that large punitive libel awards threaten self-censorship. This problem is easily solved. Marshall writes, "The threats to society's interest in freedom of the press that are involved in punitive and presumed damages can largely be eliminated by restricting the award of damages to proved, actual injuries" (84). He adds, "The victims of the defamation will be compensated for their real injuries. They will not be, however, assuaged far beyond their wounds" (84).

Marshall feels this notion avoids the problems with the two other solutions proposed in the Court's decision. He writes:

> If awards are so limited in cases involving private individuals--persons first brought to public attention by the defamation that is the subject of the lawsuit--it will be unnecessary to rely, as both the plurality and to some extent Mr. Justice Harlan do, on somewhat elusive concepts of the degree of fault, and unnecessary . . . to engage in ad hoc balancing of competing interests involved. States would be essentially free . . . to articulate whatever fault standard best suits the State's need. (86)

He concludes, "Thus, . . . I would reverse . . . and remand the case for a determination of whether Mr. Rosenbloom can show any actual loss" (87).

SIGNIFICANCE

This case is well known for developing the notion of an involuntary public person who is simply a private person caught up in a matter of public concern. According to the Court, such persons have the responsibility of showing clearly and convincingly that a journalist who falsely defamed them acted with actual malice (knowing the defamation was false or having a reckless disregard for the truth of it). The result of this notion is that the previous distinctions between public officials, public figures, and private persons are no longer important when the defamation arises out of a matter of public concern. When the interest at issue is of general concern to the public, then all three classes of persons are treated the same.

This decision had little long-lasting impact in part because it represents the opinion of only three justices. The result of such a fractured ruling--with five opinions--is that the Court soon reconsidered its conclusions and, in *Gertz*, severely restricted the "public interest" concept.

Two important issues are discussed in the dissenting opinions. First, what is the level of care the media should be required to adhere to when disseminating false defamatory statements about private persons. Secondly, what is the best way to deal with large punitive damages that encourage self-censorship.

In regard to the level of fault, it is interesting to note that Harlan's dissent is soon endorsed by the whole court in *Gertz*. He suggests that, when dealing with private libel, the states should be free to define for themselves the applicable standard of care so long as they do not impose liability without fault.

Harlan's solution is to limit the imposition of punitive damages to those situations where actual malice is proved. Moreover, he would use precisely measured actual damages as a "touchstone" for granting punitive awards. He feels that punitive damages should work as a deterrent to valueless defamatory speech, but the deterrent should be held in check by having some relationship to the actual damage suffered by the persons libeled.

Marshall feels threats to society's freedom of press interests constituted by large punitive and presumed damage awards can largely be eliminated by restricting the award of damages to proved actual injuries. He likes this solution mainly because it makes unnecessary the need first to rely on somewhat elusive concepts of the degree of fault, and secondly to engage in ad hoc balancing of competing interests involved.

St. Amant v. Thompson

Phil A. St. Amant
v.
Herman A. Thompson

Docket No. 1968-517
390 U.S. 727, 20 L.Ed.2d 262, 88 S.Ct. 1323 (1968)
Argued April 4, 1968. Decided April 29, 1968.

BACKGROUND

By 1968, attorneys were developing ways to show that false defamatory statements were published with reckless disregard for their truth. Because recklessness is such a subjective concept, however, the lower courts were not applying a consistent definition. Thus, the Court accepted this case for review, in part, so that it could reaffirm its suggestions in *Garrison* (1964), *Beckley* (1967), and *Curtis* (1967) that recklessness means more than mere failure to investigate or mere doubt about whether or not the defamatory statements published are true.

CIRCUMSTANCES

As part of his campaign for a public office, Phil A. St. Amant made a televised speech on June 27, 1962, in Baton Rouge, Louisiana. In the speech he read answers to some questions he had asked J. D. Albin, who was a member of a Teamsters Union local. Part of Albin's answers accused Herman A. Thompson, a deputy sheriff, of criminal misconduct growing out of his relationship to another union official. Thompson was called an "ex-convict," and a "labor Chieftain" who misused and stole union funds and was accused of being involved in a hit-and-run accident with a union car. Vigorously denying the assertions, Thompson filed a libel suit against St. Amant.

SUMMARY OF THE COURT'S ANALYSIS

Justice Byron R. White writes for the Court.
Chief Justice Earl Warren and Justices William J. Brennan, Jr., John M. Harlan, Thurgood Marshall, and Potter Stewart join.

Justice White states at the outset the Court's reason for review when he writes, "The question presented by this case is whether the Louisiana Supreme Court . . . correctly interpreted and applied the rule of New York Times Co. v. Sullivan" (728). He begins the analysis by writing, "We accept the determinations of the Louisiana courts that the material published by St. Amant charged Thompson with criminal conduct, that the charge was false, and that Thompson was a public official" (730). The question, though, says White, is whether the Louisiana Supreme Court was correct when it said St. Amant broadcast the false information "recklessly, though not knowingly" (730).

The Court asserts the following are facts: (1) "St. Amant had no personal knowledge of Thompson's activities"; (2) "he relied solely on Albin's affidavit"; (3) he "failed to verify the information"; (4) he "gave no consideration to whether or not the statements defamed Thompson"; and (5) "he mistakenly believed he had no responsibility for the broadcast because he was merely quoting Albin's words" (730).

In reaffirming the rulings of *Garrison* and *Curtis*, White uses these soon-to-be-well-known words:

> Reckless conduct is not measured by whether a reasonably prudent man would have published, or would have investigated before publishing. There must be sufficient evidence to permit the conclusion that the defendant entertained *serious doubts* [emphasis added] as to the truth of his publication. Publishing with such doubts shows reckless disregard for truth or falsity and demonstrates actual malice. (731)

He then turns to analyzing a common criticism of the actual malice test. He writes:

> It may be said that such a test puts a premium on ignorance, encourages the irresponsible publisher not to inquire, and permits the issue to be determined by the defendant's testimony that he published the statement in good faith and unaware of its probable falsity. (731)
>
> The defendant . . . cannot, however, automatically insure a favorable verdict by testifying that he published with a belief that the statements were true. The finder of fact must determine whether the publication was indeed made in good faith. Professions of good faith will be unlikely to prove persuasive. (732)

White ends this discussion by affirming once more the assertion that "recklessness may be found where there are obvious reasons to doubt the veracity of the informant or the accuracy of his reports" (732).

RULING

The Court concludes that, since "nothing referred to by the Louisiana courts indicates an awareness by St. Amant of the probably falsity of Albin's statement about Thompson" (732, 733), "the judgment is reversed and the case remanded for further proceedings not inconsistent with this opinion" (733).

Justices Hugo L. Black and William O. Douglas write a concurring opinion.

Black and Douglas once again concur for the reasons "set out in their concurring opinions in New York Times v Sullivan" (733, 734).

Justice Abe Fortas writes a dissenting opinion.

St. Amant did indeed publish the defamatory falsehood with reckless disregard for the truth, according to Fortas. He writes, "Petitioner's casual, careless, callous use of the libel cannot be rationalized as resulting from the heat of a campaign" (734). He continues, "The First Amendment is not a shelter for the character assassinator" (734).

Emphasizing the severity of injury inflicted by defamatory statements, Fortas supports his somewhat lower concept of recklessness. For him, failure to check on the reliability of sources who make defamatory statements is adequate evidence of reckless disregard for the truth. He writes:

> The occupation of public officeholder does not forfeit one's membership in the human race. The public official should be subject to severe scrutiny and to free and open criticism. But if he is needlessly, heedlessly, falsely accused of crime, he should have a remedy in law. New York Times does not preclude this minimal standard of civilized living.
>
> Petitioner had a duty here to check the reliability of the libelous statement about respondent. (734)

SIGNIFICANCE

This case holds significance mainly because it reaffirms the high level of proof required to show reckless disregard for the truth of a defamatory statement. In *Garrison* the Court used the words "high degree of probable falsity"; here it uses the words "serious doubts about falsity."

There is some additional interest, though, in the dissent by Fortas, who felt that St. Amant's failure to check the reliability of his sources did in fact constitute actual malice. One year earlier Chief Justice Earl Warren, concurring in *Curtis*, also asserted that poor investigative techniques are evidence of reckless disregard for the truth. Thus, the lack of uniformity in determining what actions constitute recklessness characterized opinions of lower courts partly because the members of the Court shared a similar lack of uniformity.

Time, Inc. v. Firestone

Time, Inc.
v.
Mary Alice Firestone

Docket No. 74-944
424 U.S. 448, 47 L.Ed.2d 154, 96 S.Ct. 958 (1976)
Argued October 14, 1975. Decided March 2, 1976.

BACKGROUND

In *Gertz*, the Court backed away from a subject matter test (announced earlier in *Rosenbloom*) as a condition for applying the actual malice rule and focused once again, as it did in *Sullivan*, primarily on the nature of the defamed persons. While in *Rosenbloom* persons involved in a matter of public interest would have to show that the media disseminated a false defamatory statement with actual malice, in *Gertz* only public persons would have to prove actual malice.

Coming soon after *Gertz*, this case not surprisingly again highlights the court's basic disagreement over determining whether public interest rests in public persons (*Rosenbloom*) or in public matters (*Sullivan* and *Gertz*). The level of fault or care for the media is also an important issue here. One important new distinction drawn in *Sullivan* is the level of media fault that defamed persons must show in various situations in order to collect damages. Likewise, this case focuses to a large degree not only on the problems of where to draw the line for different persons and circumstances, but also on the very notion of requiring and determining fault.

CIRCUMSTANCES

Three years after marrying, Mary Alice Firestone left her husband Russell A. Firestone and filed a lawsuit for separate maintenance. Her husband, in turn, filed "for divorce on the grounds of extreme cruelty and adultery" (450). The ambiguity of the trial judge's opinion in the divorce case is blamed by nearly everyone concerned for the multitude of confusing issues raised by *Time* magazine's reporting of it.

Parts of the relevant passages from this decision include these words:

> According to certain testimony in behalf of the defendant, extramarital escapades of the plaintiff are of an amatory nature which would have made Dr. Freud's hair curl. Other testimony, in plaintiff's behalf, would indicate that defendant was guilty of bounding from one bed partner to another with the erotic zest of a satyr. (450, 451)
>
> It is the conclusion of the court that neither party is domesticated, within the meaning of that term as used by the Supreme Court of Florida. (451)
>
> ORDERED AND ADJUDGED
>
> That the equities in this cause are with the defendant [Russell A. Firestone]; that defendant's counterclaim for divorce be . . . granted. (451)
>
> That the defendant shall pay unto the plaintiff [Mary Alice Firestone] the sum of $3,000 per month. (451)

Time magazine's press deadline for printing information about this case was "Saturday, December 16, the day after the Circuit Court rendered its decision at about 4:30 in the afternoon" (466). The New York office first learned of the divorce from an Associated Press wire story saying "that Russell A. Firestone had been granted a divorce from his third wife, whom 'he had accused of adultery and extreme cruelty'" (466). Later that evening the New York *Daily News* "carried a special bulletin . . . to the same effect as the AP dispatch" (466).

In addition, the New York office received an answer to a inquiry sent to the Miami bureau "quoting excerpts from the Circuit Court's opinion that strongly suggested adultery on the part of both parties" (466). A fourth source for the story was the *Time*'s Palm Beach stringer, who wrote in part, "'The technical grounds for divorce . . . were given as extreme cruelty and adultery [*sic*]'" (467).

On the basis of these four sources, *Time* printed the following paragraph as part of its "Milestones" feature in the December 22, 1967, issue.

> DIVORCED. By Russell A. Firestone, Jr., 41, heir to the tire fortune: Mary Alice Sullivan Firestone, 32, his third wife; a onetime Palm Beach schoolteacher; on grounds of extreme cruelty and adultery; after six years of marriage, one son; in West Palm Beach, Fla. The 17-month intermittent trial produced enough testimony of extramarital adventures on both sides, said the judge, "to make Dr. Freud's hair curl." (452)

Mary Alice Firestone sued for libel saying the divorce was not granted on the grounds of adultery. She was awarded a $100,000 judgment, which the Florida District Court of Appeals and the Supreme Court of Florida affirmed.

SUMMARY OF THE COURT'S ANALYSIS

Justice William H. Rehnquist writes for the court.
Chief Justice Warren E. Burger and Justices Harry A. Blackmun, Lewis E. Powell, Jr., and Potter Stewart join.

Justice Rehnquist begins his analysis with two important arguments advanced by the attorneys for *Time*. First, *Time* claimed Mary Alice Firestone is a public figure and so must show that the article was printed with actual malice. Secondly, *Time* proposed a new privilege that would grant the actual malice protection to reports of judicial proceedings. In other words, *Time* suggested that, in order to collect damages, persons falsely defamed by news reports from courtrooms would have to show that the stories were written with actual malice. Responds Rehnquist, "We reject both arguments" (453).

The Court says Mary Alice Firestone is not a public figure because she does not pass any of the tests set forth in *Gertz*. Rehnquist writes, "[She] did not assume any role of especial prominence in the affairs of society . . ., she did not thrust herself to the forefront of any particular public controversy in order to influence the resolution of the issues involved in it" (453).

Rehnquist then draws an important distinction when he writes, "[*Time*] seeks to equate 'public controversy' with all controversies of interest to the public" (454). The notion of applying the actual malice protection to statements about matters of "general" interest, although proposed in *Rosenbloom*, was rejected more recently in *Gertz*, according to Rehnquist.

Another reason the Court feels Mary Alice Firestone does not meet the public figure definition is that she did not "freely choose to publicize issues as to the propriety of her married life. She was compelled to go to court by the State in order to obtain legal release from the bonds of matrimony" (454). In short, she was forced to use the courts because they were the only place she could obtain a legal separation.

Earlier--in *Cox* v. *Cohn* (1975), a privacy case--the Court granted a qualified privilege to "publication of truthful information contained in official court records open to public inspection" (455). *Time*, says Rehnquist, now wants to extend that privilege to "inaccurate and false statements" (455) reported without actual malice from judicial proceedings. The Court refuses to do so, saying that such action would focus on a "subject-matter test," which was "eschew[ed]" in *Gertz* in favor of "one focusing upon the character of the defamation plaintiff" (456). Moreover, such a requirement is not allowed by the Constitution, Rehnquist asserts, because it "would effect substantial depreciation of the individual's interest in protection from such harm [injury from defamation]" (456).

What about a more narrowly defined protection limited to "focused reports of what actually transpires in the courtroom" (457)? Even this concept is too broad for the Court. Rehnquist writes, "The details of many, if not most, courtroom battles would add almost nothing toward advancing the uninhibited debate on public issues thought to provide principle support for the decision [actual malice] in New York Times" (457).

In sum, the Court says the media are adequately protected by the rule, in *Gertz*, requiring a defamed person to show that false reports from courthouses were published as the result of some sort of fault (457).

Another defense raised by *Time* is that its "Milestone" article is "factually correct" (458). The question of accuracy was given to the jury, which, because it charged damages, Rehnquist says must have felt that *Time*'s interpretation of the divorce judgment "does not exist even for laymen" (458). He writes, "We believe the Florida courts properly could have found the 'Milestones' item to be false" (458).

The main problem with the claim of truthful reporting, according to the Court, is that *Time* said adultery was one of the grounds for the divorce. Although it is true that Russell A. Firestone filed on the grounds of adultery and mental cruelty, the trial court's decision "did not specify the basis was either of the two grounds alleged" and the Florida Supreme Court "concluded that the ground actually relied upon by the divorce court was 'lack of domestication of the parties'" (458).

Even though the trial court's decision may have been unclear, Rehnquist continues, the media do not have "license" to "choose from among several conceivable interpretations" (459). Instead, the media "must be able to establish not merely that the item reported was a conceivable or plausible interpretation of the decree, but that the item was factually correct" (459).

Another argument put forth by *Time* is that defamed persons can be compensated only for injury to reputation. Rehnquist notes in this regard that *Gertz* allows for damages on several other bases, such as "'personal humiliation, and mental anguish and suffering'" (459) as long as the damages "'are a direct and natural result of the alleged libel'" (460). He adds:

> There was competent evidence introduced to permit the jury to assess the amount of injury. Several witnesses testified to the extent of respondent's [Mary Alice Firestone's] anxiety and concern over Time's inaccurately reporting that she had been found guilty of adultery, and she herself took the stand to elaborate on her fears that her young son would be adversely affected by this falsehood when he grew older. (461)

The final point addressed by the Court is the requirement in *Gertz* that private persons who are falsely defamed can collect damages only if they show that the statements were printed as the result of some sort of fault. Rehnquist points out, "No question of fault was submitted to the jury" (461) because Florida law did not require it. Still, he points out that the question of fault does not have to be settled at the trial; an appellant court could also determine fault.

The only statement mentioning some form of fault can be found in the ruling by the Florida Supreme Court. This court said the divorce judgment obviously was not grounded in adultery because Mary Alice Firestone was given alimony and, under Florida law, "a wife guilty of adultery could not be awarded alimony" (462). That court concluded, "This is a flagrant example of journalistic negligence" (463).

Does the statement about "journalistic negligence" mean that the Florida Supreme Court found *Time* was at fault because it was negligent? The answer by the Court is no. Writes Rehnquist, "Without some finding of fault by the judge or jury in the Circuit Court, we would have to attribute to the Supreme Court of Florida from the quoted language . . . an intention to find such a fact in the first instance" (463). Since the Florida Supreme Court did not make a determination of negligence by finding "the existence of . . . critical fact," then there is also no finding of fault. Moreover, the Court says it is "not inclined to canvass the record to make such a determination in the first instance" (464).

RULING

The Court rules, "Accordingly, the judgment of the Supreme Court of Florida is vacated and the case remanded for further proceedings not inconsistent with this opinion" (464).

Justice Lewis F. Powell, Jr., writes a concurring opinion.
Justice Potter Stewart joins.

Powell says he concurs with the majority in "this bizarre case . . . in order to avoid the appearance of fragmentation of the Court on the basic principles involved" (464).

First, since *Gertz* requires a showing of fault in order to win damages; secondly, since no court so far has determined whether or not *Time* was at fault; and, thirdly, since the majority opinion requires the case to be reconsidered in order to make such a determination, Powell decides to give some guidance in what he calls the "ultimate question" (465): Was *Time* at fault?

To provide guidance for answering this question, Powell first reviews the four sources of information used by *Time*. Next he notes, "The opaqueness of the Circuit Court's decree is also a fact to be considered in assessing whether Time was guilty of actionable fault" (467), a decree which he says "was hardly a model of clarity" (468).

Powell notes that, although there is "no reference whatever in the 'order' portion of the decision . . . to . . .' adultery,' . . . the divorce was granted to him [Russell A. Firestone]" after he sued on the basis of adultery, and the judge found "the equities . . . are with the husband" (469). Powell also points out, "The opinion that preceded the order was full of talk of adultery" (469). He concludes, "In these circumstances, the decision of the Circuit Court may have been sufficiently ambiguous to have caused reasonably prudent newsmen to read it as granting divorce on the ground of adultery" (469).

Powell refuses to say, however, whether or not "as a matter of law . . . Time exercised the requisite care" (469). He adds, "My point in writing is to emphasize that . . . there *was* [Powell's emphasis] substantial evidence supportive of Time's defense that it was not guilty of actionable negligence" (470).

Justice William J. Brennan, Jr., writes a dissenting opinion.

Brennan says the primary question presented in this case is the "degree of protection commanded by the First Amendment's free expression guarantee" (471). He argues for a return to the subject matter test in *Rosenbloom* as a condition for requiring the showing of actual malice.

He writes, "The extension of the relaxed standard of Gertz to news reporting of events transpiring in and decisions arising out of public judicial proceedings . . . savages the cherished values encased in the First Amendment" (476). He notes, quoting in part from *Pennekamp*:

> Error in reporting and debate concerning the judicial process is inevitable. Indeed, in view of the complexities of that process and its unfamiliarity to the laymen who report it, the probability of inadvertent error may be substantially greater. (478, 479)
>
> "In view of these facts any standard which would require strict accuracy in reporting legal events factually or in commenting upon them in the press would be an impossible one." (481) "There must be some room for misstatement of fact . . . if the press and others are to function as critical agencies in our democracy concerning courts as for all other instruments of government." (481)

Powell concludes, "In the field of reporting public judicial affairs. . . . [t]he actual-malice standard of New York Times must be met in order to justify the imposition of liability in these circumstances" (481).

Justice Byron R. White writes a dissenting opinion.

White supports the Florida Supreme Court's decision because he does not feel a fault standard is required by the First Amendment. He adds that, in any case, a fault standard should not be applied in this particular case because the requirement that some sort of fault must be shown in order to collect damages was issued after the *Firestone* case went to trial. Moreover, White feels the Florida Supreme Court "made a sufficiently 'conscious determination' . . . of the fact of negligence" (484).

Justice Thurgood Marshall writes a dissenting opinion.

Marshall dissents from the majority because he feels Mary Alice Firestone was a public figure. He offers as evidence several facts:

> She was "prominent among the '400' of Palm Beach society," and an "active [member] of the sporting set," . . . whose activities predictably attracted the attention of a sizeable portion of the public. (485) Indeed, Mrs. Firestone's appearances in the press were evidently frequent enough to warrant her subscribing to a press-clipping service. (485) The 17-month trial elicited no fewer than 43 articles in the Miami

Herald and 45 articles in the Palm Beach Post and Palm Beach Times. Far from shunning the publicity, Mrs. Firestone held several press conferences in the course of the proceedings. (485)

Marshall next applies from *Gertz* "two distinguishing features" (485) of a public figure. The first asserts "public figures have less need for judicial protection because of their greater ability to resort to self-help" (485); that is, they "usually enjoy significantly greater access to the channels of effective communication [the mass media]" (485). For Marshall, though, this is "a minor consideration in determining whether an individual is a public figure" (486).

More important is "a normative notion that public figures are less deserving of protection than private figures" (486) because they thrust themselves into a conflict in order to influence the resolution. He writes, "We must assume that it was by choice that Mrs. Firestone became an active member of the 'sporting set'--a social group with 'especial prominence in the affairs of society'" (486). She also held press conferences in the course of her lawsuit.

Marshall then asserts that terming her actions "not of the sort deemed relevant to the 'affairs of society' is, in effect, turning attention away from a person-focused test to a subject matter test. He writes, "If Gertz is to have any meaning at all, the focus of analysis must be on the actions of the individual, and the degree of public attention that had already developed" (489).

Two final points are addressed by Marshall. First, unlike the Court, he accepts "the contention that a rational interpretation of an ambiguous document is always entitled to some constitutional protection" (491). He notes the Court said in *Pape* that wrongly selecting "one of several rational interpretations of an ambiguous document" does not constitute actual malice. He then extends this notion when he writes, "The choice of one of several rational interpretations of an ambiguous document, without more, is insufficient to support a finding of fault under Gertz" (491). To Marshall, therefore, selecting a false defamatory meaning of an ambiguous document is not actual malice, negligence, nor any other fault so long as the interpretation is rational.

Interestingly, Marshall also feels, unlike the Court, that the Supreme Court of Florida did indeed find *Time* guilty of a fault. For Marshall, however, that court's "determination" is "wholly unsupportable" (292). The Florida court reasoned that Mary Alice Firestone could not have been found guilty of adultery because she was granted alimony and, under Florida law, a wife could not be given alimony if she was an adulterer. Marshall notes a flaw in the Florida court's reasoning. It overlooks the fact "that courts occasionally err in their assessment of the law" (292). In fact, the Florida Supreme Court itself found such an error when it said the "divorce had been granted for lack of 'domestication' and pointed out that lack of domestication was not one of the statutory grounds for divorce" in Florida (492, 493). Marshall is saying, in short, that *Time* would not necessarily know that one ground of the divorce could not be adultery because the trial judge may have erred when granting Mary Alice Firestone alimony.

SIGNIFICANCE

A significant distinction is drawn by the Court in this case; it said well-known persons--even if they actively seek publicity--are not necessarily public figures. In order to qualify for becoming public figures, defamed persons must in some way voluntarily thrust themselves into a controversy of public interest with an intent to affect a resolution. As noted by Marshall in his dissent, however, the Court is unable to escape completely from a subject matter test here because the controversy into which these public figures voluntarily thrust themselves must be of public, not merely social, interest. Not all controversies of interest to the public are considered by the Court to be public controversies.

Another significant result of this case is the failure to create a qualified privilege for the media to report on events at the courthouse. While the Court earlier created in *Cox* a qualified privilege for accurate reporting of courthouse news, it refused to treat false defamatory statements based on judicial proceedings any differently from news reports taken from another source. To create a privilege for reporting judicial proceedings would amount to protecting news on the basis of a particular subject matter, a concept the Court said it rejected in *Gertz*.

In addition, the Court indicated that accurate reporting means more than selecting a rational interpretation from among those available in an ambiguous document. It means the facts must be correct.

The decision hinged, though, on the Court's reaffirmation of the requirement announced in *Gertz* that damages cannot be awarded to falsely defamed private persons unless they can show some sort of fault on the part of the media. While *Time* sought to raise the level of that fault to actual malice (and thereby create a qualified privilege for reporting of judicial proceedings), the Court said the states are free to set lower levels, such as negligence. The most interesting result of the case, therefore, is that, although Mary Alice Firestone was able to show she was falsely defamed, she was unable to collect damages because she failed to show a fault on the part of Time.

Time v. Pape

Time, Incorporated
v.
Frank Pape

Docket No. 1971-109
401 U.S. 279, 28 L.Ed.2d 45, 91 S.Ct. 633 (1971)
Argued December 16, 1970. Decided February 24, 1971.
Petition for a rehearing denied April 5, 1971.
401 U.S. 1015, 28 L.Ed.2d 552, 91 S.Ct. 1248 (1971)

BACKGROUND

This case is the second in a series of three decided on the same day in an attempt to clarify yet more precisely the *Sullivan* decision. In particular attention is directed here toward the impact of publishing a rational, believed true, but nevertheless wrong, interpretation of an ambiguous document. One question addressed in this case is whether or not purposely publishing such an interpretation without using some form of the word "allege" is knowingly or recklessly publishing a falsehood; that is, does such an action constitute actual malice?

The Court first struggled with the impact of ambiguous meanings of words in *Greenbelt Coop. Pub. Asso.* v. *Bresler* (1970), when it considered the various meanings of the word "blackmail." The issue in *Greenbelt* was determining the denotations of the word, that is, the exact meaning of blackmail.

In this case, however, the gravamen is not so much the actual dictionary meaning of words as it is a writer's understanding of what words mean in a given context. The question here is this: Does the writer honestly believe the words written to be a fair and accurate description of what he is trying to communicate?

CIRCUMSTANCES

The circumstances of this case are fairly complex. Frank Pape filed a libel suit against *Time* magazine because of an article it published in November 1961. The article summarized some findings published by the United States Commission of Civil Rights in a report entitled *Justice*. The *Time* article says the report concluded that Pape was guilty of police brutality in his treatment of a James Monroe and his family when the Chicago police entered Monroe's home "ostensibly investigating a murder" (282). Pape contends that the problem with the article was that it did not indicate "in any way that the charges were those made by Monroe rather than independent findings of the Commission" (282).

Police who participated in the raid "all testified that nothing resembling the events described in the Time article as findings of the Commission had occurred" (282, 283). The author of the article "denied that the Time article was false, given the full context of the Justice report" (283). By this assertion, the author meant the report seemed to suggest that all events described in it did in fact occur. The researcher at *Time* said that, after reading several articles in other newspapers as well as dispatches from the *Time* Chicago correspondent, she too "believed the article to have been true as written" (283).

The district and appeals courts agreed that Pape was a public official "by virtue of his position as Deputy Chief of Detectives of the Chicago Police Department and that charges contained in the Monroe complaint, the Justice report, and the Time story concerned his 'official conduct'" (284). Since the story was not clearly false, the district court dismissed the case. The appeals court, however, said that *Time*'s omission of the word "alleged" constituted publishing a false report, and so a jury should decide whether or not the false statements were published with actual malice.

SUMMARY OF THE COURT'S ANALYSIS

Justice Potter Stewart writes for the Court.
Chief Justice Warren E. Burger, and Justices Harry A. Blackmun, William Brennan, Jr., Thurgood Marshall, and Bryon R. White join.

Justice Stewart says the only issue before the court was whether or not the appeals court correctly applied the actual malice test when it reversed the directed verdict of the district court in favor of *Time*. Citing the precedent of the *Sullivan* case, Stewart said the Court would review the facts of the case because a First Amendment question is at issue. The Court has a duty to determine in such cases, says Stewart, whether the record can support *Time*'s request to dismiss Pape's libel suit.

Stewart says three items make this an unusual libel suit. First, Pape did not object to *Time*'s description of what he did in Monroe's house, but to the magazine's description of what the commission said he did there. Secondly, Pape says he was damaged not by *Time*'s reporting of Monroe's accusations, but by the singular fact that *Time* attributed Monroe's accusations "to an authoritative official source" (285). The last unusual aspect is that *Time* did not deny it altered "significantly" the "wording of the Commission Report," (285), but the magazine "insisted that its [the report's] real meaning had not been changed" (285).

According to Stewart, "The Court of Appeals concluded that it was obvious that the omission of the word 'allegation' or some equivalent was a 'falsification' of the Report" (285). If the report is false, then, to determine actual malice, Stewart says Pape must show that *Time* printed the report knowing it was false or having a reckless disregard of its falsity. The appeals court said that, since falsity "might reasonably be inferred from the very act of deliberate omission" (285) of the word alleged, a jury should be allowed to determine whether or not *Time* published the falsehood with actual malice. Therefore, it overturned the district court's dismissal of the case.

The Court disagrees. The main problem with the reasoning of the appeals court, according to Stewart, is this: "The attitude of the Commission toward the factual verity of the episodes recounted was anything but straightforward. First, the episodes were presented in the context of a report which from the first page purported to be dealing with a problem of unquestionable reality and seriousness" (285). Stewart says the result of this confusing context is that "it was impossible to know whether the Commission was seeking to encourage belief or skepticism regarding the incidents about to be described" (288). He continues, "Since the series of incidents described earlier in the report was the only evidence the Commission presented in support of its finding and recommendations, there was a logically inevitable implication that the Commission must have believed that the incidents described had in truth occurred" (289).

Therefore, the Court concludes:

> *Time*'s omission of the word "alleged" amounted to the adoption of one of a number of possible rational interpretations of a document that bristled with ambiguities. . . . [T]hough arguably reflecting a misconception [this interpretation] was not enough to create a jury issue of "malice" under the New York Times. (290) To permit the malice issue to go to the jury because of the omission of a word like "alleged," . . . would be to impose a much stricter standard of liability on errors of interpretation or judgment than on errors of historic fact. (290)

In short, the Court is saying that *Time*'s interpretation of the report, although possibly in error, is not false. Making a rational, if inexact, interpretation of an ambiguous document does not constitute a falsity. Stewart writes, "Time's conduct reflected at most an error of judgment" (292).

The actual malice rule was designed, Stewart writes, to add "a constitutional zone of protection for errors of fact caused by negligence" (291). "This protection would not exist for errors of interpretation," he continues, "were the analysis of the Court of Appeals to be adopted, for once a jury was satisfied that the interpretation was 'wrong' the error itself would be sufficient to justify a verdict for the plaintiff [the defamed person]" (291). In other words, the Court is saying that purposely publishing a wrong--but believed true--interpretation of an ambiguous document without using a form of the word "allege" is not knowingly publishing a falsehood and so does not constitute actual malice.

Before issuing the ruling, though, Stewart writes these words: "We should add, however, a final cautionary note. Nothing in this opinion is to be understood as making the word 'alleged' a superfluity in published reports of information damaging to reputation" (292).

RULING

Stewart writes, "The judgment of the Court of Appeals is reversed, and the case is remanded for further proceedings consistent with this opinion" (292).

Justice Hugo L. Black writes a concurring opinion.
Justice William O. Douglas joins.

Black and Douglas say they concur for reasons set out in the *Sullivan* case.

Justice John M. Harlan writes a dissenting opinion.

Harlan objects to the Court's review because he feels there is no need to review the facts of a case when the appeals court "applied the correct standard of review in passing upon the trail judge's decision to grant a directed verdict" (294).

SIGNIFICANCE

This case turns on highly technical points of law, but, at bottom, the Court seems to have ruled out erroneous, but believed true, interpretations of documents as examples of actual malice. The Court made a similar ruling in *Bose Corp. v. Consumers Union of U.S., Inc.* (1984) where it said an engineer made a mistake when he wrote a incorrect description of the sound produced by a high fidelity speaker. In short, purposely printing an error in judgment is not an example of actual malice.

In *Time, Inc.* v. *Firestone* (1976), however, the Court ruled that accurate reporting means more than selecting a rational interpretation from among those available in an ambiguous document. It means the facts must be correct. Rehnquist said there that the media do not have "license" to "choose from among several conceivable interpretations." Instead, the media "must be able to establish not merely that the item reported was a conceivable or plausible interpretation . . ., but that the item was factually correct." Not to do so, according to Rehnquist, is negligence.

These differences can be clarified by noting that actual malice is a higher standard of fault than is negligence. It would appear that, while a rational and believed true, but erroneous, interpretation of an ambiguous document does not constitute actual malice, it could indeed constitute the lower fault of negligence.

Wolston v. Reader's Digest Assn., Inc.

Ilya Wolston
v.
Reader's Digest Association, Inc.

Docket No. 78-5414
443 U.S. 157, 61 L.Ed.2d 450, 99 S.Ct. 2701 (1979)
Argued April 17, 1979. Decided June 26, 1979.

BACKGROUND

When the Court first announced the actual malice test, many jurists felt it would give the media some financial relief from libel suits because many lower courts would dismiss in summary judgment suits brought by public officials. This case, however, is the second time the Court reversed a summary judgment on the basis that the defamed person was wrongly labeled a public figure by the lower courts. The reversal of these judgments caused much concern in the media over an escalation of libel costs necessary to defend cases that may be won ultimately, but that are not dismissed early in the litigation process.

CIRCUMSTANCES

Reader's Digest in 1974 "published a book entitled KGB, The Secret Work of Soviet Agents (KGB). The book describes the Soviet Union's espionage organization and chronicles its activities since World War II" (159). It also states that, as part of this history, Ilya Wolston was once "indicted for espionage and had been a Soviet agent" (160). Wolston sued for libel, saying the charges were false. The district court ruled him a public figure and dismissed the case in summary judgment. The appeals court upheld the judgment.

Wolston, who was born in Russia in 1918, came to the United States in 1939 and became a naturalized citizen during a tour of duty with the U.S. Army in World War II. After receiving an honorable discharge in 1946, he worked on and off as an interpreter. According to the Court, "On July 1, 1958, . . . [Wolston] failed to respond to a [New York] grand jury subpoena directing him to appear on that date" (162). Instead, Wolston, who lived then in Washington, D.C., asked to be excused from a trip to New York because "of his state of mental depression" (162). After his pregnant wife became hysterical on the witness stand in an attempt to support his request for relief from the subpoena, he "agreed to plead guilty to the contempt [of court] charge" (163).

According to the Court, "He received a 1-year suspended sentence and was placed on probation for three years. . . . [T]hereafter, he succeeded for the most part in returning to the private life he had led prior to issuance of the grand jury subpoena" (163).

SUMMARY OF THE COURT'S ANALYSIS

Justice William H. Rehnquist writes for the Court.
Chief Justice Warren E. Burger and Justices Potter Stewart, Byron R. White, Lewis F. Powell, Jr., and John Paul Stevens join.

Justice Rehnquist notes first that all concerned parties agree that Wolston did not occupy "a position of such 'persuasive power and influence' that he could be deemed one of that small group of individuals who are public figures for all purposes" (165). He adds, "[Wolston] . . . achieved no general fame or notoriety and assumed no role of special prominence in the affairs of society as a result of the contempt citation" (165) that would qualify him as a general public figure.

Reader's Digest argued with success in the lower courts, however, that Wolston "falls within the second category of public figures--those who have 'thrust themselves to the forefront of particular controversies in order to influence the resolution of issues involved'" (165). The District Court said this , for example:

> By failing to appear before the grand jury and subjecting himself to a citation for contempt, petitioner [Wolston] "became involved in a controversy of a decided public nature in a way that invited attention and comment, and thereby created in the public an interest in knowing about his connection with espionage. (165)

The appeals court said this: "By refusing to comply with the subpoena, petitioner [Wolston] 'stepped center front into the spotlight focused on the investigation of Soviet Espionage. In short, by his voluntary action he invited attention and comment in connection with the public questions involved in the investigation of espionage" (165).

The Court disagrees. Rehnquist says Wolston "was dragged unwillingly in the controversy" because the "government pursued him in its investigation" (166). Rehnquist explains:

> But the mere fact that petitioner [Wolston] voluntarily chose not to appear before the grand jury, knowing that his action might be attended by publicity, is not decisive on the question of public-figure status. [Wolston] . . . played only a minor role in whatever public controversy there may have been concerning the investigation of Soviet espionage. (167)

Rehnquist then redraws a distinction made in *Gertz*:

> Petitioner's [Wolston's] failure to appear before the grand jury and citation for contempt no doubt were "newsworthy," but the simple fact that these events attracted media attention also is not conclusive of the public-figure issue. A private individual is not automatically transformed into a public figure just by becoming involved in or associated with a matter that attracts public attention. (167)
>
> A libel defendant must show more than mere newsworthiness to justify application of the demanding burden of New York Times. (167, 168)

Another point Rehnquist makes is that Wolston did not engage "the attention of the public in an attempt to influence the resolution of the issues involved" (168). Rehnquist writes:

> His failure to respond to the grand jury's subpoena was in no way calculated to draw attention to himself in order to invite public comment or to influence the public with respect to any issue. He did not in any way seek to arouse public sentiment in his favor and against the investigation. There is no evidence that petitioner's [Wolston's] failure to appear was intended to have, or did in fact have, any effect on any issue of public concern. (168).

The Court ends its opinion by noting:

> This reasoning leads us to reject the further contention of respondents [*Reader's Digest Association, Inc.*] that any person who engages in criminal conduct automatically becomes a public figure for purposes of comment on a limited range of issues relating to his conviction. (168) To hold otherwise would create an 'open season' for all who sought to defame persons convicted of a crime. (169)

RULING

Rehnquist writes, "Accordingly, the judgment of the Court of Appeals is reversed" (169).

Justice Harry A. Blackmun writes a concurring opinion.
Justice Thurgood Marshall joins.

Blackmun objects to the Court's notion "that a person becomes a limited-issue public figure only if he literally or figuratively 'mounts a rostrum' to advocate a particular view" (169). He writes, "I see no need to adopt so restrictive a definition of 'public figures'" (170).

Nevertheless, Wolston is not a public figure in 1974 for Blackmun, who says "the lapse of the intervening 16 years renders consideration of this petitioner's [Wolston's] original public-figure status unnecessary" (170). Blackmun gives two reasons for asserting that the passage of time is important. He writes, "First, a lapse of years between a controversial event and a libelous utterance may diminish the defamed party's access to the means of counterargument" (170). He continues, "Second, the passage of time may diminish the 'risk of public scrutiny' that a putative public figure may fairly be said to have assumed" (171).

Blackmun concludes, "The lapse of 16 years between petitioner's [Wolston's] participation in the espionage controversy and respondent's [Reader's Digest, et. al.] defamatory reference to it was sufficient to erase whatever public-figure attributes petitioner once may have possessed" (171).

Justice William J. Brennan, Jr., writes a dissenting opinion.

Unlike the Court, Brennan agrees with the district court that Wolston did indeed qualify "'as a public figure for the limited purpose of comment on his connection with, or involvement in, espionage in the 1940's and '50's'" (172). Brennan goes on to say, "[Wolston] also qualified as a public figure in 1974" (172) because, as the appeals court noted, "'The issue of Soviet espionage in 1958 and of Wolston's involvement in that operation continues to be a legitimate topic of debate today'" (172).

Nevertheless, Brennan would still overrule the summary judgment because in his view "the evidence raised a genuine issue of fact respecting the existence of actual malice on his [John Barron's] part" (172).

SIGNIFICANCE

The significance of this case lies in the further refinement of the definition of a public figure. The Court reaffirmed its assertion that private persons involved in matters that attract public attention are "not automatically transformed" into public figures. Nor does a person's involvement in the criminal justice system constitute a voluntary effort to influence the outcome of a particular public controversy. Rehnquist said that such a notion of a public figure would "create an 'open season' for all who sought to defame persons convicted of a crime" (169).

Sentence Outline of Libel Issues in Each Case

1964 *New York Times Co.* v. *Sullivan*

* The actual malice privilege is created. It asserts that the First Amendment protects reporters (and presumably other citizens who disseminate false defamatory statements) from libel actions based on criticism of official conduct of public officials as long as the journalists believe what they print is true or do not hold a reckless disregard for its truth.
* Mere failure to, investigate may constitute negligence, but it does not constitute the higher fault of actual malice.
* Actual malice must be demonstrated with clear and convincing evidence. A mere preponderance of the evidence is insufficient.
* Converting criticism of the actions of government officials into personal criticism of public officials, like Sullivan, wrongly changes criticism of public actions into a personal attack.
* Where criticism of the government is concerned, the First Amendment requires some false ideas to be protected in order to guarantee that the full truth is heard. Error is inevitable in any vigorous debate, and so some error must be tolerated in public debates in order to avoid deterring attempts to express unpopular but truthful statements.
* An editorial advertisement is entitled to First Amendment protection.

1964 *Garrison* v. *Louisiana*

* The actual malice rule applies to criminal as well as civil libel.
* Nearly any action by a public official is relevant to an evaluation of official conduct; thus, almost any words criticizing these actions are likewise relevant and so protected by the actual malice rule.
* Reckless disregard of the truth does not mean negligence nor just an intent to inflict harm. Rather it means an intent to inflict harm through falsehood, and the writer must have a high degree of awareness of probable falsity.

1965 ***Henry* v. *Collins***

* Actual malice in a libel case does not mean hatred or ill will. It involves an intent to inflict harm through falsehood, not just an intent to inflict harm without more.

1966 ***Ashton* v. *Kentucky***

* Punishing persons for publishing a statement that threatens to breach the peace makes them criminal simply because their neighbors have no self-control and cannot refrain from violence.
* Vague laws in any area suffer a constitutional infirmity.
* An appeals court cannot properly narrow a broad unconstitutional ruling by taking out everything but the constitutional aspects. (See also *Shuttlesworth* v. *Birmingham*.)

1966 ***Rosenblatt* v. *Baer***

* Public officials are "government employees who have, or appear to the public to have, substantial responsibility for or control over the conduct of governmental affairs."
* Trial courts should take care to see that defamation of a public official's conduct is not made into a personal defamation of the person's private life. Defamation of a public official's conduct is close to defamation of the government, a form of speech protected by the First Amendment.
* The concurring opinions also make this case important in that they emphasize the need to protect speech related to public issues, not just speech directed at a public officials. (Eventually, in *Rosenbloom* v. *Metromedia* (1971), the Court adopts this position for a brief period.)

1966 ***St. Amant* v. *Thompson***

* Reckless conduct is not measured by whether a reasonably prudent person would have published or would have investigated before publishing. There must be sufficient evidence to permit the conclusion that the journalists entertained serious doubts about the truth of their publication. (Compare *Garrison* (1964), where the words "high degree of probable falsity," not "serious doubt," are used.)
* Journalists cannot, however, automatically insure a favorable verdict by testifying that they published with a belief that their statements were true. The finder of fact (usually a jury) must determine whether the publication was indeed made in good faith. Professions of good faith are unlikely to prove persuasive.
* Reckless disregard for the truth may be found where there are obvious reasons to doubt the veracity of informants or the accuracy of their reports.

1967 ***Beckly Newspapers Corp.*** **v.** ***Hanks***

* Actual malice does not mean "ill will," but the publishing of a known defamatory falsehood or a reckless disregard of its truth.
* Reckless disregard of the truth means more than simply a failure to investigate the truth of what is printed. It means a "high degree of awareness" that a statement is false. [Compare *Garrison* (1964) and *St. Amant* (1966).]

1967 ***Curtis Publishing Co.*** **v.** ***Butts***

* The right to communicate information of public interest is not unconditional. These conditions are related to conduct, not subject matter.
* The standard of fault required for public figures to collect damages from false defamatory statements is highly unreasonable conduct constituting an extreme departure from the standards of investigation and reporting ordinarily adhered to by responsible publishers.
* A consideration of conduct resolves the antithesis between civil libel actions and the freedoms of speech and press because impositions based on misconduct can be neutral with respect to content of the speech involved. In other words, courts can regulate the conduct of the communicators instead of the content of the communication.
* Guidelines for regulating the conduct of news gathering can be taken from general liability law, that is, from the general liability rules compensating persons injured by the improper performance of a legitimate activity by another.
* Persons who command the interest of the general public are "public figures."

  (A) Some of these persons are considered to be "public figures" just because of the public interest in the position they occupy.
  (B) Others because they seek to affect debate on public issues.
  (C) In both cases, though, these persons are considered "public figures" because they are important enough to gain access to the mass media where they can respond to any statement falsely defaming them.

* Misconduct sufficient to justify the award of compensatory damages also justifies the imposition of a punitive award. It is not necessary to show a higher fault in order to collect punitive damages.

1970 ***Greenbelt Coop. Pub. Asso.*** **v.** ***Bresler***

* Malice as "ill will" is not a proper definition when public figures, as well as when public officials, are falsely defamed.
* Accurate reporting is at least a partial defense in cases involving libel of public figures.

1971 *Ocala Star-Banner Co.* **v.** *Damron*

* A charge of criminal misconduct against an official or a candidate, no matter how remote in time or place, is always "relevant to his fitness for office" for purposes of applying the *New York Times* rule of knowing falsehood or reckless disregard of the truth.

1971 *Patriot Co.* **v.** *Roy*

* Distinctions between "private sectors" and public sectors" do not help much in resolving questions of First Amendment protection.
* For purposes of determining the need to show actual malice, a jury cannot be asked to consider whether political speech probably would touch upon or be relevant to a candidate's fitness for office. A standard of "relevance" may become a dangerous instrument for the suppression of those vehement, caustic, and sometimes unpleasantly sharp attacks protected by the First and Fourteenth Amendments.
* A standard of relevance is lower than the actual malice standard of care because showing relevance requires presenting only a preponderance of the evidence, whereas showing actual malice requires clear and convincing evidence of knowing falsity or of reckless disregard of the truth.
* As a matter of constitutional law, a charge of criminal conduct, no matter how remote in time or place, can never be irrelevant to an official's or a candidate's fitness for office for purposes of application of actual malice test. [See *Garrison* (1964).]
* The distinction between when actual malice will have to be shown and when it will not is based on two sets of factors: (1) "A class of persons"; and (2) "a type of activity."
* A reasonable person standard as a measure of care is not adequate protection for political speech about public officials.

1971 *Rosenbloom* **v.** *Metromedia*

* There is such a thing as an involuntary public person who is simply a private person caught up in a matter of public concern. Such persons have the responsibility of showing clearly and convincingly that a journalist who defamed them acted with actual malice (knowing the defamation was false or having a reckless disregard for the truth of it).
* The previous distinctions between (1) public officials, (2) public figures, and (3) private persons are no longer important when the defamation arises out of a matter of public concern. When the interest at issue is of general concern to the public, then all three classes of persons are treated the same. [This idea was soon overturned in *Gertz* (1974).]
* Part of Harlan's dissent is soon endorsed by the whole court in *Gertz* (1974). He suggests that, when dealing with private libel, the states should be free to define for themselves the applicable standard of care so long as they do not impose liability without fault.

1971 *Time* v. *Pape*

* If journalists adopt one of a number of possible rational interpretations from a document that bristles with ambiguities, then, even if the interpretation creates a misconception, such action does not constitute actual malice. It is, instead, at most, an error of judgment.
* Nevertheless, the word "alleged" is not a superfluity in published reports of information damaging to reputation.
* While a rational, but erroneous, interpretation of an ambiguous document does not constitute actual malice, it does indeed constitute the lower fault of negligence. [Compare *Time, Inc. v. Firestone* (1976).]

1974 *Gertz* v. *Welch*

* This ruling overturned the public interest standard of *Rosenbloom* (1971) and returned to the distinction between public and private persons first articulated in *New York Times* (1964).
* In addition, it classified public figures into three types and provided some guidelines for defining each type.

    (A) The involuntary public figure who engages in no purposeful action is a hypothetical possibility, but would be rare.
    (B) Voluntary public figures are persons who assume special prominence in the resolution of public questions. Public figures for all purposes and in all contexts are persons who achieve pervasive fame or notoriety.
    (C) Limited public figures are those persons who voluntarily inject themselves or who are drawn into a particular public controversy and thereby become public figures for a limited range of issues.

* States may set their own level of fault for media performance related to private figures, but punitive damages may be assessed only if actual malice can be demonstrated.
* In addition to out-of-pocket expenses, actual damages could consists of impairment of reputation and standing in the community, personal humiliation, and mental anguish and suffering.

1976 *Time, Inc.* v. *Firestone*

* A distinction can be drawn based partially on the nature of the person defamed and partially on the situation giving rise to a defamatory statement. Well-known persons--even if they actively seek publicity--are not necessarily public figures. In order to qualify for becoming public figures, defamed persons must in some way voluntarily thrust themselves into a controversy of public interest with an intent to affect a resolution. The controversy into which these public figures voluntarily thrust themselves must be of public, not merely social, interest.
* Not all controversies of interest to the public are public controversies.
* There is no such thing as a qualified privilege for the media to report on events at the courthouse. To create a privilege for reporting judicial proceedings would amount to protecting news on the basis of a

particular subject matter, a concept the Court said it rejected in *Gertz* (1974).

* Accurate reporting means more than selecting a rational interpretation from among those available in an ambiguous document. It means the facts must be correct. [For a different view see *Time* v. *Pape* (1971).]
* Damages cannot be awarded to falsely defamed private persons unless they can show some sort of fault on the part of the media. The states are free to set levels lower than actual malice, such as negligence.

1979 *Herbert* **v.** *Lando*

* There is no such thing as a First Amendment editorial privilege protecting journalists from revealing information that is part of the editorial process.
* Actual malice was designed for the specific purpose of discouraging the very part of the editorial process that may tend to result in the publication of false defamatory information.
* The rules of civil procedure require a trial judge to protect the media from requests for irrelevant information.

1979 *Hutchinson* **v.** *Proxmire*

* The "speech or debate" clause in Article I, Section 6 of the Constitution excludes information "not essential to the deliberations" of Congress. Specifically, it does not include press releases sent to the media and newsletters sent to constituents. Thus, the privilege that exempts members of Congress from libel suits does not extend beyond statements essential to congressional deliberations.
* To qualify as public figures, persons must have regular and continuing access to the media, and they must voluntarily enter a particular controversy of interest to the public with the intention of influencing others.

1979 *Wolston* **v.** *Reader's Digest Assn., Inc.*

* Private persons involved in matters that attract public attention are "not automatically transformed" into public figures. In particular, a person's involvement in the criminal justice system does not constitute a voluntary effort to influence the outcome of a particular public controversy.

1982 *Bose Corp.* **v.** *Consumers Union of U.S. Inc.*

* The "clearly erroneous" standard of the civil procedures rule [56(B)] does not preclude an independent review of the evidence in order to determine whether constitutional protection was properly considered. In other words, the procedural rule does not forbid an appeals court from reviewing evidence, including factual evidence, to determine if the constitutional concept of actual malice was properly applied by the trial court.

* Constitutional protection is extended to persons who publish knowingly a false defamatory statement if in doing so they made an honest mistake. A false defamatory statement made as the result of an unintentional "mistake" is the kind of "inaccuracy" that "fits easily within the breathing space that gives life to the First Amendment."

1984 *Calder* **v.** *Jones*

* Journalists working for a newspaper published in one state can be sued for libel in another in which the newspaper is circulated if they write an article that they know will injure in that state a resident who lives there. If a state is both "the focal point of the story and of the harm suffered," then that state is likely to be the place of sufficient "contacts" to qualify as a location where a libel suit can be brought against a newspaper published in another state.

1984 *Keeton* **v.** *Hustler Magazine, Inc.*

* Publishers who circulate on a regular basis copies of its newspaper or magazine in a certain state should expect to be held responsible in that state for defamatory statements.
* Just because a state has jurisdiction over a magazine as a corporation does not mean this same state also has jurisdiction over the magazine's employees or other persons related in some way to the magazine.

1985 *Dun & Bradstreet* **v.** *Greemoss Builders*

* A distinction may be drawn between speech by private persons about private matters and speech by private persons about public matters.
* Libeled private persons involved in private matters may collect punitive damages for showing a fault lower than actual malice.
* Although the plurality opinion did not address the request for a special privilege for media defendants, five members of the court reaffirmed a long-standing position that the media have no special First Amendment rights not accorded to the general public.

1986 *Anderson* **v.** *Liberty Lobby*

* To defeat a motion for summary judgment in a libel case involving public officials or public figures, one must demonstrate that a reasonable jury could find that there is clear and convincing evidence that defamatory statements were published with actual malice.
* Libel cases require special standards of evidence in order to meet the requirements of Rule 56 of the *Federal Rules of Civil Procedure*. Actual malice is a material fact (i.e., a relevant issue) that must be considered when evaluating a motion for summary judgment. A genuine dispute about actual malice must exist in order to defeat the motion.
* To support the assertion of a genuine dispute, and so to force a trial, one must show that a reasonable jury would find there is clear and convincing evidence of actual malice.

1986 *Philadelphia Newspapers, Inc.* **v.** *Hepps*

* Defamed persons have the burden of proving defamatory statements about them are false. (Before this case, most states ordinarily used the common-law assumption that statements about presumed upright persons therefore were presumed false, and so defamers had to prove their accusations were true.)
* The burden is limited to (1) private persons (2) who are engaged in matters of public concern (3) who have been defamed by the media.
* The existence of a shield law does not alter the nature of the burden, even though the shield law may make it a bit more difficult to obtain evidence from the media to prove that defamatory statements are false.

1988 *Hustler Magazine* **v.** *Falwell*

* In order to collect damages for outrageous speech intentionally designed to inflict severe emotional distress, one must show actual malice, which means, in part, that the speech itself must be shown to be factual.
* If speech is opinion, then it cannot be false because there is no such thing as a false idea.

1989 *Harte-Hanks Communications, Inc.* **v.** *Connaughton*

* Giving the appearance of purposely avoiding an investigation into a story can be interpreted constitutionally by a jury to constitute adequate factual evidence of reckless disregard for the truth.
* Appellate courts are to make an independent evaluation not of the facts determined by the jury, but of the value of those facts for establishing sufficient evidence to assert that the journalists involved published with actual malice.

CASES RELATED TO PRIVACY

Cantrell v. Forest City Pub. Co.

Margaret Mae Cantrell
v.
Forest City Publishing Co.

Docket No. 73-5520
419 U.S. 245, 42 L.Ed.2d 419, 95 S.Ct. 465 (1974)
Argued November 13, 1974. Decided December 18, 1974.

BACKGROUND

The courts are not isolated from events in the other two branches of government. Just as the legislature is dealing with privacy concerns at this time, so too are the courts. It is not surprising, therefore, that a media-related privacy case makes it way to the Court in 1974. False light is the form of privacy presented by this case. The Court says it is not unlike the fictionalization concept presented in *Time* v. *Hill* (1967). In both cases, the Court focuses on the question of whether or not false nondefamatory, but personally offensive, statements about private citizens must be shown to have been published with actual malice in order qualify for damages.

CIRCUMSTANCES

This case has its origins in the 1967 collapse of the Silver Bridge across the Ohio River at Point Pleasant, West Virginia. Melvin Cantrell and 43 other persons were killed. Joseph Eszterhas, a reporter, was assigned by the Cleveland *Plain Dealer*, owned by Forest City Publishing Company, to cover the story. Subsequently, he wrote a feature "focusing on the funeral of Melvin Cantrell and the impact of his death on the Cantrell family" (247).

Five months later Eszterhas proposed a follow-up story and took a photographer with him to Mrs. Cantrell's home. She was not home at any time during the 60-to-90-minute visit, but Eszterhas talked to the children and Conway took about 50 photographs.

When Eszterhas' follow-up story appeared on page 32 in the August 4, 1968 issue, it "stressed the family's abject poverty" and carried comments by Mrs. Cantrell saying she refused offers of money from townspeople. The story also contained other inaccuracies that were not contested at the trial, including descriptions of the Cantrell's poverty and the "dirty and dilapidated conditions of the Cantrell home" (248).

Margaret Cantrell sued on the basis of the false light theory of privacy, charging that Eszterhas' story was false and made her and her family "objects of pity and ridicule," "causing them to suffer outrage, mental distress, shame, and humiliation" (248). The district judge properly instructed the jury that, to win damages, Cantrell would have to show the false statements were published with actual malice. Forest City did not object to the instructions.

The district judge also struck the punitive damages because, he said, the statements were not published maliciously. The appeals court took the word "maliciously" to be a reference to actual malice, not the traditional common-law definition of "ill will," and so asserted the district judge should have ordered a verdict dismissing all of Cantrell's claims.

SUMMARY OF THE COURT'S ANALYSIS

Justice Potter Stewart writes for the Court.
Chief Justice Warren E. Burger, and Justices William J. Brennan, Jr., Byron R. White, Thrugood Marshall, Harry A. Blackmun, Lewis F. Powell, Jr., and William H. Rehnquist join.

Justice Stewart points out first, "The sole question that we need decide is whether the Court of Appeals erred in setting aside the jury's verdict" (251) on the basis that the trial judge said the evidence did not show the story was published maliciously. To answer this question, the Court must first determine whether the district judge's word "maliciously" referred to actual malice or to the traditional common-law definition of "ill will." Stewart writes, "The conclusion is inescapable that the District Judge was referring to the common law standard of malice" (252). The importance of this determination is that "in dismissing the punitive damages claims he [the district judge] was not determining that Mrs. Cantrell had failed to introduce any evidence of knowing falsity or reckless disregard for the truth" (252). Since Mrs. Cantrell did show actual malice--even though she failed to show ill-will--she, in fact, has meet the level of proof necessary to collect compensatory damages.

Stewart takes care to note that the stories were indeed published with actual malice. Describing parts of Eszterhas' feature as "calculated falsehood," he focuses on two items. Stewart says Eszterhas falsely "implied that Mrs. Cantrell had been present during his visit to her home" and that she wore "'the same mask of non-expression she wore at her husband's funeral'" (253).

In a footnote, the Court points out that the court of appeals correctly found there was "insufficient evidence to support the jury's verdict against the photographer Conway" (253). The court notes, "Conway testified that the photographs he took were fair and accurate depictions of the people and scenes he found at the Cantrell residence" (253). "In short," Stewart writes, "Conway simply was not shown to have participated in portraying the Cantrells in a false light" (253).

The Court also found Forest City Publishing Company liable "under the traditional doctrine of respondeat superior" (253) because Eszterhas wrote the story "within the scope of his employment at the Plain Dealer" (253).

RULING

Stewart writes, "The judgment of the Court of Appeals is reversed and the case is remanded to that court with directions to enter a judgment affirming the judgment of the District Court as to the respondents Forest City Publishing Co. and Joseph Eszterhas" (254).

Justice William O. Douglas writes a dissenting opinion.

Douglas says the Court's decision (to affirm the award for compensatory damages) makes the jury a "censor with broad powers . . . to lay heavy damages on the press" (255). He adds, "The installation of the Court's regime would require a constitutional amendment" (255). "There must be freedom from damages," he writes, "Lest the press be frightened into playing a more ignoble role than the Framers visualized" (255).

SIGNIFICANCE

This case gains significance because it is the only one explicitly to deal with the false light theory of privacy. The Court reaffirms its position in *Time* v. *Hill* (1967) that, in order for a private citizen to win compensatory damages from false, nondefamatory, but offensive, statements, that person must show they were written with actual malice.

The Court found that reporters who write a story saying they talked with someone not present at an interview are guilty of a "calculated falsehood" and so of actual malice. Such an action constitutes knowingly publishing a falsehood.

There is some additional significance in the Court's ruling that the newspaper is also liable when reporters, in the course of their regular duties, write falsehoods with actual malice. Nor should the disposition of the suit against the photographer be overlooked. He was held not liable because he did not participate in presenting the Cantrells in a false light.

Cox Broadcasting Corp. v. Cohn

Cox Broadcasting Corporation
v.
Martin Cohn

Docket No. 73-938
420 U.S. 469, 43 L.Ed.2d 328, 95 S.Ct. 1029 (1975)
Argued November 11, 1974. Decided March 3, 1975.

BACKGROUND

At this time the Court recognizes an explosion of interest in the concept of a right to privacy. It places this case in the category of intrusion, which is the publishing of private information that is embarrassing or offensive. In contrast, the Court says the two previous privacy cases involving the press--*Time* v. *Hill* (1967) and *Cantrell* v. *Forest City* (1974)--are concerned with the false light category, and the Court takes care to draw careful distinctions between these two forms of privacy. This case, then, is of interest because it is the first time the Court ruled on the false light theory of privacy.

CIRCUMSTANCES

Few news events are more basic to the work of the media than the reporting of actions at the courthouse. The origins of this case can be traced to a television station's broadcasting the name of a 17-year-old rape victim. Martin Cohn's daughter, Cynthia, lost her life as a result of a rape attack in August 1971. In April 1972, five youths appeared in court to plead guilty to rape or attempted rape and a sixth, who pleaded not guilty, was given a trial date. Sometime that day, Thomas Wassell, a reporter for WSB-TV, "learned the name of the victim from an examination of the indictments which were made available for his inspection in the courtroom" (472). He used her name in a news broadcast that evening.

In May, Martin Cohn sued, charging "his right to privacy had been invaded by the television broadcast giving the name of his deceased daughter" (474). Cohn relied in part on a section of the Georgia Code "which makes it a misdemeanor to publish or broadcast the name or identity of a rape victim" (472). The television station said the First and Fourteenth Amendments gave it a privilege to use the name. Disagreeing, the trial court denied there was conditional protection and said Cohn could use the civil court to remedy his injury. It also said the station was in fact liable for his injury and ordered a jury trial solely to determine damages.

The Georgia Supreme Court said the law did not provide a basis for a civil action, and so the constitutionality of the law is not in question. It also said that, although Cohn could properly base a suit on the common-law notion of a right to privacy, he would have to prove that the station "'invaded his privacy with willful or negligent disregard for the fact that reasonable men would find the invasion highly offensive'" (475). Both courts agreed that the constitution did not "require total abrogation of the right to privacy" in favor of a free press. After considering a motion for a rehearing based on the unconstitutionality of the law, the Georgia Supreme Court declared the law a "'legitimate limitation on the right of freedom of expression contained in the First Amendment'" (475).

SUMMARY OF THE COURT'S ANALYSIS

Justice Byron R. White writes for the Court.
Justices William J. Brennan, Jr., Potter Stewart, Thurgood Marshall, Harry A. Blackmun, and Lewis A. Powell, Jr., join.

The first issue addressed by the Court is jurisdiction. Justice White poses two questions in this regard. First, is the constitutional validity of the Georgia law "'drawn into question'" (476) by the Georgia Supreme Court's ruling? Secondly, is that court's decision a final judgment?

To the first question, White responds, "The statute was drawn in question in a manner directly bearing upon the merits of the action, and the decision in favor of its constitutional validity invokes this Court's appellate jurisdiction" (476). An answer to the second question is based on a law passed by the Congress in 1789, giving the Court jurisdiction "only after the highest state court in which judgment could be had has rendered a 'final judgment or decree'" (476, 477).

White says the Court had not "observed" this rule since 1789 in a "mechanical fashion," but in "'very few'" circumstances has granted exceptions. He then outlines four types. He writes that in the first category . . . are those cases in which there are further proceedings--even entire--trials yet to occur in the state courts but where for one reason or another the federal issue is conclusive or the outcome of further proceedings preordained. In these circumstances, because the case is for all practical purposes concluded, the judgement of the state court on the federal issue is deemed final" (479).

The second category concerns cases "in which the federal issue, finally decided by the highest court in the State, will survive and require decision regardless of the outcome of further state proceedings" (480).

He continues, "In the third category are those situations where the federal claim has been finally decided, with further proceedings on the merits in the state courts to come, but in which later review of the federal issue cannot be had, whatever the ultimate outcome of the case" (481). The last exception is given a long definition, but White summarizes its effect by writing, "If a refusal immediately to review the state court decision might seriously erode federal policy, the Court has entertained and decided the federal issue" (483).

Saying the Court is using a "pragmatic approach," White concludes, quoting in part from *Miami Herald Publishing Co.* v. *Tornillo*, 418 U.S. 241 (1974), "Delaying the final decision of the First Amendment claim until after trial will 'leave unanswered . . . an important question of freedom of the press under the First Amendment,' 'an uneasy and unsettled constitutional posture [that] could only further harm the operation of a free press'" (485, 486).

Having settled the question of jurisdiction, the Court moves to the constitutional issue. Stewart says the Court admits "there *is* [emphasis his] a zone of privacy surrounding every individual, a zone within which the State may protect him from intrusion by the press" (487). Georgia has, in fact, a name for the tort at issue: "'public disclosure'" (489). He describes this tort as "that in which the plaintiff claims the right to be free from unwanted publicity about his private affairs, which, although wholly true, would be offensive to a person of ordinary sensibilities" (489). When such information is "embarrassing or otherwise painful to an individual" (489), then, writes White, "It is here that claims of privacy most directly confront the constitutional freedoms of speech and press" (389).

White notes that, although in defamation cases truth is a defense, the Court here is going to evade the broader question of whether or not truthful publications can "ever be subjected [constitutionally] to civil or criminal liability" (491). Instead, it will focus "on the narrower [question] . . . of whether the State may impose sanctions on the accurate publication of the name of a rape victim obtained from public records . . . which themselves are open to public inspection" (491). He adds quickly, "We are convinced that the State may not do so" (491).

The Court's first reason for rejecting such state sanctions is that, since in our society citizens have "limited time and resources with which to observe at first hand the operations of . . . government," they rely "necessarily upon the press" (491) to inform them of these operations. Indeed, White asserts that the media have a "great responsibility . . . to report fully and accurately the proceedings of government, and official records and documents open to the public are the basic data of governmental operations" (492). In particular, reporting of "judicial proceedings . . . serve[s] to guarantee the fairness of trials and to bring to bear the beneficial effects of public scrutiny upon the administration of justice" (492).

White continues, "Judicial proceedings . . . are without question events of legitimate concern to the public and consequently fall within the responsibility of the press to report the operations of the government" (492). "[Even] the developing law surrounding the tort of invasion of privacy," White writes, "Recognizes a privilege in the press to report the events of judicial proceedings" (493).

Another important reason given by the Court is "that the interests of privacy fade when the information involved already appears on the public record" (494, 495). White writes, "The freedom of the press to publish that information [on public records] appears to us to be of critical importance to our type of government in which the citizenry is the final judge of the proper conduct of public business" (495).

The final reason given is found in these word by White, "We are reluctant to embark on a course that would make public records generally available to the media but forbid their publication if offensive to the sensibilities of the supposed reasonable man" (496). The problem with such a course of action, according to White, is this: "The rule would invite timidity and self-censorship and very likely lead to the suppression of many items that would otherwise be published and that should be made available to the public" (496). The states can protect privacy interests, the Court asserts, "by means which avoid public documentation or other exposure of private information" (496).

RULING

White writes:

> Appellant Wassell based his televised report upon notes taken during the court proceedings and obtained the name of the victim from the indictments handed to him at his request during a recess in the hearing. Appellee [Cohn] has not contended that the name was obtained in an improper fashion or that it was not on an official court document open to public inspection. Under these circumstances, the protection of freedom of the press provided by the First and Fourteenth Amendments bars the State of Georgia from making appellants' broadcast the basis of civil liability.
> Reversed. (496, 497)

Chief Justice Warren E. Burger concurs, but he does not join the Court's opinion, nor does he write a separate opinion.

Justice Lewis F. Powell, Jr., writes a concurring opinion.

Powell writes to distinguish his notion of the role of truth from that of the Court's, in which it asserted that truth as a defense is an open question when the person defamed is private. He writes, "I view that opinion [first announced in *Gertz*] as requiring the truth to be recognized as a complete defense" (500).

Justice William O. Douglas writes a concurring opinion.

Douglas writes, "There is no power on the part of the Government to suppress or penalize the publication of 'news of the day'" (501).

Justice William H. Rehnquist writes a dissenting opinion.

Rehnquist's dissent is based on the narrow issue of jurisdiction. He writes, "Because I am of the opinion that the decision which is the subject of this appeal is not a 'final' judgment or decree . . ., I would dismiss this appeal for want of jurisdiction" (501).

Rehnquist feels, quoting in part from *Gillespie* v. *United States Steel Corp.*, 379 U.S. 148, 13 L.Ed.2d 199, 85 S.Ct. 308 (1964), there are already too many exceptions to this rule and that the Court's "'pragmatic' approach" is based, at bottom, on a desire to minimize "'the inconvenience and costs of piecemeal review'" (503). He writes, "I believe that the Court has erred by simply importing the approach of cases in which the only concern is efficient judicial administration" (505).

His main line of attack against the Court's rationale for granting an exception to the "final judgment" rule is that this holding "enunciates a virtually formless exception to the finality requirement, one which differs in kind from those previously carved out" (505, 506). He particularly objects to the Court's assertion that failure to grant an exception would "leave the press in Georgia operating in the shadow of the civil and criminal sanctions of a rule of law . . . the constitutionality of which is in serious doubt" (507).

Does this mean, he asks, that the Court is setting a new standard limiting exceptions to "cases in which a First Amendment freedom is at issue" (508)? If so, then this standard "had no basis" in the congressional rule of 1789. According to Rehnquist, another problem is that the Court did not inquire to see what would be "the consequences of permitting the decision of the Supreme Court of Georgia to remain undisturbed pending final state court resolution of the case" (508).

"But the greatest difficulty with the test enunciated today," Rehnquist writes, "Is that it totally abandons the principle that constitutional issues are too important to be decided save when absolutely necessary, and are to be avoided if there are grounds for decisions of lesser dimension" (509). He says the rule encourages the Court to "virtually rush out and meet the prospective constitutional litigant as he approaches our doors" (510). "The inevitable result," he asserts, "Will be totally unnecessary additions to our docket and serious interruptions and delays of the state adjudicatory process" (512).

SIGNIFICANCE

This case firmly establishes the principle that the accurate reports of judicial proceedings are privileged from privacy suits. This privilege is, by definition, limited because the report must be accurate. Although the liability for an inaccurate report was not addressed by the Court, it did take care to note that the issue of truth as a defense is an open question.

Other governmental operations published in records open to public inspection would also seem to be covered by the privilege.

Florida Star v. B.J.F.

Florida Star
v.
B.J.F.

Docket No. 87-329; 57 Law Week 4816
491 U. S. ---, 105 L.Ed.2d 443, 109 S.Ct. 2603 (1989)
Argued March 21, 1989. Decided June 21, 1989.

BACKGROUND

The Florida law initiating this case raises several First Amendment issues. Among them are privacy, access to public information, prior censorship, and media self-censorship. In brief, statute FS # 794.03 (1987) makes it illegal to "'print, publish, or broadcast in any instrument of mass communication' the name of the victim of a sexual offense" (105 L.Ed.2d 450-451). After the *Florida Star* published the name of a rape victim, she sued both the newspaper and the Duval County Sheriff's Department.

The Court pointed out three cases especially significant to the background of this one. *Cox Broadcasting Corp*. v. *Cohn* 420 U.S. 469 (1975) is the closest parallel. In *Cox*, the Court declared unconstitutional a Georgia law forbidding the broadcasting of a rape victim's name obtained from courthouse records. Similarly, in *Oklahoma Publishing Co*. v. *District Court*, 430 U.S. 308 (1977), the Court declared unconstitutional a state court's pretrial order forbidding the publishing of a juvenile's name obtained by reporters who attended the pretrial hearing. Finally, in *Smith* v. *Daily Mail Publishing Co*. 443 U.S. 97 (1979), the Court said reporters could not be punished for publishing information about a juvenile offender if they obtained the information legally.

Another relevant case not mentioned by the Court is *Hustler Magazine* and *Larry C. Flint* v. *Jerry Falwell*, 485 U.S. ---, 99 L.Ed.2d 41, 108 S.Ct. 876 (1988). An important issue in the Falwell's argument was the outrageousness of Flint's cartoon showing Falwell making love to his mother in an outhouse. Here too B.J.F. asserts in her complaint that the newspaper's action in printing her name "constituted such outrageous conduct that was so recklessly indifferent to . . . [her] peace of mind and right of privacy so as to render it subject to the assessment of punitive damages."

The Court asked both sides to answer two questions. The first was whether a statue imposing criminal penalties for publishing truthful information obtained from a government source violates the First and

Fourteenth Amendments. The second asks whether a statute violates these two amendments if it imposes strict liability for invasion of privacy when a newspaper publishes truthful information legally obtained from records of a state agency. That is, does a law violate the Constitution if it asserts that a newspaper automatically is guilty of negligence when it publishes the private fact of a rape victim's name obtained from government records?

CIRCUMSTANCES

A woman the Court identifies as B.J.F. told the Duval County, Florida, sheriff's department on October 20, 1983 that she had been robbed and raped. After preparing a routine incident report, someone in the department mistakenly placed the report in the press room, although the newspapers in the Jacksonville area claim that these reports were routinely available there in unredacted form.

Jacqueline Lotson, a reporting intern at the *Florida Star*, "copied the police report verbatim, including B.J.F.'s full name, on a blank duplicate of the Department's form" (105 L.Ed.2d 451). Girtha Morgan, a full-time reporter, wrote a one-paragraph news story "derived entirely" from this form. Violating its own internal policy of not mentioning the names of rape victims, the *Florida Star* published the article October 29, 1983 as one of fifty-four police blotter stories. Here it is in full.

> [B.J.F.] reported on Thursday, October 20, she was crossing Brentwood Park, which is in the 500 block of Golfair Boulevard, enroute to her bus stop, when an unknown black man ran up behind the lady and placed a knife to her neck and told her not to yell. The suspect then undressed the lady and had sexual intercourse with her before fleeing the scene with her 60 cents, Timex watch and gold necklace. Patrol efforts have been suspended concerning this incident because of a lack of evidence. (105 L.Ed.2d 451).

Nearly a year later, September 26, 1984, B.J.F. sued the *Florida Star*, Sheriff Dale Carson, and the sheriff's department in the Circuit Court of Duval County for violating Florida Statute 794.03, saying she had suffered emotional distress from the publication of her name. She said the sheriff's department failed to uphold its "statutory duty to refrain from causing or allowing to be published [her name] in an instrument of mass communication." The department settled before trial for $2,500, but the newspaper sought to dismiss the suit as a violation of the First Amendment.

At the one-day trial, December 11, 1985, B.J.F., who was a nurse's aide and mother of four children, said that, after the newspaper printed her name, a man called her house while she was still in the hospital recovering from her wounds. The caller talked to her mother, who was watching the children, and threaten to rape B.J.F. again. She also said she had to change her telephone number, to seek police protection, and to obtain psychological counseling.

In her complaint, B.J.F. asserted that the news story was published "intentionally, and with reckless indifference" towards her and her well being. She said that, as a result of the article, she "was caused to suffer shame and humiliation, and emotional pain and suffering."

The trial judge ruled the law did not threaten significantly the First Amendment rights of the media because it "applied only to a narrow set of 'rather sensitive . . . criminal offenses'" (105 L.Ed.2d 452). He also granted B.J.F's motion for a directed verdict finding the newspaper negligent *per se* (on the face of it) simply because it did, in fact, violate Florida law. Although she sought only $18,000 in damages (a dollar for each subscriber), the jury awarded her $75,000 in compensatory damages and $25,000 in punitive damages, feeling the newspaper "'acted with reckless indifference to the rights of others'" (105 L.Ed.2d 452).

The First District Court of Appeals upheld the awards, noting the "private nature" of a rape victim's name (105 L.Ed.2d 452), and the Supreme Court of Florida refused to hear the case. The Court reverses.

SUMMARY OF THE COURT'S ANALYSIS

Justice Thurgood Marshall writes for the Court.
Justices William J. Brennan, Jr., Harry A. Blackmun, John Paul Stevens, and Anthony M. Kennedy join.

Focusing on the heart of the issue immediately, Justice Thurgood Marshall says that finding a newspaper "civilly liable for publishing the name of a rape victim which it had obtained from a publicly released police report" violates the First Amendment (105 L.Ed.2d 451).

He tempers this assertion, however, by pointing out that the Court refuses to endorse the newspaper's request for a privilege to report all truthful information. Such a privilege would be much too broad, he asserts, because the Court cannot anticipate what would be the effect of always allowing the press to publish truthful information. Instead, the Court would prefer to review each incident on a case-by-case basis.

Marshall says three important considerations led the Court to its conclusion that the statute violates the First Amendment. First, the victim's name was obtained legally. Since the government can control release of rape-victim names, the Court says it thereby loses most of its authority to prosecute newspapers when they print these lawfully-obtained names. According to Marshall, the enforcement of this law cannot be considered "narrowly tailored" for the purpose of safeguarding anonymity without threatening First Amendment rights because the government itself released a name. In short, the Court says that the government constitutionally cannot first give the press a rape victim's name and then prosecute a newspaper for publishing that name. The result of such practices, Marshall asserts, would be unacceptable "self-censorship" (105 L.Ed.2d 458).

The second problem with imposing liability on a newspaper for publishing the lawfully obtained name of a rape victim is the "broad sweep of the negligence per se standard" of 794.03 (105 L.Ed.2d 459). In other words, the law says a newspaper is automatically guilty of negligence when it publishes a rape victim's name. Such a rush to judgment, Marshall notes, does not consider a number of important factors, such as these. Is the victim's name already widely known? Did the victim voluntarily call the attention of the public to her name? Does the public have other legitimate reasons for wanting to know her name; for example, did she lie about the attack?

Marshall also points out that the result of this automatic assumption of negligence is that the press has less protection from a privacy suit than from a libel suit, which requires proving a fault. In brief, the Court says the First Amendment does not give the government permission to assume negligence in all cases when the media break a law to publish information.

Finally, the Court says the law expresses an "underinclusivenss" (105 L.Ed.2d 459). By this, the Court means that the law is unfair because it punishes only the media and no one else. For example, the "small time disseminator," such as a person spreading rumors, is not covered by the law. Thus, says Marshall, the law is not "evenhandedly" applied to all (105 L.Ed.2d 460). His reasoning takes this path. Since the law does not punish all disseminators of information, it cannot effectively stop the spread of the victim's identity. Therefore, the law is under inclusive. Because the law is under inclusive, it discriminates against the media and so violates the First Amendment.

RULING

In an attempt to avoid widespread misunderstanding of the Court's ruling, Marshall takes care to point out what the Court does not hold. On the one hand, he notes the Court does not hold that the First Amendment "automatically" protects publication of the truthful information (105 L.Ed.2d 460). On the other hand, he also points out that the Court does not establish a kind of "zone of personal privacy" protecting citizens from "intrusion by the press" (105 L.Ed.2d 460). In addition, he asserts that the Court does not hold "that a State may never punish publication of the name of a victim of a sexual offense" (105 L.Ed.2d 460). He writes:

> We hold only that, where a newspaper publishes truthful information which it has lawfully obtained, punishment may lawfully be imposed, if at all, only when narrowly tailored to a state interest of the highest order, and that no such interest is satisfactorily served by imposing liability under 704.03 to appellant [*Florida Star*] under the facts of this case. The decision below is therefore Reversed. (105 L.Ed.2d 460)

Justice Antonin Scalia writes a concurring opinion,
concurring fully in the judgment, but only partially in the decision.

Scalia writes because he feels "it sufficient to decide this case to rely upon the third ground set forth in the Court's opinion," specifically that the Florida law does not protect "an interest 'of the highest order'"(105 L.Ed.2d 461). Scalia's main problem with the law is that a rape victim's discomfort in having the media disseminate her name to strangers is not greater, and perhaps less, than having her friends learn her name from rumors spread by acquaintances.

He then takes up the notion of whether there is something unique about the mass media that would justify punishing only widespread dissemination of a rape victim's name. One argument put forth by B.J.F. is that mass media dissemination of a name when the rapist is still at large threatens further injury to the victim. If this threat were in fact real, Scalia says, then, to be consistent and not discriminatory, the law should be applied to victims of all crimes resulting in a similar threat and not just to rape victims.

"This law has every appearance of a prohibition that society is prepared to impose upon the press," he writes, "But not upon itself" (105 L.Ed.2d 462). Since the government did not prove that prohibiting the publication of a legally obtained rape victim's name protects "an interest 'of the highest order,'" he agrees that the lower court should be reversed (105 L.Ed.2d 463).

Justice Byron R. White writes a dissenting opinion.
Chief Justice William R. Rehnquist and Justice Sandra Day O'Connor join.

Dividing his dissent into three parts, Justice Byron R. White says he does "not accept" the Court's opinion. First, he reviews the three background cases the Court relied upon for support. Secondly, he analyzes the Court's three main points, and, last, he considers what he calls "the larger issues implicated by today's decision" (105 L.Ed.2d 461).

Cox v. *Cohn* 420 U.S. 469 (1975) is "wholly distinguishable" from the present case, White asserts, for two reasons. One difference is that the victim's name in *Cox* was disclosed as part of judicial records, which, White says, "have always been considered public information in this country" (105 L.Ed.2d 462). Another is that the source of information in *Cox* was not closed to the public by state law.

White claims *Smith* v. *Daily Mail* 443 U.S. 97 (1979) is misinterpreted by the Court. In *Smith*, the suggestion of a "need to further a state interest of the highest order" is simply an "hypothesis," a "cautious qualifier," he says, not "constitutional dogma" (105 L.Ed.2d 463). In addition, White asserts that the privacy rights of a victim are "infinitely more substantial" than those of "alleged criminals" (105 L.Ed.2d 463). Since he feels there is clearly an interest of privacy in this case, White says it is different from *Smith*, where privacy was not an issue.

Turning to an analysis of the Court's three main points, White says that one very important aspect of the present case is that the victim's name was obtained from a room with "signs making it clear that the names of rape victims were not matters of public record, and were not to be published" (105 L.Ed.2d 463). He adds, "As I see it, it is not too much to ask the press, in instances such as this, to respect simple standards of decency and refrain from publishing a victim's name, address, and/or phone number" (105 L.Ed.2d 464).

A jury finding that the newspaper "acted with 'reckless indifference towards the rights of others'" is, for White, evidence that the jury therefore determined that the newspaper was at fault. He asserts that, in effect, the negligence *per se* feature of the law means simply that the legislature determines the level of care instead of the court. In short, White says the

Florida legislature defined a fault as "reckless indifference towards the rights of others," and the jury said the newspaper committed that fault.

Looking at the third point, White says under inclusiveness is defined by the Court here differently from its definition in other cases. Ordinarily, he says, "underinclusiveness" means that the legislature wrongly "singled out one segment of the news media or press for adverse treatment" (105 L.Ed.2d 465). The relevant Florida statute here "excludes neighborhood gossips," he writes, "because the Florida legislature has determined that gossips do not pose the danger and intrusion to rape victims that 'instrument[s] of mass communication' do" (105 L.Ed.2d 465).

In point of fact, White points out, Florida does recognize a tort of publication of private facts. Thus, he says, "It is quite possible that the neighborhood gossip . . . would be subject to the same . . . liability" requirements of the mass media (105 L.Ed.2d 466).

Finally, White focuses on what he calls "the more general principles" (105 L.Ed.2d 466). "At issue in this case," he writes, "Is whether there is any information about people, which--though true--may not be published in the press" (105 L.Ed.2d 466). By holding that only a state interest of the highest order can be used to challenge publication, the Court, asserts White, in effect, obliterates "one of the most note-worthy legal inventions of the 20th-Century; the tort of publication of private facts" (105 L.Ed.2d 466).

To White, "There is no public interest in publishing the names, addresses, and phone numbers of persons who are the victims of crime" (105 L.Ed.2d 468). He also feels there is no public interest in allowing the press to publish this information in cases where the government has failed to protect its release.

SIGNIFICANCE

First, it is important to note what the Court did not do. On the one hand, the Court did not hold that the First Amendment always in all circumstances protects publication of truthful information. Instead, the Court said that, since it could not anticipate all possible effects of such a ruling, it would prefer to take up each instance on a case-by-case basis. On the other hand, the Court did not say that personal privacy can never, in any circumstances, be invaded by the press. Here too the Court said it would prefer to review invasion-of-privacy claims on a case-by-case basis.

Thirdly, the Court did not hold that a state may never punish a newspaper that published the name of a rape victim. Is is conceivable, the Court seems to suggest, that certain unforeseen circumstances could take away First Amendment rights from a newspaper that published a victim's name.

As is often the case, the Court preferred a much more narrow ruling. It held only that, if a newspaper publishes truthful information lawfully obtained, the government may constitutionally impose punishment, if at all, only when a statute is narrowly designed to support a public interest of the highest order. Preventing the press from publishing a rape victim's name obtained from the police does not constitute a state interest of the highest order.

Time v. Hill

Time, Inc.
v.
James J. Hill

Docket No. 1967-22
385 U.S. 374, 17 L.Ed.2d. 456, 87 S.Ct. 534 (1967)
Reargued October 18 and 19, 1966. Decided January 9, 1967.

BACKGROUND

The roots of this case are traced by the Court back to 1888, when Judge Cooley mentioned in *Law of Torts* a right "'to be let alone'" (412). The first mention in legal literature of the phrase "a right to privacy" is granted to a famous *Harvard Law Review* article called "The Right to Privacy" and written in 1890 by Warren and Brandeis. Fortas in dissent traces references to the concept and to the title of this right as they appear in the Court's decisions beginning in 1886, when it ruled in *Boyd* v. *United States*, 166 U.S. 616, that the sanctity of the home should be secure from "'invasions'" "'on the part of the government and its employees'" (413).

For the most part, the Court confines its history of relevant privacy law to New York State since this case came through the courts of that state and arguments were presented that the New York State privacy statute is relevant. The Court took much of the history from a decision by Judge Robert G. Keating. It seems that the Rochester Folding Box Co. put the picture of a pretty girl upon its flour bags without asking her permission. She sued, claiming a violation of her right to privacy. The appeals court denied the existence of such a right in the Constitution, but said that the legislature could create one if it wished in order that "'no one should be permitted for his own selfish purpose to use the picture or the name of another for advertising purposes without his consent'" (381). The legislature did so. Taking the name or likeness of another is a form of privacy now known as appropriation.

As slowly more legislatures and courts began to turn their attention to this right, four distinct notions of privacy began to crystallize, and they were elucidated eventually by Dean Prosser in an article on "Privacy" published in the *California Law Review* (1960). One other important event that sets the stage for this case is the Court's announcement of the actual malice rule in *New York Times Co.* v. *Sullivan*, 376 U.S. 254 (1964).

CIRCUMSTANCES

This case is filled with history. The original set of circumstances that ultimately give rise to a lawsuit occurred in 1952, fully a quarter-century before this decision was issued. For 19 hours on September 11 and 12, 1952, James Hill, his wife, son, and daughter were held hostage in their own home at Whitemarsh, Pennsylvania, by three escaped convicts. Released unharmed, they pointedly noted that the convicts treated them "courteously, had not molested them, and had not been violent" (378). The family went to great lengths to avoid publicity, eventually moving to Connecticut.

The next spring, Joseph Hayes published a novel called *The Desperate Hours*. It depicted a family of four suffering some violence at the hands of convicts who held them hostage in their own home. The book was later made into a play, which became the subject of an article by *Life* magazine in February, 1955.

The text of the *Life* article said, in part, "Three years ago Americans all over the country read about the desperate ordeal of the James Hill family, who were held prisoners in their home outside Philadelphia by three escaped convicts. Later they read about it in Joseph Hayes' novel, The Desperate Hours, inspired by the family's experience. Now they can see the story re-enacted in Hayes' Broadway play . . .. On the next page [of *Life*] scenes from the play are re-enacted on the site of the crime" (377). Among other things, the pictures showed the son being "'roughed up'" by a convict and the "daughter biting the hand of a convict to make him drop a gun" (377).

Hill sued, charging "the Life article was intended to, and did, give the impression that the play mirrored the Hill family's experience, which to the knowledge of the defendant [*Life*]'. . . was false and untrue'" (378). *Life* said it published an article of "'legitimate news interest'" "'in good faith without any malice'" (379).

The trial judge denied a motion to dismiss the case on the grounds that a jury should determine the truth of the article. A jury awarded Hill $50,000 compensatory and $25,000 punitive damages. An appeals court let the liability verdict stand, but ordered a new trial for damages. The court said that, because the article was printed "to advertise and attract further attention," it was not "mere dissemination of news" (379). At the new trial Hill won $30,000 in compensatory damages, but no punitive ones. This award was affirmed in appeal, but is reversed now by the Court.

SUMMARY OF THE COURT'S ANALYSIS

Justice William J. Brennan, Jr., writes for the Court.
Justices Potter Stewart and Byron R. White join.

Brennan begins his analysis of this complex case with a summary of salient points from a recent decision by Judge Keating writing for the Court of Appeals of New York in *Spahn* v. *Julian Messner*, 221 NE2d 543 (1966). Brennan's main interest in this history is in the broad or liberal interpretation given by the New York State courts to that state's privacy law. The trial judge found that an unauthorized biography of Warren Spahn, a well-known baseball pitcher, gave an "inaccurate and distorted" view of his "personal and private life" (386). The appeals court said that, although Spahn's public career "substantially" took away his "right to privacy," he still owned his "personality," and it could not be "fictionalized" and "exploited for . . . commercial benefit through the medium of an unauthorized biography" (386).

The heart of the issue, according to Brennan, is "fictionalization." While "'minor errors'" do not constitute fictionalization, "material and substantial falsification" does (386). Brennan notes, however, that the Court has not yet ruled whether showing actual malice is also necessary to collect damages for fictionalization. That is, does the person bringing suit have to show that an author published "material and substantial falsification" knowing it was false or having a reckless disregard for it falsity? The appeals court felt not, writing, "No public interest is served" (387) by such a requirement.

Disagreeing, Brennan writes, "We hold that the constitutional protections for speech and press preclude the application of the New York Statute to redress false reports of matters of public interest in the absence of proof that the defendant published the report with knowledge of its falsity or in reckless disregard of the truth" (388). Brennan justifies the Court's position here by saying that the First Amendment applies to a wider notion of "comment on public affairs" than just statements "essential . . . to healthy government" (388). The play was, in fact, "a matter of public interest" (388). Moreover, "Exposure of the self to others in varying degrees is a concomitant of life in a civilized community" (388). He concludes that the Court cannot "saddle the press with the impossible burden of verifying to a certainty the facts associated in news articles with a person's name, picture or portrait, particularly as related to non-defamatory matter" (389).

Nor would the requirement of proving mere negligence be adequate to protect the press. The Court writes, "A negligence test would place on the press the intolerable burden of guessing how a jury might assess the reasonableness of steps taken by it to verify the accuracy of every reference to a name, picture, or portrait" (389). Persons wishing to preserve their privacy are not without protection, however. Brennan continues, "But the constitutional guarantees can tolerate sanctions against *calculated* [Brennan's emphasis] falsehood" (389).

The Court, thus, reviews the facts of the case to see if *Life* published the article innocently, with mere negligence, or with actual malice. Book and play author Hayes, the Court feels, did not intend to reenact the Hill incident. His long-standing interest in hostage situations, which included a collection of newspaper clippings, support his claim that his book was merely "'triggered'" by Hill's tragedy. The complex series of events leading up to the *Life* article, in contrast, does not present the Court with such a clear-cut answer. Brennan writes, "The jury might [or might not] reasonably conclude . . . that Life knew the falsity of or was reckless of the truth in stating in the article that 'the story re-enacted' the Hill family's experience" (394).

Therefore, since the instructions to the jury did not require it to rule on the issue of actual malice, they were inadequate. The instructions were also inadequate because they equated "fictionalization" with "falsity," but did not include the aspects of knowing falsity or reckless disregard for the truth (396). A third inadequacy in the instructions was the charge that the jury rule on a distinction between news and commercial speech as a method for determining whether the words deserved First Amendment protection.

Nevertheless, because the New York State courts had "been assiduous in construing" that state's privacy act "to avoid invasion of the constitutional protections of speech and press," (397), the Court refused to declare it unconstitutional. Brennan assets that the ruling in this case is based narrowly on "the failure of the trial judge to instruct the jury that a verdict of liability could be predicated only on a finding of knowing or reckless falsity in the publication of the Life article" (397).

RULING

Brennan writes, "The judgment of the Court of Appeals is set aside and the case is remanded for further proceedings not inconsistent with this opinion" (398).

Justice Hugo L. Black writes a concurring opinion.
Justice William O. Douglas joins.

Black says he concurs so that the Court can muster a majority, but he does not "recede from any of the views I have previously expressed about the much wider press and speech freedoms" (398). He reaffirms his conviction that the actual malice "doctrine" is "bound to pass away as its application to new cases proves its inadequacy to protect freedom of the press from destruction in libel cases and other cases like this one" (398).

He takes the opportunity of the dissent to attack "the recently popularized weighing and balancing formula" because it "encourages and actually invites judges to choose for themselves between conflicting values, even where, as in the First Amendment, the Founders made a choice of values, one of which is a free press" (399). He laments, "If the judicial balancing choice of constitutional change is to be adopted by this Court, I could wish it had not started on the First Amendment" (400).

Black fears the Court may have "today created a right of privacy" when "Life's conduct here was at most a mere understandable and incidental error of fact in reporting a newsworthy event" (400). The right, he says, may "frighten and punish the press so much that publishers will cease trying to report news in a lively and readable fashion" (400).

Justice William O. Douglas writes a concurring opinion.

Not one to mince words, Douglas writes, "A fictionalized treatment of the event is, in my view, as much in the public domain as would be a watercolor of the assassination of a public official. It seems to me irrelevant to talk of any right of privacy in this context" (401).

Justice John M. Harlan writes a separate opinion, concurring in part and dissenting in part.

Harlan feels that a requirement to show negligence is adequate constitutional protection for the press here. A requirement to show actual malice, says Harlan, grants "a 'talismanic immunity' to all unintentional errors" (407). He feels statements about private citizens do not need that much "'breathing space'" (407).

For one thing, Harlan writes, "It would be unreasonable to assume that Mr. Hill could find a forum for making a successful refutation of the Life material or that the public's interest in it would be sufficient for the truth to win out by comparison as it might in that area of discussion central to a free society" (408). In addition, he writes, "There is a vast difference in the state interest in protecting individuals like Mr. Hill from irresponsibly prepared publicity and the state interest in similar protection for a public official" (408).

Harlan concludes, "A state should be free to hold the press to a duty of making a reasonable investigation of the underlying facts and limiting itself to 'fair comment' on the materials so gathered" (409). This "duty of reasonable care," he says, is the same that is required of "medical practitioners" and "attorneys" (410).

Justice Abe Fortas writes a dissenting opinion. Chief Justice Earl Warren and Justice Tom C. Clark join.

Fortas feels the Court's holding is "exceedingly narrow' (411), based on only one failure in the trial court judge's instructions to the jury, the failure to require a showing of actual malice. "Although they were not a textbook model," Fortas writes, "the jury instructions" were not fatally inadequate (416). The real problem with this ruling, for Fortas, is that, after 11 years in litigation, Hill will have to face yet more.

Fortas asserts, "Privacy, then, is a basic right" (415). He continues, "The First Amendment does not compel us to deny a State the right to provide a remedy for reckless falsity in writing and publishing an article which irresponsibly and injuriously invades the privacy of a quiet family for no purpose except dramatic interest and commercial appeal" (415).

For much of the remainder of his opinion, Fortas attempts to show that the trial judge's instructions were "close enough to this Court's insistence" (419) on a showing of actual malice. By refusing to recognize the adequacy of these instructions, the Court, in effect, writes Fortas, produces "not only an individual injustice, but an encouragement to recklessness and careless readiness to ride roughshod over the interests of others" (420). He continues, "For this Court totally to immunize the press . . . in areas far beyond the needs of news, comment on public persons and events, discussion of public issues and the like would be no service to freedom of the press, but an invitation to public hostility to that freedom" (420).

Fortas concludes, "This Court cannot and should not refuse to permit under state law the private citizen who is aggrieved by the type of assault which we have here . . . to recover compensatory damages for recklessly inflicted invasion of his rights" (420).

SIGNIFICANCE

Requiring a private citizen to show actual malice in order to collect damages for false nondefamatory, but offensive, statements gives significance to this case. In essence, the Court borrowed the concept of actual malice fashioned in 1964 as a requirement for public officials to win libel suits and applied it here to private persons seeking damages from nondefamatroy statements.

Libel, the Court appears to be saying, defames and so inflicts serious and to some degree reasonably measurable damages. Invading the privacy of others, however, is not an injury so clearly and commonly defined. Moreover, the Court seems to feel that injury from invasion of privacy is a lower injury than is defamation. Thus, even though the State is thought by the Court to have a greater duty to protect private citizens than it does to protect public officials, private persons must show the high fault of actual malice to win damages in a privacy case because invasion of privacy is a lower injury than is libel.

Zacchini v. Scripps-Howard Broadcasting Co.

Hugo Zacchini
v.
Scripps-Howard Broadcasting Company

Docket No. 76-577
433 U.S. 562, 53 L.Ed.2d 965, 97 S.Ct. 2849 (1977)
Argued April 25, 1977. Decided June 28, 1977.

BACKGROUND

Once again the battleground for a media-related privacy case is Ohio. Unlike the false light case of *Cantrell* v. *Forest City Publishing Co.* (1974), however, this case focuses on appropriation, the oldest form of privacy incorporated in a state statute. Featuring a classic confrontation between the right to broadcast news stories of interest to the public and the right to earn a living from one's talents, this case also highlights the conflicting values of news as entertainment and of privacy as protection from unremunerated publicity.

CIRCUMSTANCES

On August 30, 1972, George J. Masur (whose television name was Jay Bacchus), a news stringer for Scripps-Howard Broadcasting Co., filmed for television station WEWS the full 15-second act of Howard Zacchini, a "human cannonball" performing at the Geauga County Fair in Burton, Ohio. That night all 15 seconds of Zacchini being shot 200 feet into a net were shown on the 11 o'clock news along with "favorable commentary" (564). Afterwards, he sued, saying his act was "commercialized" (564) without his consent and the newscast was an "'unlawful appropriation'" of his "'professional property'" (565).

The trial court dismissed his case in summary judgment, but the Court of Appeals for Ohio reversed. One of the three appellate judges said the newscast was an "appropriation" of Zacchini's "'right of publicity'" (564). All "agreed that the First Amendment did not privilege the press to show the entire performance on a news program without compensating" Zacchini (564).

The Supreme Court of Ohio felt Zacchini's best chance for a cause of action would be based on his "'right to the publicity value of his performance'" (565). Nevertheless, it ruled against him, saying, "'A TV station has a privilege to report in its newscasts matters of legitimate public interest which would otherwise be protected by an individual's right of publicity, unless the intent was to appropriate the benefit of publicity for some non-privileged private use, or unless the actual intent was to injure the individual'" (565).

SUMMARY OF THE COURT'S ANALYSIS

Justice Byron R. White writes for the Court.
Chief Justice Warren E. Burger and Justices Potter Stewart, Harry A. Blackmun, and William H. Rehnquist join.

White says the Court agreed to hear this case in order to determine "whether the First and Fourteenth Amendments immunized respondent [Scripps-Howard Broadcasting Co.] from damages for its alleged infringement of petitioner's [Zacchini's] state-law 'right of publicity'" (565). The Court's answer is no.

Turning first to the issue of jurisdiction, White said the Ohio court rested its decision--not on the Ohio constitution, even though it could have--but on the First Amendment, thus giving the case federal concerns.

The first argument the Court proposes against the Ohio court's assertion of privilege is a perception that Zacchini "is not contending that his appearance at the fair and his performance could not be reported by the press as newsworthy items" (569). White writes, "His complaint is that respondent [Scripps-Howard] filmed his entire act and displayed that film on television . . . [which] is appropriation" (569). The main problem with the Ohio court's rationale for asserting the privilege, White says, is that it based its case on *Time* v. *Hill* (1967). That case involved "an entirely different tort," (571) White notes, and it did not "mandate a media privilege to televise a performer's entire act without his consent" (570).

"The Court was aware that it was adjudicating a 'false light' privacy case involving a matter of public interest," writes White, "Not a case involving . . . 'appropriation' of a name or likeness for the purposes of trade" (571). He then points out what he feels are important differences between the two forms of privacy. First, he notes, the interests of the state are different. In matters related to false light, the state's interest, he says quoting Prosser's famous law review article, is "'clearly that of reputation, with the same overtones of mental distress as in defamation'" (573). Contrarily, in matters related to a "right of publicity," the state's interest "is in protecting the proprietary interests of the individual in his act in part to encourage such entertainment" (573). This proprietary interest, according to White, "Is closely analogous to the goals of patent and copyright law" (573).

A second difference rests "in the degree to which they intrude on dissemination of information to the public" (573). False light cases attempt to "minimize publication of the damaging matter, while in 'right of publicity' cases the only question is who gets to do the publishing" (573). In point of fact, Zacchini did not attempt to block the broadcasting of his act; "he simply sought compensation . . . in the form of damages" (573, 574). White points out that "there is no claim" that the television station could not report "the newsworthy facts" about Zacchini's act (574). This distinction does not mean, however, White points out, that the station is "immunize[d]" from broadcasting "a performer's entire act without his consent" (575).

White says the problem with broadcasting the entire act is that it "poses a substantial threat to the economic value of that performance" (575). "If the public can see the act free on television, " he writes, "It will be less willing to pay to see it at the fair" (576). Although the broadcast may not appropriate Zacchini's reputation, White admits, it constitutes nevertheless "the appropriation of the very activity by which the entertainer acquired his reputation in the first place" (576).

White also concedes that "entertainment, as well as news, enjoys First Amendment protection," (578) and that "entertainment itself can be important news" (578). But the public and the press can have the performance available to them if they only pay for it. The point is, says White, that Zacchini "does not seek to enjoin the broadcast of his performance; he simply wants to be paid for it" (578).

RULING

White writes, "We concluded that although the State of Ohio may as a matter of its own law privilege the press in the circumstances of this case, the First and Fourteenth Amendments do not require it to do so. Reversed" (578, 579).

Justice Lewis F. Powell, Jr., writes a dissenting opinion.
Justices William J. Brennan, Jr., and Thurgood Marshall join.

Powell feels the "formula" of the court--that is, the focus on the entirety of an act--is not "clear enough" and that the Court is not "appropriately sensitive to the First Amendment values at stake" (579, 580).

First, Powell notes that the television station did not make commercial use of the broadcast. Instead, he writes, "The report was part of an ordinary daily news program" (580). The problem with the entire-act "formula," he says, is the requirement of guessing what would be and what would not be an entire act. He writes:

> When a film is used, as here, for a routine portion of a regular news program, I would hold that the First Amendment protects the station from a "right of publicity" or "appropriation" suit, absent a strong showing . . . that the news broadcast was a subterfuge or cover for private or commercial exploitation. (581) Having made the matter public . . . he [Zacchini] cannot, consistent with the First Amendment, complain of routine news reportage. (582)

Justice John Paul Stevens dissents.

Stevens dissents simply because he feels the case should be first sent to the Ohio court for "a clarification of its holding before deciding the federal constitutional issue" (583).

SIGNIFICANCE

The Court did not say Zacchini had a right to publicity; it said the First Amendment did not forbid the state from requiring the television station to pay him for broadcasting his entire act. In addition, however, the Court also said the First Amendment would allow the state legislature to grant the press a privilege exempting it from such "right to publicity" cases.

The privacy issue involved is appropriation of a person's ability to earn a living. Broadcasting for free so much of a person's entertainment that it discourages others from paying to see it in effect, said the Court, threatens the entertainer's right to benefit economically from his talents. The problem with this "formula," Powell notes in dissent, is that the media are required to know how much of an act is enough to be considered its entirety so that it constitutes an economic threat to the performer.

CASES RELATED TO FIRST AMENDMENT ISSUES

Abrams v. United States

Jacob Abrams
v.
United States

Docket No. 1919-316
250 U.S. 616, 63 L.Ed. 1173, 40 S.Ct. 17 (1919)
Argued October 21 and 22, 1919. Decided November 10, 1919.

BACKGROUND

This case is one in a series related to the Espionage Act passed at the end of World War I. The 1917 act made it a crime to attempt to cause insubordination, disloyalty, mutiny, or refusal of duty in the armed forces and to obstruct the recruitment efforts of the armed forces. The 1918 amendments made it a crime to print disloyal or profane language intended to cause contempt of the federal government, the Constitution, the flag, or the uniform of the armed forces.

CIRCUMSTANCES

Abrams and four other socialists, all born in Russia, admitted to distributing (in part by throwing them out a window in New York City) on August 22, 1918 circulars directed against the war. The circulars protested the movement of U.S. troops into the Soviet Union and called upon the American workers to stage a general strike against the production of munitions and arms.

All five socialists were convicted of four counts of conspiring to violate certain provisions of the 1917 Espionage Act and its 1918 amendments. The first count was printing "disloyal, scurrilous, and abusive language about the form of the government of the United States" (617). The second was printing language "intended to bring the form of government of the United States into contempt, scorn, contumely, and disrepute" (617). Third was printing language "intended to incite, provoke, and encourage resistance to the United States" (617). The fourth was printing words "to urge, incite, and advocate curtailment of production of things and products . . . essential to the prosecution of the war" (617).

One pamphlet was written in English, another in Yiddish. Entitled "The Hypocrisy of the United States and Her Allies," the first denounced President Wilson as a hypocrite and a coward for sending troops into

Russia. The court found the following words to be the most inflammatory: "Yes, friends, there is only one enemy of the workers of the world and that is CAPITALISM. . . . Workers of the World! Awake! Rise! Put down your enemy and mine" (620).

The title in English of the second pamphlet is "Workers--Wake up." The court found these words to be objectionable:

> Spit in the face the false, hypocritic, military propaganda which has fooled you so relentlessly, calling forth your sympathy, your help to the prosecution of the war. (620)
>
> Workers in the ammunitions factories, you are producing bullets, bayonets, cannon, to murder not only the Germans, but also your dearest, best, who are in Russia and are fighting for freedom. (621)

SUMMARY OF THE COURT'S ANALYSIS

Justice John H. Clarke writes for the Court.
Chief Justice Edward D. White, and Justices Joseph McKenna, William R. Day, Willis Van Devanter, Mahlon Pitney, and James C. McReynolds join.

It is interesting to note that Justice Clarke, writing for the Court, feels the petitioners only "faintly" (618) claimed that publishing the two works was not illegal because the act proscribing them is itself unconstitutional. He then quickly dismisses the contention on the basis that the Court discussed and "negatived" (619) it in *Schenck* v. *United States* (1918). Since the law is indeed constitutional, the only remaining question is whether there is enough evidence to convict the defendants under the act. Clarke puts it this way, "A question of law is thus presented, which calls for an examination of the record, not for the purpose of weighing conflicting testimony, but only to determine whether there was some evidence, competent and substantial, before the jury, fairly tending to sustain the verdict" (619).

At the beginning of this examination, Clarke says the words of the first pamphlet were "clearly an appeal to the 'workers' of this country to arise and put down by force the government of the United States" (620).

The Court objects to the second pamphlet even though the petitioners claim they want only to "prevent injury to the Russian cause" (621). Clarke writes, "Even if their primary purpose and intent was to aid the cause of the Russian Revolution, the plan of action which they adopted necessarily involved . . . defeat of the war program of the United States" (621).

As the Court views the pamphlets, they are not "an attempt to bring about a change of administration by candid discussion," but to "defeat the war plans of the government of the United States by bringing upon the country the paralysis of a general strike, thereby arresting the production of all munitions and other things essential to the conduct of the war" (622).

Clarke writes, "The language of these circulars was obviously intended to provoke and to encourage resistance to the United States in the war" (624). Abrams and the others, he says, "Plainly urged and advocated resort to a general strike of workers in ammunition factories for the purpose of curtailing the production of ordinance and munitions necessary and essential to the prosecution of the war, as is charged in the fourth count" (624).

RULING

The Court's ruling is succinct: "Thus, it is clear . . . that the defendants were guilty as charged in both the third and fourth counts of the indictment, and under the long-established rule of law hereinbefore stated, the judgment of the District Court must be affirmed" (624).

Justice Oliver W. Holmes, Jr., writes a dissenting opinion.
Justice Louis D. Brandies joins.

Holmes once again, this time in dissent, affirms his conviction that freedom of speech is not an absolute right. "Prosecution for the expression of opinions seems to me perfectly logical," he writes. "To allow opposition by speech seems to indicate that you think the speech impotent" (630).

He then calls forth the clear-and-present-danger rule first announced in *Schenck*: "The United States constitutionally may punish speech that produces or is intended to produce a clear and imminent danger that it will bring about forthwith certain substantive evils that the United States constitutionally may seek to prevent" (624).

Short of a clearly demonstrable clear and present danger, however, Holmes is not willing to support governmental regulation of speech. Instead, he advocates what has come to be known as the Holmesian "marketplace of ideas," a concept often traced to John Milton's *Areopagitica*. In Holmes's *laissez-faire* intellectual marketplace true thoughts defeat false ones. He writes, "But . . . the very foundations of their [human's] own conduct that the ultimate good desired is better reached by free trade in ideas--that the best test of truth is the power of the thought to get itself accepted in the competition of the market . . .. That, at any rate, is the theory of our Constitution" (630).

It cannot be said too strongly that time is of the utmost importance to Holmes. The danger must be present. He approves of controlling dangerously false speech only when there is no time to allow true speech to defeat it. He writes:

> It is only the present danger of immediate evil or an intent to bring it about that warrants Congress in setting a limit to the expression of opinion where private rights are not concerned. (625)
>
> Only the emergency that makes it immediately dangerous to leave the correction of evil counsels to time warrants making any exception to the sweeping command, "Congress shall make no law abridging the freedom of speech"(631).

SIGNIFICANCE

This case is most widely known for the marketplace-of-ideas concept used by Holmes in his dissent to justify the clear-and-present-danger test he promulgated in *Schenck*. At the center of this concept is Holmes' notion that the best test of truth is the power of an idea to achieve acceptance in an open market where it is forced to compete with all other ideas.

Brandenburg v. *Ohio*

Clarence Brandenburg
v.
State of Ohio

Docket No. 1969-492
395 U.S. 444, 23 L.Ed.2d 430, 89 S.Ct. 1827 (1969)
Argued February 27, 1969. Decided June 9, 1969.

BACKGROUND

Most scholars agree that the Court has struggled since 1918 with the degree of protection the First Amendment gives to speech. The beginning of that struggle is commonly traced to *Schenck* v. *United States* (1919), in which Justice Oliver Wendell Holmes, Jr., first issued his now-famous words that speech can be restricted constitutionally only if it presents "a clear and present danger" to the security or existence of the nation. Ever since then, the Court has attempted to refine or, in some instances, reject this formula as an adequate guide for determining when speech does or does not deserve First Amendment protection. Here, the Court does not address the clear-and-present-danger doctrine; instead it refines the distinctions made early in *Dennis* v. *United States* (1951) and *Yates* v. *United States* (1957) between advocacy and incitement.

Justice William O. Douglas's dissent in this case presents a cursory, but enlightening, survey of the Court's struggles with Holmes's words. When he completes the survey, he declares that this case finally puts the formula to rest as an inadequate protection of free speech. The Court, however, refused to address Holmes's test, and so Douglas's pronouncement may be a bit premature. Nevertheless, his criticism illustrates dramatically the Court's difficulty in applying the guarantee of this fundamental liberty to the events of history.

CIRCUMSTANCES

Clarence Brandenburg, leader of a Ku Klux Klan (KKK) chapter in Ohio, telephoned an announcer at a Cincinnati television station inviting him to attend a KKK "rally" to be held at a farm in Hamilton County. In a speech there Brandenburg announced that the rally was "an organizer's meeting" (446). Since the event was recorded with his permission by television cameras, he was convicted eventually for advocating "'unlawful television cameras, he was convicted eventually for advocating "'unlawful methods of terrorism as a means of accomplishing industrial or political reform'" (445) and for assembling with "'persons formed to teach or advocate the doctrines of criminal syndicalism'" (445), which were defined as crimes under the 1919 Ohio Criminal Syndicalism Statute.

His $1,000 fine and prison term (one to ten years) was affirmed without opinion by an appellate court in Ohio and the Ohio Supreme Court dismissed his case, saying he raised "no substantial constitutional question" (445).

SUMMARY OF THE COURT'S ANALYSIS

In a *per curiam* (by the court) opinion, the Court began its analysis with a reference to *Whitney* v. *California* (1927), in which it ruled constitutional a statute that said merely advocating "violent means to effect political and economic change involves such danger to the security of the State that the State may outlaw it" (447). Here the Court asserts that "Whitney has been thoroughly discredited by later decisions" (447), pointing out *Dennis* (1951) in particular.

According to the Court, these "later decisions" "do not permit a State to forbid or proscribe advocacy of the use of force or of law violation except where such advocacy is directed to inciting or producing imminent lawless action and is likely to incite or produce such action" (447). Therefore, the Court found fault with the trial judge's instructions to the jury because they did not "in any way refine the statue's bald definition of the crime in terms of mere advocacy not distinguished from incitement to imminent lawless action" (448, 449). Moreover, the statute itself lacks constitutional sanction, according to the Court, because it "purports to punish mere advocacy and to forbid, on pain of criminal punishment, assembly with others merely to advocate the described type of action" (449).

RULING

The Court writes, "Such a statute falls within the condemnation of the First and Fourteenth Amendments. The contrary teaching of Whitney v California, supra, cannot be supported, and that decision is therefore overruled. Reversed" (449).

Justice Hugo L. Black writes a concurring opinion.

Justice Black writes separately only to note that, like justice Douglas, he feels the Court should have rejected explicitly the clear-and-present-danger doctrine, which, he says, "should have no place in the interpretation of the First Amendment" (450).

Justice William O. Douglas writes a concurring opinion.

Justice Douglas begins his opinion cursorily reviewing the history of the Court's opinions related to the clear-and-present-danger doctrine. He writes, "Though I doubt if the 'clear and present danger' test is congenial to the First Amendment in time of a declared war, I am certain it is not reconcilable with the First Amendment in days of peace" (452).

Douglas then lists two problems with the test. He writes:

> First, the threats were often loud but always puny and made serious only by judges so wedded to the status quo that critical analysis made them nervous. Second, the test was so twisted in Dennis as to make the trial of those teachers of Marxism an all-out political trial which was part and parcel of the cold war that has eroded substantial parts of the First Amendment. (454)

He adds, "Action is often a method of expression and within the protection of the First Amendment" (454).

The important distinctions to be drawn in free speech cases, according to Douglas, lie between speech and action, not between different degrees of speech. He writes:

> The lines drawn by the Court between the criminal act of being an "active" Communist and the innocent act of being a nominal or inactive Communist mark the difference only between deep and abiding belief and casual or uncertain belief. But I think that all matters of belief are beyond the reach of subpoenas or the probings of investigators. (456)

He summarizes, "The line between what is permissible and not subject to control and what may be made impermissible and subject to regulation is the line between ideas and overt acts" (456).

In closing, he addresses Holmes's notion that one cannot yell fire in a crowded theater, saying this is one of those rare instances "where speech is brigaded with action" (446). He continues, "They are indeed inseparable and a prosecution can be launched for the overt acts actually caused. Apart from rare instances of that kind, speech is, I think, immune from prosecution" (457).

SIGNIFICANCE

Although not explicitly rejecting the clear-and-present-danger doctrine, this case has gained significance because it did explicitly overrule *Whitney* (1927). *Whitney* is seen here as wrongly denying First Amendment protection to advocacy of unlawful or violent overthrow of the government instead of restricting this denial only to speech that incites such actions.

Yet the majority opinion in *Whitney* did not directly address the notion of advocacy. Instead, it focused on membership in an organization that advocated unlawful overthrow of the government. Still, with no little irony, *Whitney* can indeed be read quite correctly to rule, by implication, that advocacy of such action is unconstitutional even though Whitney's primary defense was her claim that she opposed the California Communist Labor Party's support of revolutionary means to bring about change in governments or economies. In point of fact, it was she who proposed a plank for the party's platform, in which it was asserted that the ballot box should be used to effect political and economic change. Her criminal conviction was upheld by the Court, however, not because it was shown that she advocated wrongful actions, but because she remained a member of the party even after it substituted revolution for her much milder proposal to accomplish change through voting.

Brandeis, concurring in *Whitney*, takes care to point out that "the mere act" of becoming a member of the party was declared a crime by the Court. Moreover, he makes there the identical distinction between advocacy and incitement that the Court makes here in *Brandenberg*. It may be possible, therefore, that *Whitney* was only selectively discredited because it was selectively misunderstood by later opinions.

It is also interesting to note that Douglas, while concurring here, criticizes the clear-and-present doctrine as inadequate protection for free speech, saying the proper distinction is to be drawn not between degrees of speech, but between speech and action. Yet even Douglas agrees that, at times, speech takes on the nature of action to such a degree that it cannot be distinguished from action. This sounds very much like Brandeis's distinction in *Whitney* between "preparation and attempt," in which he asserts that restriction of speech is justified constitutionally only when action is so imminent that opposing speech alone cannot prevent grave injury to the state. Furthermore, much of Douglas's objection to the doctrine is directed not to its inherent shortcomings, but to the way it was misused by the courts.

Thus, the significance of *Brandenberg* may be misplaced to some degree. Perhaps it rests as much in its overturning of *Whitney*'s impact as it does in the overturning of its ruling.

Apart from its avowed overturning of *Whitney*, this case also gains significance because it continues a trend started in earnest implicitly with the majority opinion and explicitly with Frankfurter's dissent in *Dennis*. That trend is a movement away from refining the clear-and-present-danger formula and toward refining the border lines between speech that advocates, which is protected by the First Amendment, and speech that incites, which is unprotected.

In *Dennis*, then, the Court said, in essence, that the properties clear and present can be assumed if the danger is great enough. In other words, if the gravity of the evil (violent overthrow of the government) threatened is great enough Dennis may not constitutionally advocate doing it. Unconstitutional advocacy, though, according to *Dennis*, does not mean merely advocating a general notion that we would all be better off if our government were overthrown by force; rather it means advocating an action that would accomplish this goal. In addition, there must be present an intent to take the action advocated. The distinction between Constitutional and unconstitutional advocacy, therefore, depends upon the speaker's intent. Intent to carry through an unconstitutional action, that is, takes away the First Amendment protection to advocate that action.

In *Yates* the Court said it clarified this distinction. The point at issue became what does it mean to advocate action. The answer given is that advocating forceful overthrow of the government as a general principle even though engaged in with an evil intent is, after all, not enough to qualify as unconstitutional speech. An intent to act is said not to be the same as an urging to act. The key to defining action in *Yates* is the presence of "an effort to instigate" action. This notion has sometimes been called an "incitement" standard because the key point is whether or not an audience is urged or incited to do something.

The result of all of this complex reasoning is summarized by the Court here with the assertion that advocacy is constitutional, but incitement to imminent lawless action is not. The notion of intent, so important in *Dennis* and termed irrelevant in *Yates*, is, interestingly enough, ignored.

Chaplinsky v. New Hampshire

Walter Chaplinsky
v.
State of New Hampshire

Docket No. 1942-255
315 US 568, 86 L.Ed. 1031, 62 S.Ct. 766 (1942)
Argued February 5, 1942. Decided March 9, 1942.

BACKGROUND

Although the Court did not address directly the clear-and-present-danger doctrine in this case, attorneys for Chaplinsky (Mr. Hayden C. Covington and Mr. Joseph F. Rutherford of Brooklyn, New York) argued that the New Hampshire Supreme Court erroneously approved his conviction even though there was no evidence of a clear and present danger to breach of the peace.

In the main, this case focused on two amendments, the First and the Fourteenth. Once again the Court reaffirmed its stance that the First Amendment does not make freedom of speech absolute, and so certain classes of words, including fighting words, are deprived of First Amendment protection. Secondly, since the New Hampshire statute in question set the test of a word's offensiveness as the definition commonly used by the average person, the law is therefore drawn narrowly enough to meet the Fourteenth Amendment's requirement of due process of law.

CIRCUMSTANCES

Chaplinsky was distributing Jehovah's Witness tracts in Rochester, New Hampshire, when he ran afoul of a state statute reading, in part:

> No person shall address any offensive, derisive or annoying word to any other person who is lawfully in any street or other public place, nor call him by any offensive or derisive name . . . with intent to deride, offend or annoy him, or to prevent him from pursuing his lawful business or occupation. (569)

Because his actions stirred up the crowd against him, a traffic officer decided to take him to the police station for his own safety when the city marshal passed by going to what he thought was a riot. According to the complaint, Chaplinsky directed these words, among others, to the marshal: "'You are a God damned racketeer;'" "a damned Fascist'" (569). He admitted he said all the words with the exception of the "name of the Deity" (570).

Chaplinsky was eventually convicted in the Rochester municipal court. He was found guilty a second time when he was tried *de novo* (a new, a fresh) before a jury in the superior court, and the New Hampshire Supreme Court affirmed his conviction.

SUMMARY OF THE COURT'S ANALYSIS

Justice Frank Murphy writes for the Court.
Chief Justice Charles E. Hughes and Justices James C. McReynolds, Harlan F. Stone, Owen J. Roberts, Hugo L. Black, Stanley F. Reed, Felix Frankfurter, and William O. Douglas join.

Justice Murphy notes at the outset that Chaplinsky's appeal raised three Fourteenth Amendment issues related to the First. As Murphy sees it, Chaplinsky claimed that, because the law was "vague and indefinite" (a Fourteenth Amendment concern), it "placed an unreasonable restraint on freedom of speech, freedom of the press, and freedom of worship" (three First Amendment concerns) (569).

Quoting in part from *Lovell* v. *Griffin* 303 U.S. 444, 82 L.Ed. 949, 58 S.Ct. 666 (1938), Murphy asserts that the First Amendment freedoms of speech and press "are among the fundamental personal rights and liberties which are protected by the Fourteenth Amendment from invasion by the state" (570, 571). The Court immediately dismisses two of these three bases, however, because spoken words do not involve the press, and "cursing of a public officer is [not] the exercise of religion in any sense of the term" (571). This dismissal leaves only freedom of speech for analysis here.

Reaffirming the long-standing stance of the Court first stated by Justice Oliver Wendell Holmes, Jr., in *Schenck* v. *United States* 249 U.S. 47 (1919) that "the right of free speech is not absolute," Murphy lists categories of unprotected speech: "The lewd and obscene, the profane, the libelous, and the insulting or 'fighting' words--those which by their very utterance inflict injury or tend to incite an immediate breach of the peace" (572). The problem with these kinds of speech, Murphy says, in reference to the thoughts of Zachariah Chafee in *Free Speech in the United States*, "Such utterances are no essential part of an exposition of ideas, and are of such slight social value as a step to truth that any benefit that may be derived from them is clearly outweighed by the social interest in order and morality" (572).

The issue to be resolved now becomes whether or not, as Chaplinsky argues, the law is too vague and indefinite to meet the Fourteenth Amendment requirements of due process. To this argument, the Court notes that the statute forbids only those words having "'a direct tendency to cause acts of violence by the persons to whom, individually, the remark is addressed'" (573). Nor is the definition of offensiveness determined,

Murphy points out, by the person to whom the offensive remark is addressed. Such a definition, one would presume, would be too vague because the offensiveness of a word could never be determined in advance of its being spoken to a particular person. Moreover, the offensiveness of a word in such a case would come and go depending upon the values of the person to whom it is spoken. Instead, the test, according to the Court, is "'what men of common intelligence would understand would be words likely to cause an average addressee to fight'" (573). By general consent, the Court asserts, certain specific words are thought by common citizens to be "'fighting words'" (573).

Consequently, Murphy writes, "It is a statute narrowly drawn and limited to define and punish specific conduct lying within the domain of state power, the use in a public place of words likely to cause a breach of peace" (573). He continues, "A statute punishing verbal acts, carefully drawn so as not to unduly impair liberty of expression, is not too vague for a criminal law" (574).

Finally, Murphy points out that the words "'damned racketeer'" and "'damned Fascist'" need no evidence or argument to prove they "are epithets likely to provoke the average person to retaliation, and thereby cause a breach of peace" (574). He also notes, however, that, since two of Chaplinsky's arguments--the truth of his words and the existence of provocation--do not raise constitutional issues, the Court cannot address them.

RULING

Murphy writes, "Our function is fulfilled by a determination that the challenged statute, on its face and as applied, does not contravene the Fourteenth Amendment. Affirmed" (574).

SIGNIFICANCE

Upholding the notion that so-called "fighting words" do not qualify for First Amendment protection gives this case significance. It also gains significance because the Court ruled that properly drawn narrow statutes making the utterance of fighting words a crime do fulfill the Fourteenth Amendment's requirement of due process.

At bottom, the main problem the Court seems to find with fighting words is that they incite. Just as the Court took away constitutional protection from words that incite through encouragement the unlawful overthrow of the government, so too does it take away here constitutional protection of words that incite through offensive language a violent breach of the peace.

In *Schenck*, Holmes says that, because words can have the effect of force, they are in some instances tantamount to action. Thus, if the states can outlaw constitutionally a particular action, then they can likewise outlaw words having the effect of these actions. When do words have the effect of action? Holmes said this effect occurs when there is a clear and present danger that a constitutionally outlawed action will result as a consequence of no more than their being spoken. The Court here says this effect also occurs when offensive words are spoken because these words by consensus are so inherently provocative that they ineluctably elicit a violent response. Indeed, Murphy refers to fighting words as "verbal acts."

Dennis v. United States

Eugene Dennis, John B. Williamson, Jacob Satchel,
Robert G. Thompson, Benjamin J. Davis, Jr.,
Henry Winston, John Gates, Irving Potash,
Gilbert Green, Carl Winter, and Gus Hall
v.
United States

Docket No. 1951-336
341 U.S. 494, 95 L.Ed 1137, 71 S.Ct. 857 (1951)
Argued December 4, 1950. Decided June 4, 1951.

BACKGROUND

The statute known today as the Smith Act was enacted shortly before this country entered World War II. Like the 1917 Espionage Act passed at the end of World War I, Sections 2 and 3 of the Smith Act were directed against forceful and violent overthrow of the government. The primary target, however, was the U.S. Communist party. When the Cold War replaced World War II, the attention of many government prosecutors turned toward the activity of the U.S. Communist party headed then by Eugene Dennis.

CIRCUMSTANCES

In July 1948, 12 members of the national board of the Communist party in the United States were indicted for violating the Smith Act during the period from April 1945 to July 1948. In the main, the leaders were convicted of organizing the Communist party and so, the government asserted, of thereby teaching and advocating the violent and forceful overthrow of the United States. The Supreme Court limited its review of the convictions to questions about the constitutionality of Sections 2 and 3 of the Smith Act.

The relevant passages of the act are these:

> Sec. 2.(a.) It shall be unlawful for any person--
>
> (1) to knowingly or willfully advocate, abet, advise, or teach the duty, necessity, desirability, or propriety of overthrowing or destroying any government in the United States by force or violence . . .;
>
> (2) with the intent to cause the overthrow or destruction of any government in the United States, to print, publish, edit, issue, circulate, sell, distribute, or publicly

> display any written or printed matter advocating, advising, or teaching the duty, necessity, desirability, or propriety of overthrowing or destroying any government in the United States by force or violence;
>
> Sec. 3. It shall be unlawful for any person to attempt to commit or to conspire to commit, any of the acts prohibited by the provisions of . . . this title. (495)

The trial took nine months and produced 16,000 pages of evidence. The decision, also very long, reflected the inability of even these nine wise jurists to resolve the conflicts between free speech and the security of the government. Only three justices joined the majority opinion. Two wrote concurring opinions, two wrote dissenting opinions. Justice Tom C. Clark did not participate.

SUMMARY OF THE COURT'S ANALYSIS

Chief Justice Fred M. Vinson writes for the court.
Justices Stanley F. Reed, Harold H. Burton, and Sherman Minton join.

At bottom, the decision of the Court affirms the trial court's ruling that the activities of Dennis and the other petitioners represented a clear and present danger of an evil that Congress constitutionally could prevent.

Since it was very difficult for the Court to define just exactly why organizing the Communist party violated a Constitutional statute, long passages are devoted to coming up with a viable definition. A good summary of the Court's conclusions are these words of Justice Vinson: "The literature of the Party and the statements and activities of its leaders, petitioners here, advocate, and the general goal of the Party was, during the period in question, to achieve a successful overthrow of the existing order by force and violence" (498).

One of the main problems the court faces is distinguishing between the Communist party's teaching and, say, a college professor's teaching the mainline Communist doctrine of the inevitable violent overthrow of all non-Communist governments. This distinction is drawn by relying on the concept of intent. In short, the court says that persons could teach the doctrine of violent overthrow of our government as long they do not intend to take this action. Writes Vinson, "We hold that the statute requires as an essential element of the crime proof of the intent of those who are charged with its violation to overthrow the Government by force and violence" (499, 500).

A second way that the court distinguishes between legal and illegal teaching under the act is to focus on the difference between advocacy and discussion. Vinson writes, "Thus, the trial judge properly charged the jury that they could not convict if they found that petitioners did 'no more than pursue peaceful studies and discussions or teaching and advocacy in the realm of ideas'" (502).

In other words, the act does allow persons to discuss the merits of violent overthrow of our government and even to advocate the abstract benefits of such an action, but it does not permit advocacy of the action itself. Here is how the trial judge puts it, "It is not the abstract doctrine of overthrowing or destroying organized government by unlawful means which is denounced by this law, but the teaching and advocacy of action for the accomplishment of that purpose, by language reasonably and ordinarily calculated to incite persons to such action" (511).

Next, the Court turns its attention to the clear-and-present-danger concept by reviewing at some length the free speech and press cases it had considered from *Schenck* v. *United States* (1919) to the present. The first point Vinson makes in this review is that "Speech is not an absolute, above and beyond control by the legislature" (508).

He goes on to examine the three central words in the phrase "(1) clear and (2) present (3) danger." The Court asserts that the danger threatened in the present instance holds enough importance to warrant regulation of speech: "Overthrow of the Government by force is certainly a substantial enough interest for the Government to limit speech" (509). The opinion continues, "Certainly, an attempt to overthrow the Government by force, even though doomed from the outset because of inadequate numbers or power of the revolutionists, is a sufficient evil for Congress to prevent"(509).

In addition, the Court considers the danger to be present even though the actual overthrow attempt is not near, but somewhere in the indefinite future. Vinson explains, "Obviously, the words cannot mean that before the Government may act, it must wait until the putsch is about to be executed, the plans have been laid and the signal is awaited" (509).

Moreover, the danger here is clear to the majority. According to the Court, "The revolutionists would strike when they thought the time was ripe. We must therefore reject the contention that success or probability of success is the criterion. . . . [T]he requisite danger existed" (510).

Two other issues are disposed of briefly before the Court issues its ruling. The petitioners (Dennis and the others) claimed that the jury, not the judge, should decide whether or not a clear and present danger existed, but the Court rejects this contention.

The Court also takes pains to defend the clear-and-present-danger rule:

> We think it well serves to indicate to those who would advocate constitutionally prohibited conduct that there is a line beyond which they may not go . . . . But we are not convinced that because there may be borderline cases at some time in the future, these convictions should be reversed because of the argument that these petitioners could not know that their activities were constitutionally proscribed by the statue. (516)

In other words, the Court says that the rule provides a clear, if not exact, warning about what is and what is not acceptable speech under the Smith Act.

RULING

The portions of the Smith Act in question are held constitutional; the Court asserts that, because the petitioners conspired to organize the Communist party, they intended to overthrow the United States government "as speedily as the circumstances would permit" (516). Thus, their teaching and advocacy of this action did indeed create a "clear and present danger" of an "attempt to overthrow the Government by force and violence" (517). Consequently, Vinson writes, "They were properly and constitutionally convicted for violation of the Smith Act. The judgments of conviction are Affirmed" (517).

Justice Felix Frankfurter writes a concurring opinion.

Frankfurter's 44 page concurring opinion--including a 4-page appendix in which he summarizes eight previous, related court rulings--is double the length of the Court's. His opinion is in many ways an attack upon the clear and present danger rule and an apology for using a balancing-of-conflicting-interests concept as the basis for deciding free speech and press cases. He also asserts that the legislature, not the courts, has the right to do the balancing.

Frankfurter begins by setting out what he sees are the two sides or interests of the conflict at issue in this case:

> The appellants maintain that they have a right to advocate a political theory, so long, at least, as their advocacy does not create an immediate danger of obvious magnitude to the very existence of our present scheme of society. On the other hand, the Government asserts the right to safeguard the security of the Nation by such a measure as the Smith Act. Our judgment is thus solicited on a conflict of interests. (518, 519)

According to Frankfurter, both sides claim absolute importance, but both are, in reality, relative: "Just as there are those who regard as invulnerable every measure for which the claim of national survival is invoked, there are those who find in the Constitution a wholly unfettered right of expression" (521).

The way to approach this problem of conflicting absolutes, he asserts, is not to announce a rule (like the clear-and-present-danger doctrine) because the rule will itself become an absolute. Frankfurter writes:

> The demands of free speech in a democratic society as well as the interest in national security are better served by candid and informed weighing of the competing interests, within the confines of the judicial process, than by announcing dogmas too inflexible for the non-Euclidian problems to be solved. (524, 525)

The only question remaining, then, is who is to do the balancing, and the answer for Frankfurter is Congress.

> History teaches that the independence of the judiciary is jeopardized when the courts become embroiled in the passions of the day and assume primary responsibility in choosing between competing political, economic and social pressures.
>
> Primary responsibility for adjusting the interests which compete in the situation before us of necessity belongs to Congress. (525)

After laying out the basis for his decision, Frankfurter then attempts to justify it by a long review of what he feels are all the important relevant cases since *Schenck* (1919). From this review, he draws three conclusions.

"Free speech cases," he writes first, "Are not an exception to the principle that we are not legislators, that direct policy-making is not our province. How to best reconcile competing interests is the business of legislatures, and the balance they strike is a judgment not to be displaced by ours, but to be respected unless outside the pale of fair judgment" (539, 540).

His second point focuses on the basis that the Court should use to make free speech and press decisions. He writes, "A survey of the relevant decisions indicates that the results which we have reached are on the whole those that would ensue from careful weighing of conflicting interests" (542).

He then quotes a scholar's criticism of the clear-and-present-danger rule:

> The truth is that the clear-and-present-danger test is an oversimplified judgment unless it takes account of a number of other factors: the relative seriousness of the danger in comparison with the value of the occasion for the speech or political activity; the availability of more moderate controls than those which the state has imposed; and perhaps the specific intent with which the speech or activity is launched. (542) (From Freund, *On Understanding the Supreme Court*.)

Frankfurter's third point is that "not every type of speech occupies the same position on the scale of values" (544). To illustrate, he draws a distinction "between the statement of an idea which may prompt its hearers to take an unlawful action, and advocacy that such action be taken" (545). Consequently, even though it is not always easy to draw the line between the two forms of speech, we can still attempt to regulate the one (advocacy of unlawful actions) that is not as valuable as the other (statements of ideas that may lead to unlawful actions).

Frankfurter closes by questioning the wisdom of the action that he so strongly asserts Congress has a right to take. It appears from this section, that, if a legislator, Frankfurter would have voted against the Smith Act. He writes:

> The mark of a truly civilized man is confidence in the strength and security derived from the inquiring mind. We may be grateful for such honest comforts as it supports, but we must be unafraid of its uncertitudes. Without open minds there can be no open society. And if society be not open the spirit of man is mutilated and becomes enslaved. (556)

In short, it appears that Frankfurter supports the constitutionality of an act he disapproves of.

Justice Robert H. Jackson writes a concurring opinion.

Justice Jackson asserts in the main that conspiracy to advocate overthrow of the government in itself (regardless of any clear or present danger) does not violate the right of free speech.

He argues that the clear-and-present-danger test wrongly requires the Court to make a prophecy when dealing with the complex issue of a conspiracy. He beings his argument this way:

> When the issue is criminality of a hot-headed speech on a street corner, or circulation of a few incendiary pamphlets . . ., it is not beyond the capacity of the judicial process to gather, comprehend, and weigh the necessary materials for decision whether it is a clear and present danger of substantive evil or a harmless letting off of steam. It is not a prophecy, for the danger in such cases has matured by the time of trial or it was never present. (568)
>
> If we must decide that the Act and its application are constitutional only if we are convinced that petitioner's conduct creates a "clear and present danger" of violent overthrow, we must appraise imponderables, including international and national phenomena which baffle the best informed foreign officers and our most experienced politicians. We would have to [for example] foresee and predict the effectiveness of Communist propaganda, opportunities for infiltrations, whether, and when, a time will come that they consider propitious for action. (570)
>
> If applied as it [clear-and-present-danger test] is proposed here, it means that the Communist plotting is protected during its period of incubation; . . . the Government can move only after imminent action is manifest, when it would, of course, be too late. (570)

This analysis leads to the conclusion for Jackson that, if the goal of a conspiracy can be constitutionally forbidden, then so can the advocacy of that goal. He writes, "But it is not forbidden to put down force or violence, it is not forbidden to punish its teaching or advocacy, and the end being punishable, there is no doubt of the power to punish conspiracy for the purpose" (575).

Justice Hugo L. Black writes a dissenting opinion.

Interestingly, although the concurring opinions reject the majority's usage of the clear-and-present-danger test, the two dissenting opinions accept it. Both dissenting opinions differ from the majority's, though, by asserting that the actions of the petitioners do not present a clear and present danger.

Black dissents mainly because he feels that the petitioners (Dennis and the others) never actually advocated, in speech or writing, violent overthrow of the U.S. government. He sees the situation this way:

> The indictment is that they conspired to organize the Communist Party and to use speech or newspapers and other publications *in the future* [emphasis added] to teach and advocate the forcible overthrow of the Government. No matter how it is worded, this is a virulent form of prior censorship of speech and press, which I believe the First Amendment forbids. (579)

Justice William O. Douglas writes a dissenting opinion.

Douglas begins by agreeing with the majority that "freedom to speak is not absolute; the teaching of methods of terror and other seditious conduct should be beyond the pale along with obscenity and immorality" (581).

He continues:

> There comes a time when even speech loses its constitutional immunity. That is the meaning of the clear and present danger test. When conditions are so critical that there will be no time to avoid the evil that the speech threatens, it is time to call a halt. (585)
>
> Free speech--the glory of our system of government--should not be sacrificed on anything less than plain and objective proof of danger that the evil advocated is imminent. (590)

To Douglas, no clear and present danger exists because "Communism has been so thoroughly exposed in this country that it has been crippled as a political force. Free speech has destroyed it as a political force" (588).

He concludes, "How it can be said that there is a clear and present danger that this advocacy will succeed is, therefore, a mystery" (588).

SIGNIFICANCE

This case is significant for a number of reasons. The first is the Court's attempt to define what is a clear and present danger. It says that overthrow of government by force is a substantial enough evil to count as a danger that could take speech out from the protective cover of the First

Amendment. The danger is clear even though an attempt appears unable to succeed. Moreover, the danger is present, even though it may not occur until sometime in the indefinite future. In the Court's view, if government waits until the danger is absolutely clear and all doubt is gone, then it will be too late. In short, the Court seems to be saying that the gravity of the evil (violent overthrow of the government) is so great that one may not constitutionally advocate doing it.

What does it mean, then, to advocate this goal? The Court's definition of advocacy is the second reason this decision is significant for free speech and press cases. The majority says it does not mean advocating a general notion that we would all be better off if our government were overthrown by force; rather it means advocating an action that would accomplish this goal. In addition, there must be present an intent to take the action advocated.

A third reason this case is important arises out of Frankfurter's concurring opinion. He challenges the clear-and-present-danger test, and suggests a substitute: a balance-of-issues approach. When two extremely important goods come into conflict, then he says the interests must be weighed to see which is the more important. Although he asserts that Congress must do the weighing, not the courts, he seems to suggest at the end of his opinion that the Congress made an error in this case by giving too little weight to the interest of free speech.

Gitlow v. New York

Benjamin Gitlow
v.
People of the State of New York

Docket No. 1925-19
268 U.S. 652, 69 L.Ed. 1138, 45 S.Ct. 625 (1925)
Argued April 12, 1923. Reargued November 23, 1923.
Decided June 8, 1925.

BACKGROUND

Until this case, the First Amendment protected citizens only from the actions of the federal government. Since the amendment begins with the words "Congress shall make no law," it was thought that only Congress (i.e., the federal government), and not the states, was constrained by the rights listed in this part of the Bill of Rights. Indeed, the Supreme Court specifically ruled in 1833 (*Barron* v. *Baltimore*) that the first ten amendments protected citizens from the actions of the federal, but not state, government.

In 1868, however, the Fourteenth Amendment was adopted. Among other things, it attempted to eliminate what has sometimes been called "dual citizenship"; that is, simultaneous state and federal citizenship. One important passage reads, "No State shall . . . deprive any person of life, liberty, or property, without due process of law."

Gitlow's attorneys asserted that the word "liberty" in the Fourteenth Amendment imposed on the states the free press and speech restrictions of the First Amendment. The court agreed, but Gitlow still lost his appeal because a majority said Gitlow broke the law and the New York State law did not violate the First Amendment.

CIRCUMSTANCES

Benjamin Gitlow, a member of the left-wing section of the Socialist party, and three others were convicted of violating a New York State statute making it a crime to promote anarchy. The statute defined criminal anarchy as "the doctrine that organized government should be overthrown by force or violence, or . . . by any unlawful means" (654). It also stated, "The advocacy of such doctrine . . . is a felony" (654).

As business manager for *The Revolutionary Age*, the official organ of this group, Gitlow arranged for the printing of the first issue, which contained *The Left Wing Manifesto*. Gitlow's indictment charged that the *Manifesto* "advocated, advised, and taught the duty, necessity, and propriety of overthrowing and overturning organized government by force, violence, and unlawful means" (656). The indictment also said he "printed, published, and knowingly circulated" it (656).

Gitlow's appeal was two pronged. First, he claimed that, because the Fourteenth Amendment applied the First Amendment to the states, the *Manifesto* was protected from the New York State law by the free press clause. More specifically, Gitlow said one of the liberties referred to in the Fourteenth Amendment is the liberty of free speech and press mentioned in the First.

Secondly, he claimed that the *Manifesto* did not violate the statute anyway. This argument had two points. Both points rested on the proposition that, in order to violate the statute, the *Manifesto* had to advocate the violent or unlawful overthrow of the government. Indeed, the trial judge agreed and told the jury the following: "A mere statement that unlawful acts might accomplish such a purpose would be insufficient, unless there was a teaching, advising, and advocacy for the purpose of overthrowing government" (661).

Gitlow said that one good reason the *Manifesto* did not so advocate was because it did not urge "some definite or immediate act or acts" (661). Another reason was that the *Manifesto* did not "incite certain persons" to unlawful or violent acts. In short, Gitlow claimed that advocacy meant the words were to be directed towards (1) a specific act, and (2) a specific person or group of persons.

SUMMARY OF THE COURT'S ANALYSIS

Justice Edward T. Sanford writes for the Court.
Chief Justice William H. Taft and Justices Joseph McKenna, Willis Van Devanter, James C. McReynolds, George Sutherland, and Pierce Butler join.

Justice Sanford accepts almost casually Gitlow's argument that the Fourteenth Amendment applies the First to the states. He writes:

> For present purposes we may and do *assume* [emphasis added] that freedom of speech and of the press--which are protected by the 1st Amendment from abridgment by Congress--are among the fundamental personal rights and "liberties" protected by the due process clause of the 14th Amendment from impairment by the states. (666)

Sanford also agrees with Gitlow that the statute "does not penalize the utterance or publication of abstract 'doctrine' or academic discussion having no quality of incitement to any concrete action" (664).

This said, Sanford begins to develop the case against Gitlow. First, he notes that "the Constitution does not confer an absolute right to speak or publish, without responsibility, whatever one may choose" (666). He continues, "It does not protect publications prompting the overthrow of government by force . . . In short, this freedom does not deprive a state of the primary and essential right of self-preservation" (668). In other words, the government can regulate some forms of speech. One of these forms is speech threatening destruction of government.

The main point in Sanford's argument is that the gravity of the substantive evil threatened is so great (namely, the death of the state) that the government does not have to show a clear and present danger in order to prohibit or punish it. He asserts that the point at which the government can be certain there exists a clear danger is the very point at which it is too late to avoid being overthrown. He uses the analogy of a spark. A person concerned with public safety, he argues, would not have to wait until the spark has been kindled into a flame until making an effort to put it out. Likewise, he writes, "A single revolutionary spark may kindle a fire that . . . may burst into a sweeping and destructive conflagration" (669).

So, he concludes:

> It was not necessary . . . that the defendant should have advocated "some definite [clear] or immediate [and present] act or acts" of force, violence, or unlawfulness [danger]. It was sufficient if such acts were advocated in general terms; and it was not essential that their immediate execution should have been advocated. (671)

RULING

Since the statute itself is not unconstitutional, and since Gitlow did violate the statue, the court upheld his conviction.

Justice Oliver W. Holmes, Jr., writes a dissenting opinion.
Justice Louis D. Brandeis joins.

The two dissenters agree with the majority that the word "liberty" in the due process clause of the Fourteenth Amendment does indeed include free speech. Nevertheless, they feel that the clear-and-present-danger test of the *Schenck* case should be applied to Gitlow.

Holmes writes:

> It is said that this Manifesto was more than a theory, that it was an incitement. Every idea is an incitement. It offers itself for belief, and, if believed, it is acted on unless some other belief outweighs it, or some failure of energy stifles the movement at its birth. The only difference between the expression of an opinion and an incitement in the narrower sense is the speaker's enthusiasm for the result. (673) If the publication of this document had been laid as an attempt to induce an uprising against government at once, and not at some indefinite time in the future, it would have presented a different question. (673)

Therefore, the question, for Holmes and Brandeis, becomes this: Is there any danger that action would indeed result immediately? In contrast, the question for the majority is not clear and present danger, but only is there publication of words advocating action.

SIGNIFICANCE

Without doubt, the significance of this case is the Court's unequivocal statement that the Fourteenth Amendment does apply the First Amendment to the states.

In addition, some scholars feel the majority decision weakened Holmes's idea of clear and present danger by putting too much emphasis on the magnitude of the danger and too little on the importance of clear and present. Sanford argued, for example, that the gravity of a substantive evil threatened can be so great (namely, the death of the state) that the government does not have to show a clear and present danger in order to prohibit or punish it. The point at which the government can be certain there exists a clear danger, he asserts, is the very point at which it is too late to avoid being overthrown. Thus, he seems to be saying that government constitutionally can presume a danger to be clear and present if the danger threatened is the very existence of the nation.

Hazelwood School Dist. v. Kuhlmeier

Hazelwood School District
v.
Cathy Kuhlmeier

Docket No. 86-836
484 U.S. ---, 98 L.Ed.2d 592, 108 S.Ct. 562 (1988)
Argued October 13, 1987. Decided January 13, 1988.

BACKGROUND

For many years one decision [*Tinker* v. *Des Moines Independent Community School District*, 393 U.S. 503, 21 L.Ed.2d 731, 89 S.Ct. 733 (1969)] dominated discussions of the First Amendment rights of students in high schools. The most influential idea from that decision was the notion that schools could not infringe on the First Amendment rights of students unless there was a reasonable chance that such speech would substantially disrupt or materially interfere with school activities. During the 1980s, however, the Court came to grips with a number of other complex First Amendment issues in secondary education. For the first two centuries of the existence of this country, however, the Court had not taken an opportunity to rule on a case related to student newspapers. Enters *Hazelwood*.

CIRCUMSTANCES

When Robert Stergos left on April 29, 1983 Hazelwood East High School in St. Louis County, Missouri, and his job as teacher and adviser to the student newspaper, Howard Emerson, another teacher in the Hazelwood School District, was named adviser to the *Spectrum*.

Following past practice, Emerson took the May 13 edition of the *Spectrum* to Principal Robert Eugene Reynolds, who objected to two news stories. One story described three students' experiences with pregnancy and, the other, the impact on students of parental divorce.

His concerns about the pregnancy story were that, in spite of aliases, the girls quoted would be identified and that some of the references to sexual activity and birth control were "inappropriate" for younger students. He was also concerned that parents criticized in a story by a named student were not given an opportunity to reply. Because Reynolds thought there was not enough time to make changes in the story before the printing deadline, he simply cut out the two pages on which the stories appeared.

Distributing more than 4,500 copies every three weeks or so during the 1982-3 academic year, the students published the paper as part of the Journalism II class with $4,668.50 from the school board and $1,166.84 from advertising revenue.

The district court said no violation of the First Amendment occurred, mainly because the newspaper was published as part of the regular school curriculum, but the court of appeals reversed, saying the paper was a public forum.

SUMMARY OF THE COURT'S ANALYSIS

Justice Byron R. White writes for the Court.
Chief Justice William H. Rehnquist and Justices John Paul Stevens, Sandra Day O'Connor and Antonin Scalia join.

The primary issue in this case is whether or not Reynolds' actions violated the First Amendment rights of the student journalists. Writing for the Court, Justice Byron R. White said that, although students do have First Amendment rights according to *Tinker*, these rights are not equal to those of adults because of the special characteristics of the school environment. Quoting in part from *Bethel School District No. 403* v. *Fraser*, 478 U.S. ---, 92 L.Ed.2d 549, 106 S. Ct. 3159 (1988), White writes, "'The determination of what manner of speech in the classroom or in school assembly is inappropriate properly rests with the school board' . . . rather than with the federal courts" (L.Ed.2d 602).

The Court then takes up several implications of this ruling. Writes White, "We deal first with the question whether the Spectrum may appropriately be characterized as a forum for public expression" (L.Ed.2d 602). Here White says that, since public schools are in some ways unlike public streets or parks, school facilities can be considered public forums only if they meet conditions set forth by the Court in previous decisions. In *Perry Education Assn.* v. *Perry Local Educator*'s *Assn.*, 460 U.S. 37, 74 L.Ed.2d 794, 103 S.Ct. 948 (1983), the Court said, according to White, "School facilities may be deemed to be public forums only if school authorities have 'by policy or practice' opened those facilities' for indiscriminate use by the general public'" (L.Ed.2d 603). *Widmar* v. *Vincent*, 454 U.S. 263, 70 L.Ed.2d 440, 102 S.Ct. 269 (1981) refined general public to take note of "'some segment of the public, such as student organizations'" (L.Ed.2d 603). Thus, the Court rules that "no public forum has been created" so "school officials may impose reasonable restrictions on the speech of students, teachers, and other members of the school community" (L.Ed.2d 603).

As evidence that the school facilities were not indiscriminately opened to students who wanted to publish a newspaper, the Court notes that participation on the paper was limited to students in the Journalism II course. White concludes, quoting in part from *Perry*, that, since the school "'reserve[d] the forum for its intended purpose'. . . as a supervised learning experience for journalism students . . . school officials were entitled to regulate the contents of the Spectrum in any reasonable manner" (L.Ed.2d 605).

The Court then draws a distinction between the *Tinker* case, in which the school was asked to allow student speech to occur, and this case, in which the school was asked to promote a particular student speech. White makes two points about this distinction. First, school-promoted speech or expression brings up the issue of the authority of educators over school-sponsored activities. He notes three reasons for supporting this authority. He writes:

> Educators are entitled to exercise greater control over this . . . form of student expression to assure that [1] participants learn whatever lessons the activity is designed to teach, [2] that readers or listeners are not exposed to material that may be inappropriate for their level of maturity, and [3] that the views of the individual speaker are not erroneously attributed to the school. (L.Ed.2d 605)

The Court then introduces the idea that schools may "disassociate" themselves for three main reasons from school-sponsored student speech. White says first, "A school must be able to set high standards for the student speech that is disseminated under its auspices" (L.Ed.2d 605-060). Secondly, "a school must be able to take into account the emotional maturity of the intended audience" (L.Ed.2d 606). Finally, quoting in part from *Fraser*, White writes, "A school must also retain the authority to refuse to sponsor student speech that might reasonably be perceived to advocate drug or alcohol use, irresponsible sex, or conduct otherwise inconsistent with 'the shared values of civilized social order' . . . or to [avoid] any position other than neutrality on matters of political controversy" (L.Ed.2d 606).

The Court concludes as a result of this analysis that the *Tinker* standard does not apply here because the words in the *Spectrum* speak to some degree for the school as well as for the students. Therefore educators could constitutionally control the editorial content of the newspaper as long as their actions are "reasonable and related to legitimate pedagogical concerns" (L.Ed.2d 606).

Given this conclusion, the only remaining question, then, is whether or not Principal Reynolds acted reasonably and for valid educational reasons. The Court rules that he did. Three particular actions were held to be reasonable. First, since a teacher at the school was able to identify one of the pregnant students quoted in the newspaper, White says, "Reynolds therefore could reasonably have feared that the article violated whatever pledge of anonymity had been given to the pregnant students" (L.Ed.2d 607). Secondly, Reynolds "could reasonably have been concerned that the article was not sufficiently sensitive to the privacy interests of the students' boyfriends and parents, who were discussed in the article but who were given no opportunity to consent to its publication or to offer a response" (L.Ed.2d 607). Finally, White writes, "It was not unreasonable for the principal to have concluded that such frank talk [of birth control usage] was inappropriate in a school-sponsored publication distributed to 14-year-old freshmen and presumably taken home to be read by students' even younger brothers and sisters" (L.Ed.2d 607).

In regard to Reynold's "legitimate pedagogical concerns," White writes:

> Reynolds could reasonably have concluded that the students who had written and edited these articles had not sufficiently mastered those portions of the Journalism II curriculum that pertained to the treatment of controversial issues and personal attacks, the need to protect the privacy of individuals whose intimate concerns are to be revealed in the newspaper, and "the legal, moral, and ethical restrictions imposed upon journalists within [a] school community" that includes adolescent subjects and readers. (L.Ed.2d 608)

RULING

The Court states, "No violation of First Amendment rights occurred" (L.Ed.2d 608). White writes, "We hold that educators do not offend the First Amendment by exercising editorial control over the style and content of student speech in school sponsored expressive activities so long as their actions are reasonably related to legitimate pedagogical concerns (L.Ed.2d 606). The decision ends with these words, "The judgment of the Court of Appeals for the Eighth Circuit is therefore *reversed*" (L.Ed.2d 608).

Justice William J. Brennan, Jr., writes a dissenting opinion.
Justices Thurgood Marshall and Harry A. Blackmun join.

The tone for Justice Brennan's dissent is set by the opening sentence, "When the young men and women of Hazelwood East High School registered for Journalism II, they expected a civics lesson" (L.Ed.2d 609). The lesson they received was not palatable to Brennan.

He begins by criticizing what he calls the Court's "taxonomy of school censorship" (L.Ed.2d 612), referring to the distinction between a "student's personal opinion that happens to occur on the school premises" and expression that "arises in the context of 'school-sponsored . . . expressive activities'" (L.Ed.2d 612). He writes:

> The Court offers no more than an obscure tangle of three excuses to afford educators "greater control" over school-sponsored speech than the Tinker test would permit: the public educator's prerogative to control curriculum; the pedagogical interest in shielding the high school audience from objectionable viewpoints and sensitive topics; and the school's need to dissociate itself from student expression. None of these excuses, once disentangled, supports the distinction that the Court draws. (L.Ed.2d 612,613)

In reference to the curriculum, Brennan says the school can indeed "censor" a newspaper with poor "grammar, writing, or research" because these items are part of the curriculum. In contrast, the school cannot "censor" information simply to "shield the *audience* or dissociate the *sponsor* from the expression" because this action "in no way furthers the curricular purposes of a student *newspaper* [emphases in original text]" (L.Ed.2d 613).

Brennan also opposes the notion of a legitimate pedagogical interest in shielding a high school audience from objectionable viewpoints and sensitive topics. He writes, "'potential topic sensitivity' is a vaporous nonstandard--like 'public welfare, peace, safety, health, decency, good order, morals or convenience' . . . that invites manipulation to achieve ends that cannot permissibly be achieved through blatant discrimination and chills student speech to which school officials might not object" (L.Ed.2d 616). He adds, "School officials (and courts) can camouflage viewpoint discrimination as the 'mere' protection of students from sensitive topics" (L.Ed.2d 616).

Next, Brennan responds to the Court's support of the value of disassociating the school from inferior student work by suggesting that methods other than the extreme of "brutal censorship" can be used. He notes, "It could, for example, require the student activity to publish a disclaimer. . . . [o]r it could simply issue its own response clarifying the official position on the matter and explaining why the student position is wrong" (L.Ed.2d 617).

In addition, Brennan objects to the method the principal used to correct what may have been in fact objectionable material. Brennan writes, "He did not so much as inquire into obvious alternatives, such as precise deletions or additions . . . rearranging the layout or delaying publication. Such unthinking contempt for individual rights is intolerable from any state official" (L.Ed.2d 617).

He concludes, "The young men and women of Hazelwood East expected a civics lesson, but not the one the Court teaches them today" (L.Ed.2d 618).

SIGNIFICANCE

The mere fact that this is the first and only opinion given by the Court on student newspapers makes it a significant case. In the main, the opinion appears on the face of it to be important for drawing a distinction between school speech that is part of the curriculum and school speech that is not. Since school authorities and educators do have the constitutional right to control the curriculum, the Court says, then they also have more authority to regulate speech that is part of the curriculum than they do speech that is not. Although journalists are viligant in monitoring the impact of this case, it appears that administrators in high schools--and not colleges where students are thought to be adults--that produce the school newspaper as part of the curriculum do enjoy strong editorial control.

Near v. Minnesota Ex Rel. Olson

J. M. Near
v.
State of Minnesota Ex Rel. Floyd B. Olson

Docket No. 1931-91
283 U.S. 697, 75 L.Ed. 1357, 51 S.Ct. 625 (1931)
Argued January 30, 1931. Decided June 1, 1931.

BACKGROUND

There are always times when some citizens feel that the police do not enforce particular laws as energetically as possible. After the Eighteenth Amendment was ratified on January 16, 1919, law enforcement officers were required to arrest all persons engaged in "the manufacture, sale, or transportation of intoxicating liquors within . . . the United States." Enforcement of this prohibition against the sale and manufacture of alcoholic beverages was not easy and not always enthusiastic. A common target of crusading reporters and editors during the 1920s and early 1930s (until the Twenty-First Amendment repealed the Eighteenth in 1933), consequently, was failure by the police and government officials to enforce what came to be known simply as Prohibition.

CIRCUMSTANCES

Jay M. Near seems to have considered himself a reformer. On September 24, 1927 he and Howard Guilford published in Minneapolis the first issue of a weekly newspaper called the *Saturday Press*. The ostensible purpose of the paper was to expose graft, corruption, and all other forms of wrong doing especially in local government. Critics claimed, though, that Near and Guilford were in reality blackmailers who intended to make money by offering their "news makers" an opportunity to purchase the bad news that the two entrepreneurs said they intended to publish. Butler takes note in his dissenting opinion that the defendants admitted a man named Bevans did, in fact, use another newspaper (the *Twin City Reporter*) they were associated with for blackmail purposes.

That the newspaper was born in controversy is clear. In fact, the two claimed they received threats when they announced their intention to publish, and Guilford was shot and wounded soon after publication did occur. Guilford said he was also carrying a gun at the time.

The 1925 Minnesota statute that Near was accused of violating is extremely unusual, if not unique. At bottom, it gives the courts permission to abate as a public nuisance a "malicious, scandalous, and defamatory newspaper." The purpose of the statute, according to the Minnesota State Supreme Court, was to protect the public from material "'detrimental to public morals and to the general welfare'" because it tended "'to disturb the peace of the community'" and "'to provoke assaults and the commission of crime'" (709).

Floyd B. Olson, county attorney of Hennepin County, Minnesota, brought suit charging the newspaper was a public nuisance because of anti-Semitic articles attacking, among others, the mayor and police chief of Minneapolis. The articles said, "A Jewish gangster was in control of gambling, bootlegging and racketeering in Minneapolis, and that law enforcement officers and agencies were not energetically performing their duties" (704).

The district court made a finding of fact that "the editions in question were 'chiefly devoted to malicious, scandalous, and defamatory articles' concerning the individuals named" (705). The court then "adjudged" the paper a public nuisance and enjoined the defendants "'from producing, editing, publishing, circulating . . . any publication whatsoever which is a malicious, scandalous or defamatory newspaper as defined by law'" (706). Near appealed the judgment, asserting, among other things, that the statute was unconstitutional.

SUMMARY OF THE COURT'S ANALYSIS

Chief Justice Charles Evans Hughes writes for the Court.
Justices Louis Brandies, Oliver Wendel Holmes, Harlan Stone, and Owen J. Roberts join.

Justice Hughes begins by stating that, on the one hand, the First Amendment does indeed apply to the states through the Fourteenth. On the other hand, he says, "Liberty of speech and of the press is also not an absolute right, and the state may punish its abuse" (708). The question at issue, then, becomes whether the state statute constitutionally regulates the Minnesota press.

Hughes outlines four points. First, he notes that, since "the statute is not aimed at the redress of individual or private wrongs," the truth of the scandalous information is irrelevant to enforcement of the law. In other words, the law allows the newspaper to be abated as a public nuisance even if the scandalous material truthfully accuses persons of scandalous acts.

Secondly, Hughes points out that "the statute is directed not simply at the circulation of scandalous and defamatory statements with regard to private citizens, but at the continued publication . . . of charges against public officers of corruption, malfeasance in office, or serious neglect of duty" (710). Thus, the law would seem to discourage any attempt to ferret out corruption among public officials because those very officials being investigated could convict their accusers of printing scandalous information.

The third point Hughes makes is that the statute does not attempt to "punish" the offending publication, but to suppress it, to eliminate it. He writes, "It is the continued publication of scandalous and defamatory matter that constitutes the . . . declared nuisance" (711). Hughes's final point is that the statute, in effect, operates "to put the publisher under an effective censorship" (712). He writes:

> If we cut through mere details of procedure, the operation and effect of the statute in substance is that public authorities may bring the owner or publisher of a newspaper or periodical before a judge upon a charge of conducting a business of publishing scandalous and defamatory matter--in particular that the matter consists of charges against public officials of official dereliction--and unless the owner or publisher is able and disposed to satisfy the judge that the charges are true and are published with good motives and for justifiable ends, his newspaper or periodical is suppressed and further publication is made punishable as a contempt. This is the essence of censorship. (713)

Hughes now uses these four points to determine if Near has constitutional protection from the Minnesota statute. He suggests at once that most persons consider prevention of previous restraint to be the primary goal of the First Amendment. He writes, "In determining the extent of the constitutional protection, it has been generally, if not universally, considered that it is the chief purpose of the guaranty to prevent previous restraints upon publication" (713).

Next, he quotes a famous passage from Blackstone's *Commentaries*:

> The liberty of the press is indeed essential to the nature of a free state; but this consists in laying no *previous* restraints upon publication, and not in freedom from censure for criminal matter when published. Every Freeman has an undoubted right to lay what sentiments he pleases before the public; to forbid this, is to destroy the freedom of the press; but if he publishes what is improper, mischievous or illegal, he must take the consequences of this own temerity. (713, 714) (4 *Bl. Com.* 151,152)

Hughes then proceeds to limit Blackstone's proposed protection from previous restraint when he writes, "The protection even as to previous restraint is not absolutely unlimited. But the limitation has been recognized only in exceptional cases" (716). Among those exceptions, he lists the following: "publication [during war time] of the sailing dates of transports or the number and location of troops;" "obscene" materials; "incitements to acts of violence and the overthrow by force of orderly government" (716). Quoting in part from *Schenck*, he summarizes, "The constitutional guaranty of free speech does not 'protect a man from an injunction against uttering words that may have all the effect of force'" (716).

Nevertheless, the bottom line, as Hughes sees it, is contained in this famous passage: "The fact that the liberty of the press may be abused by miscreant purveyors of scandal does not make any the less necessary the immunity of the press from previous restraint in dealing with official misconduct" (720).

Hughes deals with a few more issues before pronouncing judgment. One is the notion that the statute does not fall under the purview of the First Amendment because the law deals, not with information, but with the newspaper as a business. To this argument he replies succinctly, "Characterizing the publication as a business, and the business as a nuisance, does not permit an invasion of the constitutional immunity against restraint" (720). He adds, "[A publisher] . . . does not lose his right [to publish] by exercising it" (720).

Another issue is the threat to public order. To this, Hughes replies:

> Equally unavailing is the insistence that the statute is designed to prevent the circulation of scandal which tends to disturb the public peace and to provoke assaults and the commission of crime. Charges of reprehensible conduct, and in particular of official malfeasance, unquestionably create a public scandal, but the theory of the constitutional guaranty is that even a more serious evil would be caused by authority to prevent publication. (722)

In dispensing with this argument, Hughes points out that there is "nothing new in the fact that charges of reprehensible conduct may create resentment and the disposition to resort to violent means of redress" (722). To the Court, this tendency to strike out at persons who publish notorious information is not sufficient to justify governmental regulation of the press.

RULING

The Court finds the relevant section of the statute "to be an infringement of the liberty of the press guaranteed by the 14th Amendment" (723). Its decision rests, according to Hughes, on the inevitable effect of the law, which could work to punish a newspaper that prints truthful, if scandalous, charges against public officials. Thus, he says, "The statute imposes an unconstitutional restraint upon publication. Judgment reversed" (723).

Justice Pierce Butler writes a dissenting opinion.
Justices Willis Van Devanter, James C. McReynolds, and George Sutherland join.

Butler notes in his dissent, "The act was passed in the exertion of the state's power of police . . ., and there exists in Minnesota a state of affairs that justifies this measure for the preservation of the peace and good order of the state" (731). To the dissenters, then, this statute is not an attack on free speech, but an attempt to preserve law and order.

After reviewing the context of Blackstone's comments quoted by the Court, Butler asserts:

> The Minnesota statute does not operate as a previous *restraint* on publication within the proper meaning of that phrase. It does not authorize administrative control in advance such as was formerly exercised by the licensers and censors but prescribes a remedy to be enforced by a suit in equity. (735) The restraint authorized is only in respect of continuing to do what has been duly adjudged to constitute a nuisánce. (735)
> It is fanciful to suggest similarity between the granting or enforcement of the decree authorized by this statute to prevent *further* publication of malicious, scandalous and defamatory articles and the *previous restraints* upon the press by licensers as referred to by Blackstone.(736)

He feels existing libel laws are "inadequate" to "suppress evils resulting from the kind of business and publications that are shown in this case" (737). To declare this law unconstitutional, Butler asserts, "Exposes the peace and good order of every community and the business and private affairs of every individual to the constant and protracted false and malicious assaults of any insolvent publisher who may have purpose and sufficient capacity to contrive and put into effect a scheme or program for oppression, blackmail or extortion" (737, 738).

At bottom, the dissenters say the law constitutionally regulates a business and does not censor information. The Court, in contrast, objects to the law because it feels that the effect of this business regulation is censorship of the press.

SIGNIFICANCE

This case is widely celebrated as a clear victory for those who oppose any form of previous (or prior) restraint upon the press. A close look, however, reveals only a partial victory against previous restraint. The Court listed several forms of speech that, under certain conditions, could be subjected constitutionally to previous restraint. Among these exceptions are the following: publication during wartime of the sailing dates of transports or the number and location of troops; obscene materials; and incitements to acts of violence and the overthrow by force of orderly government.

Schenck v. United States

Charles T. Schenck v. United States of America
Docket No. 1919-437

Elizabeth Baer v. United States of America
Docket No. 1919-438

249 U.S. 47, 63 L.Ed. 470, 39 S.Ct. 247 (1919)
Argued January 10 and 11, 1919. Decided March 3, 1919.

BACKGROUND

This case marks the beginning of modern mass communications case law. For the most part, the Supreme Court of the United States was simply too busy with other topics in the first 130 years or so of its existence to address at any length serious First Amendment issues. The passage of the 1917 Espionage Act, however, inexorably brought a series of freedom of speech and press cases through the appellate system to the country's highest court. This law made it a crime to attempt overthrow of the government through unlawful or violent means or to advocate doing so.

CIRCUMSTANCES

As general secretary of the Socialist party in 1917, Charles Schenck supervised the printing of 15,000 leaflets that, among other things, urged young men to resist the draft. Although the leaflet was so loosely organized and the arguments within bounced around disjunctively from point to point, Schenck and Baer (who was apparently a member of the party's executive board) in fact did not deny in their appeal that a jury might agree that the effect of the publication would be to encourage young men to object to the draft.

The two were convicted of "causing and attempting to cause insubordination, etc., in the military and naval forces of the United States, and to obstruct the recruiting and enlistment of the United States, when the United States was at war" (48, 49).

SUMMARY OF THE COURT'S ANALYSIS

Justice Oliver W. Holmes, Jr., writes for the Court.
Chief Justice Edward D. White and Justices Joseph McKenna, William R. Day, Willis Van Devanter, Mahlon Pitney, James C. McReynolds, Loius D. Brandeis, and John H. Clarke join.

The case centers for the most part on two closely related points. First, does the First Amendment allow Congress to outlaw some forms of speech? Secondly, it if does, then does this Socialist leaflet contain such speech?

Justice Holmes, writing for a unanimous court, begins to address the first issue by agreeing with Schenck and Baer that the First Amendment is relevant to free press issues other than prior restraint. He writes, "It may well be that the prohibition of laws abridging the freedom of speech is not confined to previous restraints, although to prevent them may have been the main purpose" (51, 52).

His next words are so tightly woven that they need to be read as a unit.

> We admit that in many places and in ordinary times the defendants, in saying all that was said in the circular, would have been within their constitutional rights. But the character of every act depends upon the circumstances in which it is done. The most stringent protection of free speech would not protect a man in falsely shouting fire in a theater, and causing a panic. It does not even protect a man from an injunction against uttering words that may have all the effect of force. The question in every case is whether the words are used in such circumstances and are of such a nature as to create a clear and present danger that they will bring about the substantive evils that Congress has a right to prevent. It is a question of proximity and degree. When a nation is at war many things that might be said in time of peace are such a hindrance to its effort that their utterance will not be endured so long as men fight, and that no court could regard them as protected by any constitutional right. It seems to be admitted that if an actual obstruction of the recruiting service were proved, liability for words that produced that effect might be enforced. (52)

Holmes now begins his main argument by saying that the right of free speech is not absolute; there do indeed exist certain words a person cannot speak in certain contexts at certain times and still receive constitutional protection.

He goes on to point out that, because words can have the effect of force, they are in some instances and conditions tantamount to an action. Thus, if Congress can outlaw constitutionally a particular action, then it can likewise outlaw words having the effect of these actions. When do words have the effect of action? Holmes seems to say that this effect occurs when there is a clear and present danger that a constitutionally outlawed action will result as a consequence of their being spoken.

RULING

The ruling in this case is succinct: "Judgments affirmed." The Court, in short, upholds Schenck and Baer's conviction on three counts of violating the 1917 Espionage Act. The first count was causing insubordination in the armed forces; the next two charge illegal use of the mails.

SIGNIFICANCE

The announcement of the clear-and-present-danger rule for the very first time has given this case its special significance.
Holmes based this rule on the assumption that the right of free speech is not absolute because, in fact, there exist certain words a person cannot speak in certain contexts at certain times and still receive First Amendment protection.

He explains that, because words can have the effect of force, they are in some instances and conditions tantamount to an action. Therefore, he reasons, if Congress can outlaw constitutionally a particular action, then it can likewise outlaw words having the effect of these actions. In short, words produce the effect of action when there is a clear and present danger that a constitutionally outlawed action will result as a consequence of their being spoken. The distinction between protected and unprotected speech, then, is, to Holmes, a question of proximity and degree.

Texas v. Johnson

Texas
v.
Gregory Lee Johnson

Docket No. 88-155; 57 LW 4770
491 U.S. ---, 105 L.Ed.2d 342, 109 S.Ct. 2533 (1989)
Argued March 21, 1989. Decided June 21, 1989.

BACKGROUND

The exact location of the border line between action and speech has long been debated in the courts of this country. Such a distinction is extremely important to jurists because the First Amendment protects speech, but not action. Thus, the government constitutionally can restrict a citizen's actions, but may not restrict a person's speech without first satisfying the demands of the First Amendment.

Burning the American flag raises a question related to this conflict. Is this burning an action, or it is speech? At bottom, the court says it is speech when it communicates a message, but action when it is done as a mindless form of behavior unrelated to a political purpose or belief. In other words, if a flag burner intends to make a political statement, then burning the flag may be a form of speech protected by the First Amendment. In contrast, if a flag burner simply lacks common respect for a piece of private property, then the burning is an action that constitutionally can be punished. For example, the government could punish such burning if it threatens harm to others, if the flag does not belong to the burner, or if it pollutes the air.

A complex, almost metaphysical, additional question is raised, however, when the flag, and not some other symbol of this country, is burned. Is the flag uniquely so intimately associated with the values of our country that it, in effect, not only symbolizes our nation but actually in some very real sense becomes the nation? If so, then burning the flag might be thought identical in many important ways to attacking the nation itself. These similarities, in turn, suggest that flag burning, even if it represents an intentional and unmistakable form of political protest, is essentially action, not speech. They further suggest that, while speech attacking the flag is protected by the First Amendment, the act of burning the flag is not because burning this unique representation of the essence of America is like burning America itself.

Rarely are conflicts brought to the Court conceived in a vacuum, and this one is no exception. The Court cites numerous relevant previous decisions, but three of them are particularly helpful and important in understanding the position taken by the slim majority. The first is *United States* v. *O'Brien*, 391 U.S. 367 (1968). This case produced the O'Brien tests, which assert that (under certain conditions) the government can punish actions having elements of speech. The tests are a series of "ifs" that need to be satisfied. .Chief Justice Earl Warren writes for the Court:

> We think it clear that a government regulation [of an action combining speech and non-speech aspects] is sufficiently justified if it is within the constitutional power of the government; if it furthers an important or substantial governmental interest; if the governmental interest is unrelated to the suppression of free expression; and if the incidental restriction on alleged First Amendment freedoms is no greater than is essential to the furtherance of that interest. (*United States v. O'Brien*, 391 U.S. at 377)

In *Spence* v. *Washington*, 418 U.S. 405 (1974), the Court ruled that the First Amendment prevents a state from punishing a person who would hang the flag upside down as an expression of political protest. In a *per curiam* opinion, the Court writes:

> His [Harold Omand Spence's] message was direct, likely to be understood, and within the contours of the First Amendment. Given the protected character of his expression and in light of the fact that no interest the State may have in preserving the physical integrity of a privately owned flag was significantly impaired on these facts, the conviction must be invalidated. (*Spence* v. *Washington*, 418 U.S. at 415)

The last case to be considered is *Boos* v. *Berry* 485, U.S. 312 (485 U.S. --- (1988). Here the Court said, in effect, that a law directed at only the nonspeech aspects of behavior, but which combines both speech and nonspeech aspects, does not satisfy First Amendment requirements.

CIRCUMSTANCES

While participating in a demonstration during the Republican party's national convention in Dallas, Texas, during the summer of 1984, Gregory Johnson burned "an American Flag handed to him by a fellow protestor who had taken it from a flag pole outside one of the targeted buildings" (105 L.Ed.2d 350). Although he doused the flag with kerosene before setting it afire, no one was injured or even threatened with injury. While the flag burned, his cohorts shouted, "America, the red, white, and blue, we spit on you" (105 L.Ed.2d 350).

Charged with violating a Texas statute that prohibited desecration of a venerated object, Johnson was eventually convicted and sentenced to a year in prison and fined $2,000. Although the Court of Appeals for the

Fifth District of Texas at Dallas affirmed the conviction, the Texas Court of Criminal Appeals reversed.

In the main the reversal was based on the assertion that Johnson's burning of the flag was, in effect, the kind of symbolic speech that is protected by the First Amendment. In contrast, the State argued it had two interests to support an argument that his actions were not speech and so not protected by the First Amendment. First, the state has an interest in preserving the flag "as a symbol of national unity" (105 L.Ed.2d 351). Secondly, the state has an interest in preventing breaches of the peace that could result from flag burning. The appeals court rejected both arguments, saying that the Texas statute was unconstitutional.

SUMMARY OF THE COURT'S ANALYSIS

Justice William J. Brennan, Jr., writes for the Court.
Justices Thurgood Marshall, Harry A. Blackmun, Antonin Scalia, and Anthony M. Kennedy join.

Justice Brennan says the first thing the Court must do is "determine whether Johnson's burning of the flag constituted expressive conduct, permitting him to invoke the First Amendment" (105 L.Ed.2d 352). Once this question is answered, the Court should decided whether the Texas statute regulated his behavior or his right to free speech.

The first question addressed by the Court, then, is whether Johnson's flag burning is enough like communication so that it can be considered free speech. One point to be addressed here is whether Johnson intended to convey a message. A second is whether the audience would understand his action as a form of communication.

Brennan says that, although the flag is "pregnant with expressive content," actions using the flag are not automatically symbolic speech and so would not be protected automatically by the First Amendment. Here, however, the State of Texas conceded "that Johnson's conduct was expressive conduct" (105 L.Ed.2d 354). Brennan adds, "The expressive, overtly political nature of this conduct was both intentional and overwhelmingly apparent" (105 L.Ed.2d 354).

Concerning the second point, Brennan asserts that the crux of the issue is not the distinctions between speech and behavior, but the legitimacy of the government's interest in restricting the expressive conduct. Where one action combines elements of speech and nonspeech, Brennan says the Court has ruled that, the First Amendment notwithstanding, a strong enough government interest in regulating the nonspeech part constitutionally justifies restricting the speech part.

The O'Brien tests, first announced in *United States* v. *O'Brien*, 391 U.S. 367 (1968), is directed at determining precisely when the government interest reaches the point at which it is, in fact, strong enough constitutionally to justify restricting speech. So, Brennan says the Court should now determine whether the Texas statute relates to the speech or the nonspeech parts of Johnson's expressive conduct. In other words, in order to see if the O'Brien test should be applied, Brennan says the Court must decide first whether or not the Texas law is directed at the speech or nonspeech aspect of burning a flag.

The state says the law is aimed at behavior, not speech, because it seeks to prevent breaches of the peace and because it seeks to "preserve the flag as a symbol of nationhood and national unity" (105 L.Ed.2d 357). Brennan gives two short replies to these arguments. First, the record does not show any attempt to prevent breaches of speech. Secondly, preserving a symbol is indeed regulating speech.

Brennan then presents a more detailed discussion of each point. Although he expresses surprise that the state did not claim Johnson's actions were likely to incite others to disturb the peace, he asserts, nevertheless, that the State's position, at bottom, is that persons watching a flag burning may be so incensed that it is likely they would breach the peace. To this argument, he responds, "The function of free speech . . . is to invite dispute" (105 L.Ed.2d 356). He adds, "We have not permitted the Government to assume that every expression of a provocative idea will incite a riot" (105 L.Ed.2d 356,7). Nor does Brennan agree that Johnson's actions fit the definition of "fighting words" as expressed in *Chaplinsky* v. *New Hampshire* (1942) because the burning is not "a direct personal insult or an invitation to exchange in fisticuffs" (105 L.Ed.2d 357).

An interest in preserving the flag as a symbol of national unity arises only if the flag is viewed as capable of communicating a message. Thus, this interest is an interest in speech, not action. Brennan concludes, therefore, that both interests of the state are related to speech and so are outside the authority of the O'Brien test, which is concerned only with the nonspeech parts of expressive conduct.

The final, and most difficult, question is whether or not the state's interest in preserving the flag as a symbol of nationhood and national unity is sufficient to deny First Amendment protection to burning the flag in order to make a political statement. Brennan writes, "If there is a bedrock principle underlying the First Amendment, it is that the Government may not prohibit the expression of an idea simply because society finds the idea itself offensive or disagreeable" (105 L.Ed.2d 360). He adds, "Nor may the Government, we have held, compel conduct that would evince respect for the flag" (105 L.Ed.2d 360).

Government cannot use laws to dictate the symbolic meaning that citizens must give to the flag or to any other symbol of the nation. If it could, then, Brennan asks, could not persons be punished constitutionally for burning copies of the constitution or of the presidential seal and so forth?

In addition, Brennan says the Court is convinced that burning the flag to make a political statement "will not endanger the special role played by our flag or the feelings it inspires" (105 L.Ed.2d 363). In fact, he says it may strengthen, not weaken, "the flag's deservedly cherished place in our community today" (105 L.Ed.2d 363). He adds, "We can imagine no more appropriate response to burning a flag than waving one's own, no better way to counter a flag-burner's message than by saluting the flag that burns, no surer means of preserving the dignity even of the flag that burned than by--as one witness here did--according its remains a respectful burial" (105 L.Ed.2d 364).

RULING

Brennan summarizes the Court's opinion when he writes the following:

> Johnson was convicted for engaging in expressive conduct. The State's interest in preventing breaches of the peace does not support his conviction because Johnson's conduct did not threaten to disturb the peace. Nor does the State's interest in preserving the flag as a symbol of nationhood and national unity justify his criminal conviction for engaging in political expression. The judgment of the Texas Court of Criminal Appeals is therefore affirmed. (105 L.Ed.2d 364)

Justice Anthony M. Kennedy writes a concurring opinion.

Although Justice Kennedy says he joins the Court's opinion "without reservation," he writes to add a" few remarks" (105 L.Ed.2d 364). He notes, "It is poignant but fundamental that the flag protects those who hold it in contempt" (105 L.Ed.2d 364). "But whether or not he [Johnson] could appreciate the enormity of the offense he gave," Kennedy continues, "The fact remains that his acts were speech, in both the technical and the fundamental meaning of the Constitution. So I agree with the Court that he must go free" (105 L.Ed.2d 365).

Chief Justice William H. Rehnquist writes a dissenting opinion. Justices Byron R. White and Sandra Day O'Connor join.

Chief Justice Rehnquist begins his opinion by asserting that the flag holds "a unique position as the symbol of our Nation" (105 L.Ed.2d 365). He then supports this assertion with a number of historical and literary references to the flag, concluding, "The American flag, then, throughout more than 200 years of our history, has come to be the visible symbol embodying our Nation" (105 L.Ed.2d 369). "Millions and millions of Americans regard it with an almost mystical reverence," he writes, "Regardless of what sort of social, political, or philosophical beliefs they may have" (105 L.Ed.2d 369,70).

Unlike the Court, Rehnquist feels "the public burning of the American flag by Johnson was no essential part of any exposition of ideas, and at the same time it had a tendency to incite a breach of the peace" (105 L.Ed.2d 371). Rehnquist concedes that Johnson constitutionally could have verbally abused the flag. Quoting from *Chaplinsky v New Hampshire* (1942), Rehnquist says the act of burning, however, "'is of such slight social value as a step to truth that any benefit that may be derived from [it] is clearly outweighed' by the public interest in avoiding a probably breach of peace" (105 L.Ed.2d 371).

Equating the burning with "an inarticulate grunt or roar," Rehnquist says, "It was Johnson's use of this particular symbol, and not the idea that he sought to convey by it or by his many other expressions, for which he was punished" (105 L.Ed.2d 371).

In the end, Rehnquist assigns Johnson's action to the area of conduct, not speech. He writes, "Surely one of the high purposes of a democratic society is to legislate against conduct that is regarded as evil and profoundly offensive to the majority of people--whether it be murder, embezzlement, pollution, or flag burning (105 L.Ed.2d 374).

Justice John Paul Stevens writes a dissenting opinion.

Justice Stevens begins his dissent with a discussion of the various symbolic meanings residing in the flag. In addition to nationhood and national unity, he sees freedom, equal opportunity, religious tolerance, and goodwill for others who share our aspirations. He admits that it is theoretically possible that burning the flag as a means of political protest could in fact enhance its value. The likelihood, however, is that such action "will tarnish its value" (105 L.Ed.2d 375). Thus, he writes, "That tarnish is not justified by the trivial burden on free expression occasioned by requiring that an available, alternative mode of expression--including uttering words critical of the flag--be employed" (105 L.Ed.2d 375).

Stevens also notes that the Texas Statute "does not compel any conduct or any profession of respect for any idea or any symbol" (105 L.Ed.2d 375). Like Rehnquist, Stevens feels that Johnson was punished not for "his expression of dissatisfaction with the policies of this country" but "because of the method he chose to express his dissatisfaction with those policies" (105 L.Ed.2d 376). He notes that spray painting the Lincoln Memorial, for example, would not be permitted.

He concludes, "It cannot be true that the flag that uniquely symbolizes their [democratic ideals] power is not itself worthy of protection from unnecessary desecration" (105 L.Ed.2d 376).

SIGNIFICANCE

Few would question the notion that the significance of this case is that it forbids the government to punish persons who, without harming or threatening to harm others, burn an American flag in order to communicate a political message. In effect, this case says such burning has enough elements of speech to invoke the protection of the First Amendment. When burning the American flag is not the result of an attempt to communicate a message, however, then, according to the Court, it may have too few elements of speech to qualify for constitutional protection.

Whitney v. California

Charlotte Anita Whitney
v.
People of the State of California

Docket No. 1927-03
274 U.S. 357, 71 L.Ed. 1095, 47 S.Ct. 641 (1927)
Argued October 6, 1925. Reargued March 18, 1926.
Decided May 16, 1927.

BACKGROUND

After World War I, fear of Communism produced a number of federal and state syndicalism laws designed to check what was perceived as a Communist conspiracy to conquer the free world. The California Criminal Syndicalism Act of 1919 made it a crime not only to teach or to advocate "unlawful acts of force and violence or unlawful methods of terrorism as a means of accomplishing change in industrial ownership or control of effecting any political change" (360), but also to "organize or assist in organizing" or to become a member of "any organization" that advocates "criminal syndicalism" (360).

In short, this statute made criminals out of persons who, even though they themselves did not proactively teach or advocate anything, nevertheless belonged to a group that espoused violent or unlawful overthrow of the government. Such a notion raised the question of how important is a member's dissent from the avowed teachings of an organization. Could it not be the case that a member who selectively does not support those organizations' official goals that are defined by statute to be illegal or who works within an organization to change illegal goals should not, therefore, be punished for such goals? This question draws a distinction between passive advocation of illegal activities (such as belonging to an organization that espouses some illegal goals) and active advocation, inciting others to illegal activity. The Court, however, recognized no such distinction.

CIRCUMSTANCES

At the 1919 national Socialist party convention held in Chicago, Illinois, the Socialist party found itself split between the "old-wing Socialists" and a newer, more radical group. After the radicals, including the delegation from Oakland, California, were ejected, they "went to another hall, and formed the Communist Labor Party of America" (363). The CLP adopted a constitution that had two important provisions relevant to this case. First, it asserted that members subscribe to the official "Platform and Program," which included, among other things, a statement saying the purpose of the organization is "to create a unified revolutionary working class" with the goal of overthrowing "capitalist rule" (363).

The second provision made possible "the formation of state organizations conforming to its platform as the supreme declaration of the party" (363). Charlotte Anita Whitney, upon her return to California, became a delegate to a November 1919 convention in Oakland where the California branch of the CLP was organized. As a member of the resolution committee, however, she prepared for the platform a plank that "urged workers who are possessed of the right of franchise to cast their votes for the ... C.L.P." (365). This plank was rejected by the membership and replaced with a statement affirming the national party's more revolutionary goals.

Eventually, Whitney and others were charged with violating the 1919 California Criminal Syndicalism Act. She was tried, convicted, and sentenced to imprisonment for one count. This count charged that "on or about November 28, 1919, in Alameda County" she "did . . . wrongfully . . . organize . . . and knowingly became a member of an organization . . . designed to advocate, teach, aid and abet criminal syndicalism" (360). The district court of appeals affirmed her conviction.

SUMMARY OF THE COURT'S ANALYSIS

Justice Edward T. Sanford writes for the Court.
Chief Justice William H. Taft and Justices George Sutherland, Pierce Butler, Harlan F. Stone, James C. McReynolds, and Willis Van Devanter join.

Before addressing the free speech issues, the Court faces the problem of jurisdiction. In the main, it searches for a constitutional issue raised in the state courts and finds only one. Because the state appeals court issued an order refusing to consider "'the question of whether the California Criminal Syndicalism Act . . . and its application is repugnant to the provisions of the 14th Amendment'" (361), the Court asserts that the lower court did thereby raise a constitutional issue. Notes Sanford, "Of course, our review is to be confined to that question" (362).

The Court divides the Fourteenth Amendment issue into four parts. First, Sanford notes that Whitney does not deny the jury did have sufficient evidence to convict her of helping to organize and of being a member of the Communist labor party of California (CLPC). Nor does she deny that the CLPC "was organized to advocate, teach, aid or abet criminal syndicalism as defined by the act" (366), Instead, Whitney claims the application of the act deprived her "of her liberty without due process of law" (366) because it was the actions of the other members who acted against her will by overruling her proposed platform plank that constituted the violation of the law. Writes Sanford, "The argument is, in effect, that the character of the state organization could not be forecast when she attended the convention" (366, 367).

To this argument, Sanford asserts that this particular determination of the jury "is one of fact merely which is not open to review in this court, involving as it does no constitutional question whatever" (367). Nevertheless, he proceeds to outline three reasons stating why she would not win this point even if the Court would choose to rule on it. First, she was a member of the national party prior to the state convention. Secondly, her resolution "did not advocate the use of the ballot to the exclusion of violent and unlawful means of bringing about the desired change" (367). Finally, she remained a member after her resolution was defeated, indicated her acquiescence in the group's action.

Sanford states the second issue this way: "It is clear that the Syndicalism Act is not repugnant to the due process clause [of the Fourteenth Amendment] by reason of vagueness and uncertainty of definition" (368). He adds succinctly, "The language of . . . the act under which the plaintiff [Whitney] in error was convicted is clear; the definition of 'criminal syndicalism' specific" (368).

Nor, says the Court, is the act repugnant to the equal protection clause of this amendment simply because only those advocating a change in--as opposed to those seeking to maintain--industrial and political conditions by violent and unlawful means, are declared criminals. To win this argument, Sanford asserts, the "one who assails the classification must carry the burden of showing that it does not rest upon any reasonable basis, but is essentially arbitrary" (369). He states that not to be "all embracing" or failure to cover "the whole field of possible abuses" (370) is not evidence of arbitrariness. Moreover, there is no reason to believe, Sanford continues, that "those desiring to maintain existing industrial and political conditions did or would advocate such [violent or unlawful] methods" (370).

Finally, Sanford asserts that the act is not "repugnant to the due process clause as a restraint of the rights of free speech, assembly, and association" (371). Paraphrasing *Gitlow* v. *New York* (1925), Sanford writes, "Freedom of speech . . . does not confer an absolute right to speak, without responsibility, whatever one may chose . . .; a state in the exercise of its police powers may punish those who abuse this freedom by utterances inimical to the public welfare" (371). He states that the "essence of the offense . . . is the combining with others . . . for the accomplishment of . . . criminal and unlawful methods" (371, 372). He adds that, since "such united and joint action involves even greater danger to the public peace and security than the isolated acts of individuals," (372) "the act is [not] an unreasonable or arbitrary exercise of the police power of the state" (372).

RULING

Sanford writes:

> We find no repugnancy in the Syndicalism Act as applied in this case to either the due process or equal protection clause of the 14th Amendment, on any of the grounds upon which its validity has been here challenged.

> The order dismissing the writ of error will be vacated and set aside, and the judgment of the Court of Appeals affirmed. (372)

Justice Louis D. Brandeis writes a concurring opinion.
Justice Oliver W. Holmes joins.

Brandeis summarizes the Court's views when he writes, "The mere act of assisting in forming a society for teaching syndicalism, [or] of becoming a member of it . . . is given the dynamic quality of crime" (373). He continues, "Thus the accused [Whitney] is to be punished, not for attempt, incitement, or conspiracy, but for a step in preparation, which, if it threatens the public order at all, does so only remotely" (373).

Next, Brandeis agrees with the Court that, "although the rights of free speech and assembly are fundamental, they are not . . . absolute," (373) and that speech may be restricted "in order to protect the state from destruction or from serious injury, political, economic, or moral" (373).

Such restrictions, according to Brandeis, can be justified only upon a showing of a clear and present danger. Therefore, the central question becomes for Brandeis how to develop a "standard by which to determine when a danger shall be deemed clear; how remote the danger shall be and yet be deemed present; and what degree of evil shall be deemed sufficiently substantial to justify resort to abridgement of free speech and assembly as a means of protection" (374).

Brandeis begins his answer to this question with these words: "Fear of serious injury cannot alone justify suppression of free speech and assembly. Men feared witches and burned women. It is the function of speech to free men from the bondage of irrational fears" (376). He then outlines three reasons sufficient to justify restriction of free speech. In a word, each of the three reasons are a (1) clear and (2) present (3) danger. First, he asserts, "there must be reasonable grounds to fear that serious evil will result if free speech is practiced" (376). Secondly, he feels, "There must be reasonable ground to believe that the danger apprehended is imminent" (373). Finally, he says, "There must be reasonable ground to believe that the evil to be prevented is a serious one" (376).

Having set forth the three conditions, Brandeis proceeds to draw a series of distinctions between actions that do and actions that do not meet these conditions. He writes, "Advocacy of violation, however reprehensible morally, is not a justification for denying free speech where the advocacy falls short of incitement" (376). There is a "wide difference," according to Brandeis, "between advocacy and incitement, between preparation and attempt, between assembling and conspiracy" (376).

A danger is not clear and present, Brandeis argues, if "there be time to expose through discussion the falsehood and fallacies" so that "the evil" (377) can be averted by education. Ordinarily, he asserts, "The remedy to be applied is more speech, not enforced silence" (377).

In addition, the danger or evil must be "relatively serious" before speech can be restricted constitutionally. He writes, "The fact that speech is likely to result in some violence or in the destruction of property is not enough to justify its suppression. There must be the probability of serious injury to the state" (378).

Considered from the perspective of the clear-and-present-danger formula, therefore, Whitney's actions of "assembling with a political party, formed to advocate the desirability of a proletarian revolution by mass action at some date necessarily far in the future" are protected by the Fourteenth and First Amendments from punishment by the state.

Nevertheless, Brandeis concurs with the Court's ruling because "there was other testimony which tended to establish the existence of a conspiracy . . . to commit present serious crimes" (379).

SIGNIFICANCE

The primary significance of this case is the Court's holding that mere membership in a group espousing goals that call for the violent or unlawful overthrow of our government or society can constitutionally constitute a crime that the state may punish. A member of such a group does not have to teach or advocate such actions in order to be convicted of a crime. Membership alone is illegal.

There is secondary significance, however, in Brandeis's concurring opinion. Although the Court did not address the notion of clear and present danger--first stated in Schenck by Holmes who joins Brandeis here--the concurring opinion gains importance because it elucidates this formula to some degree. In particular, Brandeis asserted that a danger of injury to the state is not clear and present if there is time to use discussion in order to counter speech calling for the violent or unlawful overthrow of the government. Certainly, speech that places the overthrow in the distant, unspecified future does not constitute a danger that is clear and present. Moreover, the danger must be "substantial." Substantial appears to mean for Brandeis and Holmes more than mere injury to life and property; it means a threat to the very existence of the state.

Not to be overlooked is the Court's unanimous acceptance of the radical notion announced only a year earlier in *Gitlow* v. *New York* (1926). In *Gitlow* the Court asserted that the Fourteenth Amendment can be used to apply constitutional requirements to the states. The word "liberty" in particular, at least according to Brandeis, applies the First Amendment to the states.

Yates v. United States

Oleta O'Connor Yates, Henry Steinberg, Loretta Starvus Stack v. United States of America
Docket No. 1957-06

William Schneiderman v. United States of America
Docket No. 1957-07

Al Richmond and Philip Marshall Connelly v. United States of America
Docket No. 1957-08

354 U.S. 298, 1 L.Ed.2d 1356, 77 S.Ct. 1064 (1957)
Argued October 8 and 9, 1956. Decided June 17, 1957.

BACKGROUND

Because the Court in the *Dennis* v. *United States* (1951) case upheld the constitutionality of the Smith Act, government prosecutors began to file charges against other Communists. In fact, the defendants in the *Dennis* case were named as coconspirators in this prosecution, but were not indicted. According to Justice Tom C. Clark, the persons charged in this case of conspiring to organize the Communist party include "the same group of defendants as in the Dennis case though petitioners here occupied a lower echelon in the party hierarchy" (345).

CIRCUMSTANCES

Fourteen persons were charged with violating the Smith Act. They were then convicted, after a jury trial in the Southern California District Court, of "a single count indictment charging them with conspiring (1) to advocate and teach the duty and necessity of overthrowing the Government of the United States by force and violence, and (2) to organize . . . the Communist Party of the United States" (300). They were sentenced to five year's imprisonment and fined $10,000.

After the *Dennis* case was decided and before this case was granted review, Justices Fred M. Vinson, Stanley F. Reed, Robert H. Jackson, and Sherman Minton left the Court, and Justices Earl Warren, John M. Harlan, Charles E. Whittaker, and William J. Brennan, Jr., were added, although Brennan and Whittaker did not participate in the decision. It is interesting to note, however, that Justice Harlan's majority opinion includes several statements explaining what the Court meant in the *Dennis* decision, even though he did not participate in that case because he was not then on the court.

SUMMARY OF THE COURT'S ANALYSIS

Justice Harlan writes for the Court.
Chief Justice Earl Warren and Justices Felix Frankfurter, Harold H. Burton, John M. Harlan, and William J. Brennan, Jr., join.

The main portion of the Court's decision focuses on four issues. The first is a definition of the word "organize." If it means, as the defendants contend, something close to establish, found, or create, then the three-year statute of limitations has run out because the U.S. Communist party is generally thought to have been organized (or reorganized) in 1945 at the latest. If it means, as the government contends, "a continuing process which goes on throughout the life of an organization," (304) then there is, in effect, no statute of limitations because the organizing never stops.

Justice Harlan accepts a notion like "starting" as the general meaning of organizing:

> We should follow the familiar rule that criminal statutes are to be strictly construed and give to "organize" its narrow meaning, that is, that the word refers only to acts entering into the creation of a new organization, and not to acts thereafter performed in carrying on its activities, even though such acts may loosely be termed "organizational." Such indeed is the normal usage of the word "organize." (310)
>
> We conclude, therefore, that since the Communist Party came into being in 1945, and the indictment was not returned until 1951, the three-year statute of limitations had run out on the "organizing" charge, and required the withdrawal of that part of the indictment from the jury's consideration. (312)

The second major part of the decision considers the instructions given to the jury. The petitioners, the government, and all members of the Court except Clark were dissatisfied with the trial court's instructions. Although nearly everyone had a different reason for disapproving the instructions, they all agreed that the controversy revolved around drawing distinctions among various forms of speech.

As the Court saw it, the defendants felt that the essential distinction rests between advocating an idea and advocating an action. Harlan writes:

> Petitioners contend that the instructions to the jury were defective . . . [because] the jury must find that the advocacy which the defendants conspired to promote was of a kind calculated to "incite" persons to action for the forcible overthrow of the Government. It is argued that advocacy of forcible overthrow as mere *abstract doctrine* is within the free speech protection of the First Amendment. (312, 313)

The government, which took at the trial a position similar to the defendant's, takes a different position in the appeal. Now the government draws the distinction between mere discussion and advocacy itself. One either discusses or one advocates. Writes Harlan of the government's position, "The true constitutional dividing line is not between inciting and abstract advocacy of forcible overthrow, but rather between advocacy as such, irrespective of its inciting qualities, and the mere discussion or exposition of violent overthrow as an abstract theory" (313).

"We are thus faced, " Harlan concludes, "With the question whether the Smith Act prohibits advocacy and teaching of forcible overthrow as an abstract principle, divorced from any effort to instigate action to that end, so long as such advocacy or teaching is engaged in with evil intent. We hold that it does not" (318).

To the Court, then, the important distinction rests where Yates argues it is located: between advocating ideas and advocating action.

Harlan asserts, "The statute [Smith Act] was aimed at the advocacy and teaching of concrete action for the forcible overthrow of the government, and not of principles divorced from action" (319, 320). After reviewing the faults of the notions about these distinctions held by the district court and the appeals court, Harlan gets to the nub of the matter. He writes:

> The essential distinction is that those to whom the advocacy is addressed must be urged to *do* something, now or in the future, rather than merely to *believe* in something. (324, 325) It was . . . incumbent on the court to make clear in some fashion that the advocacy must be of action and not merely abstract doctrine. (325) [Thus] . . . we must regard the trial court's charge in this respect as furnishing wholly inadequate guidance to the jury on this central point in the case. (327)

The third major issue is the evidence. After looking at the record of the trial, the Court draws an important distinction between two classes of defendants. Harlan writes:

> On this basis we have concluded that the evidence against petitioners Connelly, Kusnitz, Richmond, Spector, and Steinberg is so clearly insufficient that their acquittal should be ordered, but that as to petitioners Carlson, Dobbs, Fox, Healey (Mrs. Connelly), Lambert, Lima, Schneiderman, Stack, and Yates, we would not be justified in closing the way to their retrial. (328, 329)

Harlan then gives the Court's reasons for keeping open the possibility of convicting the nine remaining defendants in a re-trial. He writes:

> In short, while the record contains evidence of little more than a general program of educational activity by the Communist Party which included advocacy of violence as a theoretical matter, we are not prepared to say, at this stage of the case, that it would be impossible for a jury . . . to find that advocacy of action was also engaged in when the group

> involved was thought particularly trustworthy, dedicated, and suited for violent tasks. (332)
>
> And finally, all of these nine petitioners were shown either to have made statements themselves, or apparently approved statements made in their presence, which a jury might take as some evidence of their participation with the requisite intent in a conspiracy to advocate illegal action. (333)

Before leaving the notion of evidence, Harlan comments on the petitioners' claim that an overt act is necessary for conviction of conspiracy. He writes:

> It is not necessary that an overt act be the substantive crime charged . . . . The function of the overt act in a conspiracy prosecution is simply to manifest "that the conspiracy is at work" . . . and is neither a project still resting solely in the minds of the conspirators nor a fully completed operation no longer in existence. The substantive offense here charged as the object of the conspiracy is speech. (334)

A technical issue of law called "collateral estoppel" forms the fourth major part of the decision. This point is relevant only to one defendant: Schneiderman. He claims that some rulings made in his favor during a denaturalization hearing held earlier should govern some of the issues in this case. Among those rulings is the determination that "the teaching of Marxism-Leninism by the Communist Party was not necessarily the advocacy of violent overthrow of government" (335). The Court unanimously rejects his claim.

RULING

The ruling is clear, if a bit complex. Harlan writes, "We conclude that these convictions must be reversed and the case remanded to the District Court with instructions to enter judgments of acquittal as to certain of the petitioners, and to grant a new trial as to the rest. (303) The judgment of the Court of Appeal is reversed" (338).

Justice Hugo L. Black writes a separate opinion, concurring in part and dissenting in part.
Justice William O. Douglas joins.

Justices Black and Douglas agree with much of the Court's analysis of the term organize and that the trial judge erred in giving the jury instructions. They disagree with the Court, however, about what instructions should have been given. Black writes, "Under the Court's approach, defendants could still be convicted simply for agreeing to talk as distinguished from agreeing to act. I believe that the First Amendment forbids Congress to punish people for talking about public affairs" (340).

These two jurists would set free all the defendants, not just the five acquitted by the Court. They feel that there is a "pitiful inadequacy of proof to show beyond a reasonable doubt that the defendants were guilty of conspiring to incite persons to act to overthrow the Government" (341).

In summarizing their position, Black seems to be saying that there should be an absolute prohibition against punishing any speech that is confined to communicating ideas evaluating the government. He writes, "Unless there is complete freedom for expression of all ideas, whether we like them or not, concerning the way government should be run, I doubt if any views in the long run can be secured against the censor" (344).

Justice Tom C. Clark writes a dissenting opinion.

Justice Clark asserts plainly, "I would affirm the convictions. I agree with the Court of Appeals, the District Court, and the jury that the evidence showed guilt beyond a reasonable doubt" (345). (This statement stands in stark contrast to Black's words that there existed a "pitiful inadequacy of proof.") Clark also disagrees with the Court's understanding of the word organize. He feels that, when Congress passed the law, "It was concerned with the new Communist fronts, cells, schools, and other groups, which were being created nearly every day under the aegis of the Party to carry on its purposes" (319). In his opinion, therefore, organizing does not mean something like starting or founding, but it refers to ongoing activities.

Finally, he alone has praise for the trial court's instructions: "As I see it, the trial judge charged in essence all that was required under the Dennis opinions" (350). In regard to the distinctions between forms of speech that the Court said the trial judge should have drawn, Clark says, "I find . . . that the distinctions are too 'subtle and difficult to grasp'" (350).

SIGNIFICANCE

The Court made it quite clear that the kind of speech made illegal in the Smith Act is advocacy of action, not advocacy of ideas. The audience must be urged to do something, not just to believe.

The point at issue, then, becomes what does it mean to advocate action. In a "clarification" of the *Dennis* ruling, the Court says here that advocating forceful overthrow of the government as a general principle even though engaged in with an evil intent is not enough to qualify as unconstitutional speech. An intent to act is not the same as an urging to act. The key to defining action is the presence of "an effort to instigate" action.

In *Dennis*, the Court used the clear-and-present-danger test to assert that advocating an action is a clear danger, even though it may not be possible to be accomplished, and a present danger, even though the action is to take place sometime in the indefinite future. Here the Court is saying that the "capacity to stir listeners to forcible action" (315) must be considered. If the words are "uttered with the hope" (321) of revolution, then they are "too remote from concrete action" (321, 322) to be termed unconstitutional.

This notion has sometimes been called an "incitement" standard because the key point is whether or not an audience is urged or incited to do something.

In short, the Court in *Yates* did not focus on the clear-and-present-danger test as a method for distinguishing between constitutional and unconstitutional speech. Instead, it drew a line between advocacy of action and advocacy of ideas. This line seems to place unconstitutional speech much closer to the urging of the accomplishment of a probable illegal action than did *Dennis*.

Selected Bibliography

LIBEL

Abrams, Floyd. "Why We Should Change the Libel Law." *New York Times Magazine* (29 September 1985): 34.

Adler, Renata. *Reckless Disregard*: *Westmorland* v. *CBS*, *Sharon* v. *Time*., *Inc*. New York: Knopf, 1986.

Anderson, David. "Libel and Press Self-Censorship." *Texas Law Review* 53 (1975): 422.

Bezanson, Randall P., Gilbert Cranberg, and John Soloski. *Libel and the Press*: *Myth and Reality*. New York: Free Press, 1987.

Denniston, Lyle. "Libeling Teachers: It's Chaos." *Washington Journalism Review* (July/August 1988): 47.

---. "Challenging Big Money Verdicts." *Washington Journalism Review* (January/February 1989): 44.

Dill, Barbara. "Bad Journalism Caused $3 Million Libel Verdict." *Publishers Auxiliary* (22 August 1988): 7.

---. "Courts Order Reimbursement of Libel Suit Costs." *Publishers' Auxiliary* (20 February 1989): 7.

Fleming, John G. *The American Tort Process*. New York: Oxford University Press, 1988.

Forer, Lois. *A Chilling Effect*: *The Mounting Threat of Libel and Invasion of Privacy Actions to the First Amendment*. New York: W. W. Norton, 1987.

Franklin, Marc A. "Good Names and Bad Law: A Critique of Libel Law and a Proposal." *University of San Francisco Law Review* (Fall 1983): 1.

---. "Suing the Media for Libel: A Litigational Study." *American Bar Foundation Research Journal* 3 (1981): 455.

Gillmor, Donald M. "Justice William Brennan and the Failed 'Theory' of Actual Malice." *Journalism Quarterly* (Summer 1982): 249.

Helle, Steven. "Judging Public Interest in Libel: The *Gertz* Decision's Contribution." *Journalism Quarterly* Spring 1984: 117.

Hill, Alfred. "Defamation and Privacy Under The First Amendment." *Columbia Law Review* 76 (1976): 1205.
Hopkins, W. Wat. "Negligence 10 Years After Gertz." *Journalism Monograph* 93 (1985).
---. *Actual Malice: Twenty-Five Years After Times v. Sullivan.* New York: Praeger, 1989.
Hughes, Robert L. "Rationalizing Libel Law in the Wake of Gertz: The Problem and a Proposal." *Journalism Quarterly* 62 (1989): 540.
Kaufman, Henry R. "Libel 1980-1985: Promises and Realities." *Communications Lawyer* 3 (1986): 4.
Lawhorne, Clifton O. *The Supreme Court and Libel.* Carbondale, Ill.: Southern Illinois University Press, 1981.
Lewis, Anthony. "Annals of the Law (Libel)." *The New Yorker* (5 November 1984): 44.
Lynch, Judy D. "Public Officials, the Press, and the Libel Remedy: Toward a Theory of Absolute Immunity." *Oregon Law Review* 67 (1988): 611-7.
McGaffey, Ruth. "Group Libel Revisited." *Quarterly Journal of Speech* 65 (1979): 157.
Mauro, Tony. "Critics Gang Up on The Annenberg Plan." *Washington Journalism Review* (April 1989): 36.
Mollenhoff, Clark. "Twenty Five Years of *Times* v. *Sullivan*." *Quill* (March 1989): 9.
Novak, Viveca and William E. Francois. "Fighting Back on the Libel Front." *Columbia Journalism Review* (March/April 1989): 6.
Radloff, Andrew. "Defining the 'Sullivan' Decision." *Editor and Publisher* (15 April 1989): 9.
Rosenberg, Norman L. *Protecting the Best men: An Interpretive History of the Law of Libel.* Chapel Hill, N.C.: University of North Carolina Press, 1986.
Saad, Henry W. and Lisa R. Mikalonis. "The New Michigan Law on Libel." *Editor and Publisher* (11 March 1989): 24.
Sack, Robert D. *Libel, Slander and Related Problems.* New York: Practising Law Institute, 1980.
Sanford, Bruce. "High Court's Lone Libel Case May be Less Than it Seems." *Quill* (December 1988): 47.
---. *The Law of Libel and the Right of Privacy.* New York: World Almanac Publications, 1984.
---. "*Times* v. *Sullivan*: The Music Still Plays Sweetly." *Quill* (March 1989): 7.
Simon, Todd F. "Libel as Malpractice New Media Ethics and the Standard of Care." *Fordham Law Review* 53 (1984): 449.
Smolla, Rodney A. *Suing the Press.* New York: Oxford University Press, 1986.
Stein, M. L. "Libel Resolution Program Off to Slow Start." *Editor and Publisher* (10 December 1989): 18.
---. "Newspapers' Right to Report Both Sides is Upheld." *Editor and Publisher* (28 January 1989): 31.
Stevens, George E. "Negligence in Defamation Before Gertz." *Journalism Quarterly* 56 (1979): 832.
Stonecipher, Harry W. and Robert Trager. "The Impact of Gertz on the Law of Libel." Journalism Quarterly 53 (1976): 609.

Watkins, John J. "The Demise of the Public Figure Doctrine." *Journal of Communication* 27 (1977): 47.
White, G. Edward. *Tort Law in America: An Intellectual History*. New York: Oxford University Press, 1980.
Winfield, Richard N. *New York Times* v. *Sullivan*: *The New Twenty Years*. New York: Practising Law Institute, 1984.

PRIVACY

Bloustein, Edward J. "Privacy, Tort Law, and the Constitution: Is Warren and Brandeis' Tort Petty and Unconstitutional as Well?" *Texas Law Review* (April 1968): 611.
Bollinger, Lee C. *The Tolerant Society*. New York: Oxford University Press, 1986.
Franklin, Marc A. "A Constitutional Problem in Privacy Protection: Legal Inhibitions on Reporting of Fact." *Stanford Law Review* 16 (1963): 107.
Glassner, Theodore L. "Resolving the Press-Privacy Conflict: Approaches to the Newsworthiness Defense." *Communications and the Law* 4 (1982): 23.
Hixson, Richard F. *Privacy in Public Society*: *Human Rights in Conflict*. New York: Oxford University Press, 1987.
Kalven, Harry, Jr. "Privacy in Tort Law--Were Warren and Brandeis Wrong?" *Law and Contemporary Problems* 31 (1966): 326.
Pember, Don R. *Privacy and the Press*. Seattle: University of Washington Press, 1972.
Plante, Bill. "It took Willie Horton to Raise Massachusetts' Privacy Curtain." *ASNE Bulletin* (March 1989): 12.
Prosser, William. "Privacy." *California Law Review* 48 (1960): 383.
Wacks, R. I. *Personal Information*: *Privacy and the Law*. New York: Oxford University Press, 1989.
Warren, Samuel D. and Louis D. Brandeis. "The Right to Privacy." *Harvard Law Review* 4 (1890): 193.

FIRST AMENDMENT

Baker, C. Edwin. *Human Liberty and Freedom of Speech*. New York: Oxford University Press, 1989.
Barron, Jerome. *Public Rights and the Private Press*. Toronto: Buttersworths, 1981.
Black, Hugo L. *A Constitutional Faith*. New York: Alfred Knopf. 1969.
Blasi, Vincent. "The Checking Value in First Amendment Theory." American Bar Association Journal 3 (1977): 521.
Bogen, David A. *Bulwark of Liberty*: *The Court and the First Amendment*. New York: Associated Faculty Press, 1984.
Bollinger, Lee. *The Tolerant Society*: *Freedom of Speech and Extremist Speech in America*. New York: Oxford University Press, 1986.
Bork, Robert. "Neutral Principles and Some First Amendment Problems." *Indiana Law Journal* 47 (1971): 1.

Chafee, Zechariah, Jr. *Free Speech in the United States*. Cambridge, Mass.: Harvard University Press, 1954.
Clayton, James P. *The Making of Justice: The Supreme Court in Action*. New York: E. P. Dutton & Co., 1964.
Countryman, Vern, ed. *The Douglas Opinions*. New York: Random House, 1977.
Cox, Archibald. *The Warren Court*. Cambridge, Mass.: Harvard University Press, 1968.
Dennis, Everette, Donald M. Gillmor and David Grey. *Hugo L. Black and the First Amendment*. Ames, Iowa: Iowa State University Press, 1978.
Devol, Kenneth S. *The Mass Media and the Supreme Court*. 2nd ed. New York: Hastings House, 1976.
Emerson, Thomas I. *The System of Freedom of Expression*. New York: Random House, 1970.
---. *Toward a General Theory of the First Amendment*. New York: Random House, 1966.
Franklin, Marc A. *The Dynamics of American Law: Courts, the Legal Process and Freedom of Expression*. Mineola, NY: Foundation Press, 1968.
Georgetown Law Journal. *Media and the First Amendment in a Free Society*. Amherst, Mass.: University of Massachusetts Press, 1973.
Hidgon, P. R. "The Burger Court and the Media: A 10-year Perspective." *West New England Law Review* 2 (1980): 593.
Levy, Leonard W. *Legacy of Suppression: Freedom of Speech and Press in Early American History*. Cambridge, Mass.: The Belknap Press, 1960.
McClosky, Robert G. *Essays in Constitutional Law*. New York: Alfred A. Knopf, 1957.
Meiklejohn, Alexander. "The First Amendment is an Absolute." *Supreme Court Review* (1961): 245.
---. *Political Freedom*. New York: Harper and Brothers, 1960.
Murphy, Paul L. *The Meaning of Freedom of Speech*. Westport, Conn.: Greenwood Publishing Co., 1972.
Nelson, Harold L., ed. *Freedom of the Press from Hamilton to the Warren Court*. New York: Bobbs-Merrill, 1967.
Posner, Richard A. "Monopoly in the Marketplace of Ideas." *Yale Law Review* 86 (1977): 567.
Rawls, John. *A Theory of Justice*. Cambridge, Mass.: Belknap Press, 1971.
Ray, Garrett. "Hazelwood Comes to Fort Collins." *Publishers Auxiliary*. (13 June 1988): 9.
Rehnquist, William H. "The First Amendment: Freedom, Philosophy, and the Law." *Gonzaga Law Review* 12 (1976): 1.
Scanlon, Thomas. "Freedom of Expression and Categories of Expression." *University of Pittsburgh Law Review* 40 (1979): 519.
Schauer, Frederick. *Free Speech: A Philosophical Inquiry*. New York: Cambridge University Press, 1982.
Schmidt, Benno C., Jr. *Freedom of the Press v. Public Access*. Springfield: Praeger, 1976.
Shapiro, Martin. *Freedom of Speech: The Supreme Court and Judicial Review*. Englewood Cliffs, N.J.: Prentice Hall, 1976.

Index